26(10-92)0

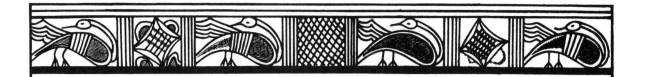

PEOPLE
OF THE SEA

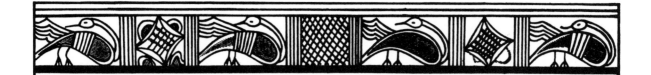

PEOPLE OF THE SEA

The Search for the Philistines

TRUDE DOTHAN   MOSHE DOTHAN

Macmillan Publishing Company   *New York*

Maxwell Macmillan Canada   *Toronto*

Maxwell Macmillan International
New York   Oxford   Singapore   Sydney

Macmillan Publishing Company
866 Third Avenue, New York, NY 10022

Maxwell Macmillan Canada, Inc.
1200 Eglinton Avenue East, Suite 200
Don Mills, Ontario M3C 3N1

Macmillan Publishing Company is part of the Maxwell Communication Group of Companies

Library of Congress Cataloging-in-Publication Data
Dothan, Trude Krakauer.
    People of the sea: the search for the Philistines/Trude Dothan
and Moshe Dothan.
        p.   cm.
    Includes bibliographical references and index.
    ISBN 0-02-532261-3
    1. Philistines.   2. Middle East—Antiquities.   3. Excavations
(Archaeology)—Middle East.   4. Ashdod (Israel)—Antiquities.
5. Excavations (Archaelogy)—Israel.   6. Israel—Antiquities.
I. Dothan, M. (Moshe) II. Title.
DS90.D63   1992   91-47880   CIP
933—dc20

Macmillan books are available at special discounts for bulk purchases for sales promotions, pre-miums, fund-raising, or educational use. For details, contact:

                    Special Sales Director
                    Macmillan Publishing Company
                    866 Third Avenue
                    New York, NY 10022

DESIGN BY ERICH HOBBING

10 9 8 7 6 5 4 3 2 1

Printed in the United States of America

To Dani and Uri, with love

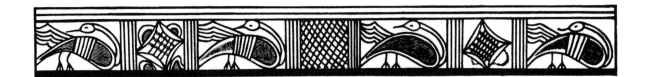

Contents

CONTENTS

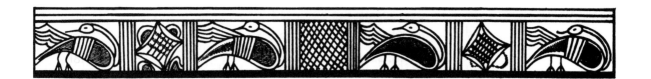

Acknowledgments

For many years we have been searching for answers to one of the most compelling enigmas of biblical and Near Eastern ancient history—the identity and origins of the Philistines, the foreign invaders whose protracted wars with the ancient Israelites made their name synonymous with barbarity and lack of culture. If we have succeeded to some extent in discovering the true nature of the Philistines, their material culture, and their pivotal role in the social, cultic, and commercial intercourse between the various Mediterranean peoples in the ancient Near East, it has not been our success alone. We are indebted, first of all, to an extraordinarily large army of professional and volunteer archaeologists and diggers, surveyors, heavy-machine operators, local workers (both Jewish and Arab), cooks and watchmen, funding organizations, and government offices—all of whose efforts are required to make a single dig possible, not to mention forty years of digging. Many of them are mentioned in the pages of this book.

To write academic reports and professional or even popular articles on archaeology is one thing. But to attempt to produce a comprehensive book on such a complex subject and long-running project—the four-hundred-year-long history of Philistine archaeology and our own four decades of explorations and findings—is something else. It was Neil Silberman, an archaeologist himself and an archaeological writer, who conceived of the idea of the book and was the main force in getting us to do it. His erudition and talents as well as his familiarity with the subject matter were invaluable to us in giving shape and substance to the book. Tamar Nahmias-Lotan was of great help in organizing and assembling the illustrations and the bibliography and in tying up a lot of loose ends. We are grateful to Beth Elon and Deborah Harris not

ACKNOWLEDGMENTS only for promoting the book but for putting us in touch with a skillful editor, Chaya Amir, who succeeded in cutting through a lot of extraneous matter and putting the manuscript in its final form. We would also like to thank Natalie Chapman, Andrew Attaway, Erich Hobbing, Nancy Cooperman, and the other staff members at Macmillan in New York, who supervised and facilitated the final stages of the work.

Thanks to our colleagues and friends at the Institute of Archaeology, Hebrew University; the Berman Center for Biblical Archaeology, Hebrew University; the Center for Maritime Studies, Haifa University; the Israel Museum; the Israel Authority of Antiquities; and Yosef Aviram from the Israel Exploration Society, for their help and advice.

Special thanks to the photographers Zeev Radovan, Ilan Sztulman, and Douglas Guthrie; to Avriel Adler for her assistance in the preparation of charts and drawings; and to Sara Halbreich for drawings.

We are fortunately exempt from that final paragraph in most acknowledgments in which the "long-suffering" wife or husband receives a porton of gratitude. But we are not entirely exempt; our two sons, Dani and Uri, have had to contend with the Philistines throughout their lives. They did not conquer them, but neither did they allow themselves to be vanquished by them, and for this we are grateful.

—Trude and Moshe Dothan
Jerusalem, 1992

Prologue

One can't dig in April in Israel, especially not when the rains have been so late. But we set out from Jerusalem one spring morning with friends whose curiosity about our work was as good a reason as any to retrace our steps in places where, for over forty years, we have been inquiring into the life and times of that enigmatic people, the Philistines.

From biblical and ancient Egyptian historical accounts, we know that the Philistines strongly influenced the history and culture of Palestine. At that time, the two major powers, Egypt and the Hittites, were politically weak and militarily impotent, and the Sea Peoples, among them the Philistines, exploited this power vacuum by invading areas previously subject to Egyptian and Hittite rule. In wave after wave of land and sea assaults they attacked Syria, Palestine, and even Egypt. According to Egyptian sources, Ramesses III defeated the invaders, who subsequently settled on the southern coastal plain of Palestine. There they developed into an independent political entity of major importance and constituted a threat to the disunited Canaanite city-states.

During the same period the Israelites, who had invaded Palestine from the east, were settling in the hill country. From the middle of the twelfth to the end of the eleventh century B.C., they fought with the Philistines for the cultural and political domination of the country. Both historically and culturally, this was the Philistines' most flourishing era. From the early tenth century on, the Philistines declined in importance until they played no more than a minor role in the history of the country. They succumbed to assimilation and gradually lost their cultural distinctiveness, merging with the Canaanites. But during their period of ascendancy, they produced a flourishing material culture.

The plains of Philistia, that April morning, were thickly covered with vegetation. Fields of wild wheat and clover, interlaced with splotches of crimson, yellow, and violet flowers, masked what was

only eight months ago the uniformly drab summer garb of this lush region. The smell of freshly cut hay lying in the neighboring fields was intoxicating. Endless rows and varieties of vegetables and fruit trees stretched away as far as the eye could see. What was so easily identifiable as Area D or Field 4 in last summer's excavations was hidden beneath nature's bounty. There were certain places where the contours of the land blocked out the not-too-distant skyline of modern Israel and one could see only land, sea, and sky. If one narrowed one's field of vision and enlarged one's field of imagination, one might almost have been in a time warp.

The beauty of the natural landscape and its evident fruitfulness no doubt appealed to the immigrant Philistines, who had left home and hearth somewhere in the Aegean over three thousand years ago for strange new lands. From their ancient harbor town of Tel Mor, near Ashdod, they could see, as we did, the expanse of the Mediterranean at their feet and the nearby tidal river of Lachish, which served them as a protected anchorage. From their capital cities of Ashdod and Ashkelon, they could view, as we did, the fruited plain, or the city walls within which they carried on their industrial and commercial enterprises. In Ekron, farther inland, they no doubt walked through the streets of the large city, much as we now walked over the mound; and, if it were as delightful a spring day as ours was, they probably walked out into the surrounding countryside, to picnic under the olive trees or to cool off in the waters of the Timna Stream nearby.

Olive trees must have been in abundance to support the impressive oil industry of Ekron, for over a hundred oil presses were later unearthed in the area, inside the massive city walls. There must have been sheep grazing over the rolling countryside to provide wool for the looms, if we are to account for all the loomweights found there. And they were only one product of the thriving potters' complex which made cooking and storing utensils in a great variety of shapes, sizes, and decoration, for home and commercial use. What precisely were their feast days and fast days it is hard to know. But the white-plastered altars and votive vessels testify to the fact that they thanked their gods or goddesses for having made them prosperous in their newfound land, and perhaps they toasted them with a juglet of wine from their own vineyards.

Today, the olive trees are few and far between. No sheep dot the countryside here where Israeli husbandry practices are different. No smoke rises from the abandoned kilns. Only the stones remain—stones, mudbrick, and potsherds, telling a story to those who have learned to read them. Some of their story we told our friends that day as we strolled together in Philistia. The rest follows.

PART I

THE ENIGMA
OF THE PHILISTINES

Trude Dothan   Moshe Dothan

CHAPTER 1

Goliath's Legacy

Phil'istine, n. & a. 1. One of an alien warlike people in S. Palestine who harassed the Israelites; (joc.) enemy into whose hands one may fall, e.g., bailiff, critic, etc.; non-student, outsider; uncultured person, one whose interests are material and commonplace, whence phil'istinism n. 2. adj. Uncultured, commonplace, prosaic.

—*Oxford Dictionary of Current English*

If the modern meaning of the word "Philistine" can be said to have a birthplace, it would not be in ancient Canaan during the biblical period, but in the German university town of Jena in 1693. It sprang from a violent encounter between a group of students and a group of townspeople.

The students apparently had been out on the town, drinking at a tavern, when they were assaulted by some local workmen who objected to their presence. Flaring tempers led to blows, and when several badly beaten students stumbled back to the safety of the university, news of the fracas reached the academic authorities.

Pastor Götz, the university chaplain, was particularly outraged by the violence and decided to raise the subject at his coming Sunday sermon. The text he used was Judges 16:20–21, which describes Delilah's betrayal of Samson into the hands of the Philistines. His congregation was, no doubt, familiar with the story of how the Nazarite Samson paid a heavy price for frolicking among the heathen. But if

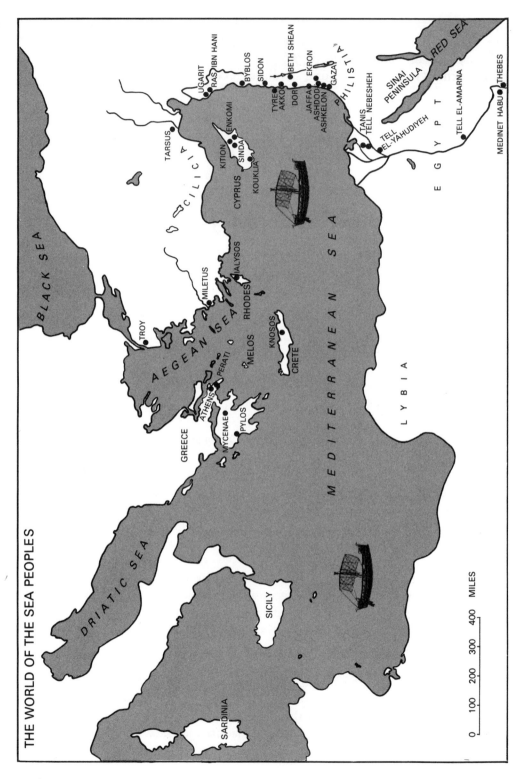

THE WORLD OF THE SEA PEOPLES

RED SEA

SINAI
PENINSULA

E G Y P T

TELL EL-AMARNA

MEDINET HABU • THEBES

UGARIT • • IBN HANI
RAS
BYBLOS •
SIDON •
TYRE • • BETH SHEAN
AKKO • • EKRON
DOR • • GAZA
JAFFA • • ASHDOD
ASHKELON •
P H I L I S T I A

TANIS •
TELL NEBESHEH
TELL
EL-YAHUDIYEH

TARSUS •

C I L I C I A

ENKOMI •
KITION •
SINDA •
CYPRUS
KOUKLIA •

MEDITERRANEAN SEA

BLACK SEA

MILETUS •

IALYSOS •
RHODES •

TROY •

KNOSOS •
MELOS •
CRETE

AEGEAN SEA

PERATI •

ATHENS •
MYCENAE •
PYLOS •

GREECE

L Y B I A

DRIATIC SEA

SICILY

SARDINIA

MILES

0   100   200   300   400

the students thought that their pastor was going to rebuke them for carousing among the townsfolk, they were in for a surprise. Instead, he cast the blame entirely on the crude, unlettered townspeople, who, by attacking God-fearing young scholars, revealed themselves as nothing better than "philistines."

Any student or scholar of the seventeenth century versed in the Holy Scriptures knew the Philistines as one of the most villainous peoples mentioned in the Bible. They were violent, scheming barbarians, sinful pagans who worshiped, among other abominations, a mysterious god called Dagon. And though the precise facts of Philistine history often got lost in the moralizing tone of the biblical narrative, the terrorizing invaders from the distant land of Caphtor seemed to deserve their evil reputation.

The Philistines' encounter with Samson was merely the opening chapter in a long tale of intense hostility. Under the command of *seranim*, or warlords, according to the biblical story, the Philistine forces with their specialized units of foot soldiers, horsemen, archers, and charioteers proved themselves to be a ruthless army of conquest, with unlimited potential for sheer brutality.

After easily crushing a short-lived Israelite rebellion at the time of King Saul and occupying Israelite territory, the Philistines laid waste to the Israelites' sanctuary at Shiloh and, adding desecration to destruction, carried off the Ark of the Covenant as booty. Then to ensure their continued control, they imposed a ban on Israelite metalworking, "lest the Hebrews make themselves swords or spears" [1 Samuel 13:19].

These vivid descriptions of Philistine evil were, of course, merely the prelude to the story of their eventual fall. For just as the Lord had given the Israelites into the hands of the Philistines, the Lord raised up a young shepherd lad of the tribe of Judah to give the Philistines their quietus. A single well-aimed pebble from David's sling suddenly shattered Philistine invincibility. David and his descendants inherited the military, political, and religious control of the country, while Goliath's descendants, consigned to oblivion, inherited only the burden of biblical scorn.

By the seventeenth century, the Philistines were so well established as legendary evildoers that even before Pastor Götz they had begun to appear in the literary idiom of Europe. Cockeram's English lexicon of 1623, for example, defined a "Phylistean embrace" as an attempt "to picke one's purse and cut his throat." Miège's French dictionary of 1688 went a step further and defined the *Philistin* as "a lewd and drunken person, des Debauchez." But after Pastor Götz's sermon, the word *Philister* became a popular item of undergraduate jargon. It served as a handy insult against anyone whose cultural or educational attainments the speaker happened to frown upon. And with that all-embracing connotation of the uncultured barbarian, the word "Philistine" quickly gained currency on the Continent.

Despite Cockeram's lexicon of 1623, however, it took another two centuries before the word was "properly" assimilated into the English language. In 1863 the noted English educator, poet, and social critic Matthew Arnold, in an essay on Heine, wrote: "*Philistinism!*—we have not the expression in English. Perhaps we have not the word because we have so much of the thing." In all his subsequent writings he used the term to mean "an inaccessibility to ideas," a dull-witted materialism and conformity.

PILGRIMS, TRAVELERS, AND DIGGERS

Happily for historical accuracy, there was another dimension to the Philistines' story. With the growth of modern learning, European linguists, historians, and antiquarians initiated the long process of speculation and exploration that would eventually provide a new and more realistic understanding of this ancient people.

Curious European pilgrims, traders, and travelers to the Holy Land found that the Philistines' influence had never really been forgotten there. According to Islamic tradition, the wars of the Israelites and the Philistines were merely a prefiguration of the later victories of the Muslims over the infidels. Islamic legend went so far as to locate the site of the battle between David and Goliath (Daoud and Jalud in Arabic) in the Valley of Esdraelon at the precise spot where the Mamluk armies won a miraculous victory over the invading Mongols in 1263.

The name "Palestine" was itself derived from the Hebrew designation of the Land of Philistines—that is, *Paleshet*, through the ancient Greek *Palaistine*, to the Latin *Palaestina*, and finally to the Arabic *Filastin*. Furthermore, the names of three of the ancient Philistine capitals still clung to their original sites: Ashdod, Ashkelon, and Gaza.

Any traveler of yore making his way along the sandy highway and caravan routes toward Egypt would pass the small village of Esdud, about twenty miles south of Jaffa, whose name and location perfectly matched the ancient Philistine capital of Ashdod. And a few yards to the west of the crumbling village was a mound that the local inhabitants knew as er-Ras Jalud, "Goliath's Head."

The city of Ashkelon, farther down the coast, was easier to find. Its commanding position, perched on the cliffs above the seashore, had ensured its existence as a thriving coastal city well into Crusader times. And though it was reduced to rubble in 1192 on orders from Saladin in his struggle against the armies of Richard the Lionheart during the Third Crusade, it still bore the Arabic version of its Philistine name, Askalan.

At Gaza, or Ghazzeh, the southernmost of the Philistine capitals,
pilgrims could visit the "House of Delilah" in the Jewish Quarter and,
for a few coins, be taken by guides to see a tumble of ruins known as
the Temple of Dagon, which, according to tradition, the desperate,
blind Samson pulled down on the heads of the Philistines gathered
inside. And it was there in Gaza, not long before Pastor Gotz's famous
sermon, that the first halting steps were taken in a new search for the
Philistines.

In 1659 the Chevalier Laurent D'Arvieux, an inquisitive and well-
traveled French merchant, received permission from the Ottoman authorities in Gaza to excavate the Temple of Dagon. A passionate
antiquarian, he eventually compiled six volumes detailing his journeys
throughout the Middle East. Aware that many relics and architectural
monuments had already been dug up by European travelers in the lands
of the Hellenes and Romans, he assumed that he might be able to
uncover vestiges of an even more ancient civilization in the Land of
the Philistines.

D'Arvieux did not consider that in a continuously occupied city like
Gaza, many feet of earth, stones, and debris separated the surface level
from the remains of the Philistine period. Consequently, his pioneering
excavations failed to unearth any meaningful traces of Philistine civilization. Nonetheless, they represented at least the beginning of a new
method of research: D'Arvieux's was the first attempt literally to probe
beneath the surface of biblical myth.

In the self-confident intellectual atmosphere of the Enlightenment, **THE RIDDLE**
when the French Encyclopedists were busily at work reorganizing **OF CAPHTOR**
human knowledge, the Bible was no longer seen only as Holy Scripture.
It was one of several sources that could be used to reconstruct the rise
and development of the entire ancient world. Since the Bible describes
the Philistines as "uncircumcised" aliens, and their system of federated
government under the rule of *seranim* was unique among all the peoples
of Canaan, some scholars believed that in seeking the origins of the
Philistines they might be able to illuminate cross-cultural connections
within the ancient world.

One of them was Dom Calmet, an early eighteenth-century French
linguist and biblical authority who was well versed in the literature and
history of Greece and Rome. He had been in the process of compiling
what he hoped would be the definitive encyclopedia of biblical knowledge when he came up against the problem of the origin of the Philistines. The geographical evidence in the Bible was both obscure and
contradictory.

To begin with, there were two quite distinct origins ascribed to them.

The first, in the "Table of the Nations" [Genesis 10:14], listed the Philistines among the sons of Egypt, not through direct descent but, marginally, in association with an obscure group known as the Caphtorim. In Deuteronomy [2:23] the Caphtorim are said to have occupied part of the coastal strip of southern Canaan that was later to become the Land of the Philistines; and in Amos [9:7], God asks: "Did I not bring up Israel from the land of Egypt and the Philistines from Caphtor?" Nowhere does the Bible offer evidence about the nature of the Caphtorim or the location of their homeland. To make matters even more confusing, as Calmet noted, in Ezekiel [25:16] the Philistines are linked to an equally obscure tribe called the Cherethites, dwelling along the coast. The reference in Zephaniah [2:5] is more direct: after prophesying the destruction of the Philistine capitals of Gaza, Ashkelon, Ashdod, and Ekron, the prophet addresses the Philistines thus: "Woe to you inhabitants of the seacoast, you nation of Cherethites." In other passages the Cherethites are portrayed as mercenaries in the service of the Israelite kings, a description that corresponds to the Philistines' martial image. The origins of both Caphtorim and Cherethites, however, remain geographically obscure. Had Calmet no more evidence than that of the Hebrew Bible to rely on, his investigation might have ended in the same confusion that had plagued earlier scholars. But he was an erudite linguist and had further textual resources.

Turning to the Greek translation of the Old Testament, the Septuagint, compiled in Alexandria in the second century B.C., Calmet discovered that the translators had substituted some well-known geographical place-names for the mysterious Caphtor and Chereth, both with morphological similarities. Caphtor became Cappadocia, an inland region of eastern Asia Minor, and "the nation of Cherethites" became "the nation of Cretans."

Having solved one problem, Calmet was faced with another: Crete and Asia Minor were certainly not the same; for the purpose of his biblical encyclopedia, he had to make a choice. Calmet turned to a nonbiblical source, the *Ethnika*, a voluminous collection of Greek and Latin place-names compiled in the sixth century A.D. by a Greek grammarian named Stephanus of Byzantium. There he discovered that Gaza, the Philistine city, was also called Minoa because Minos and his brothers Aiakos and Radamanthys "went there and gave his name to the city. For this reason there is a sanctuary of the Cretan Zeus, which even now is called Zeus Marnas, an epithet which can be translated Zeus Cretagenes, 'Zeus the Crete-born'. . . ."

This did not yet solve the problem of Caphtor, the other possible Philistine homeland. But Calmet recalled that in Jeremiah 47:4 the Philistines are referred to as "the remnant of the isle of Caphtor."

Cappadocia was no island, but Crete was; perhaps the Septuagint translators had been mistaken. In any case Calmet threw in his lot with Stephanus, Ezekiel, and Zephaniah. When he published his biblical encyclopedia in 1720, modestly entitled *Treatises Serving as an Introduction to the Holy Scripture*, his verdict was that the Philistines had migrated to Canaan from Crete.

The next contribution to the identity of the Philistines was made by another French linguist and historian, a younger contemporary of Calmet, Étienne Fourmant. Fourmant's extraordinary talent for languages—he compiled the first French-Chinese dictionary—was legendary and, convinced that the peoples of ancient Greece and Canaan were related, he attempted a correlation between the biblical genealogies and the royal and mythological lineages provided by the historians of Greece and Rome. When in 1747, under the patronage of Louis XV, he published his widely acclaimed seminal work, *Reflections on the Origin, History, and Genealogy of Ancient Peoples*, Fourmant propounded a surprising theory about the origin and identity of the Philistines.

There was, he noted, a strange passage in the postbiblical Second Book of the Maccabees [5:9] in which Arius, king of Sparta, declares that the Jews and his people are related since both are descended from Abraham. Consequently, Fourmant traced the Spartan family tree back to their first king, Lelex, whose origins in Greek myth were obscure. Fourmant theorized that Lelex was an early leader of the Hebrews who had abandoned home and religion in search of other, more fertile lands. Arriving in Greece, he and his followers adopted the name Pelasgians, which was, according to Fourmant, derived from the same Semitic root as the word "Philistine," that is, פלש, or *p-l-sh*, "to wander" or "to invade."

The Pelasgians, Fourmant continued, were mentioned in the *Iliad* and in other Greek legends as an extremely ancient people, allies of the Trojans, who inhabited discrete areas on the Greek mainland, Asia Minor, and Crete. This would explain, he thought, the contradictions between the various Philistine origins mentioned in the Bible. On the basis of this hypothesis, Fourmant traced the subsequent wanderings of the Pelasgians/Philistines, explaining that after the fall of Troy they returned to Canaan, bringing back with them some of the attributes of Greek culture.

Fourmant's theory marked the beginning of a dramatic change in attitudes toward the character of the Philistines, and as more scholars began to investigate the possible cross-cultural connection, Fourmant's hypothesis began to flesh out. Biblical scholars had little difficulty in pointing out Hellenic elements in Philistine life recorded in the Bible:

the name of one of the late Philistine kings of Gath, Achish, seemed uncannily similar to that of the Trojan prince Anchises; the Philistine title *seren* seemed related to the Greek word *tyrannos*, "tyrant"; and the Philistines' interurban confederacy demanded comparison with the city-state leagues of Greece.

Even more intriguing were the mythic connections. The story of Samson and Delilah closely corresponded to the story of the Megaran king Nisus, whose power-giving lock of red hair was shorn by his deceitful daughter Scylla, when she betrayed him to King Minos of Crete. The famous Goliath was compared in name to Alyattes, founder of the Lydian Empire, and in armor to warriors in the Greek epics. In 1 Samuel 17:5–7 there is a detailed description of his coat of mail, his bronze greaves, helmet and javelin, and his spear with an iron point. The way in which Goliath carried his javelin, "slung between his shoulders" [ibid.], was precisely the way Greek warriors in the *Iliad* fastened their swords. Furthermore, single combat, the mode of Goliath's battle with David, was an accepted, time-honored custom in the Aegean, as in the famous struggle between Hector and Achilles before the walls of Troy.

By the end of the eighteenth century, the Philistines were beginning to be seen by some scholars as a historical people with a definite place in the broader, secular history of the ancient world.

ARYANS OR PHOENICIANS?

In 1845 a German biblical scholar named Ferdinand Hitzig, at work on an ambitious long-term project, *The Ethnic and Mythological History of the Old Testament*, unexpectedly published a slim volume on the Philistines. He noted in the foreword, almost apologetically, that he had often been hindered in his studies by a lack of information about the Israelites' most prominent enemy. His conclusions about the Philistines had proved so startling that he had resolved to publish them without delay.

Hitzig asserted that the Philistines were Pelasgians, and their language derived from Sanskrit and Greek. Their name, originally a racial designation, came from the Sanskrit word *valaxa*, or "white." From Sanskrit and related Indo-Aryan languages, he traced such words as *seren* to *carana*, that is, "house" or "town"; Ashdod to *azada*, meaning "free"; Ashkelon to *ashkalan*, "not wavering"; and Goliath to *galajat*, "magician."

Hitzig rejected out of hand any early familial relations between the Philistines and the Israelites, theorizing that the former were a band of Indo-Aryan mercenaries who migrated from the southern coast of the Black Sea to Crete, and then on to Canaan, speaking a unique dialect of Sanskrit and bringing with them a complete pantheon of Aryan

gods. Marna, for example, the god of Gaza mentioned by Stephanus,
was none other than the Vedic god Varuna, the celestial king. In fact,
he continued, all of Philistine history and culture could be understood
only in the light of its close correspondence with Aryan history and
culture. The real reason for the Philistines' conquest and subjugation
of the Israelites, he implied—ominously—was their racial superiority.
Seductive as this might have been for certain nineteenth-century north
European scholars, the Indo-Aryan explanation was not the only one
put forth.

Another German biblical authority, K. B. Stark, proposed a radically
different interpretation of Philistine history and genealogy. In *Gaza and
the Philistine Coast* he averred that the Philistines were not Indo-Aryans
at all, nor was their language derived from Sanskrit. They were, rather,
a branch of the seafaring Phoenicians, renowned for their overseas
expansion, their culture, and their trade. He offered dozens of equally
probable etymologies from the Hebrew, among them *seren*, from the
Hebrew word for prince, *sar*. Caphtor, he believed, could be located
in the Nile delta.

Despite Stark's dismissal of Hitzig's Indo-Aryan theories, there were
some significant similarities in their approach to the subject. Both had
meticulously analyzed the details of the biblical accounts of the Philistines' wars with the Israelites without any reference to the Bible's
moral judgment of them. And both agreed that the Philistines' complex
military organization, their federated form of government, their monopoly of metalworking, and their elaborate religious rituals were clear
signs of an advanced civilization.

It should be mentioned here that Stark was professor of philology
at the University of Jena and assistant director of the university's archaeological museum. Jena had indeed changed from the times of Pastor
Gotz. No longer was the Bible the sole source of information about
the Philistines. But even imaginative scholars like Hitzig and Stark,
with access to a much broader range of literary evidence, could do little
but speculate without substantial supportive evidence from more detailed ancient records. And although it would take time for the importance of the discovery to be recognized and appreciated, such ancient
records had already been found—about three hundred miles south of
Cairo on the western bank of the Nile.

CHAPTER 2

Invaders from the Sea

Some fifty years before Stark and Hitzig published their speculative theories about the origins of the Philistines, a French scientific expedition uncovered the key to the solution in the ruins of the ancient Egyptian capital of Thebes. In the spring of 1798 a massive French force under Napoleon Bonaparte landed on the beaches near Alexandria. While Napoleon's main intention was to acquire a valuable colony for the young French Republic, hopes for scientific conquest also played some part in his considerations. Along with the cavalry and artillery that quickly overwhelmed the Mamluk rulers of Egypt, Napoleon had also brought along a "Scientific and Artistic Commission." Composed of 167 distinguished scholars and scientists, they immediately began to record and catalog the impressive vestiges of the ancient civilization they found there. For the next three years, Napoleon's cadre of imported savants found evidence that revealed a whole new perspective on the history of the ancient Mediterranean world.

The number of ancient Egyptian monuments mapped and recorded by the team in their southward trek from the Nile delta into the unexplored regions of Upper Egypt was enormous. But what proved to be most important to archaeology was the vivid descriptive nature of ancient Egyptian art. By carefully copying hundreds of ancient reliefs carved on the walls of the monuments, the members of the commission were able to reproduce the gods, king, armies, battles, and everyday life of remote antiquity with an immediacy that written evidence could never provide.

The copious notes, sketches, and architectural studies compiled by the French expedition were later published as an eighteen-volume work entitled *Description de l'Égypte*, and provided later scholars with an independent source of information on the world of biblical times.

The progress of the French explorations of 1798–1803 was determined, naturally, by the pace of Napoleon's military operations. For the first six months, operations were restricted to the northern part of the country. But with the defeat of the Mamluks at the Battle of the Pyramids, and the flight of their leader, Murad Bey, into the inaccessible regions of Upper Egypt, Napoleon assigned General Desaix the task of pursuing him and eliminating this last vestige of opposition to French rule.

One of the most prominent members of the commission was Dominique Vivant Denon. An artist, former diplomat, and man of letters, he was instructed to accompany Desaix's forces into Upper Egypt and record any significant ruins that might be encountered along the way. Although the military objective of this expedition ultimately proved unattainable, scientifically it was a great triumph. Denon was the first modern scholar to examine—and carefully sketch—the monuments of the ancient Egyptian capital of Thebes.

In the late eighteenth century, Thebes was a city enshrouded in legend. Homer had immortalized its magnificence in his description of the "hundred-gated Thebes" in the *Odyssey*. The fifth-century B.C. Greek historian Herodotus had recorded his impressions of a visit to the city, even then still a center of Egyptian tradition. With the arrival of the French troops, after a difficult march of three hundred miles up the Nile from Cairo, the ruins of ancient Thebes were found to be even more impressive than the myths.

On the eastern bank of the river stood the massive Temples of Luxor and Karnak, their gates and walls covered with elaborate carvings of gods, kings, and hieroglyphic inscriptions, their papyrus bud columns towering above the modern mudbrick houses huddled in the ancient temple precincts.

On the western bank were equally impressive ruins, which Denon tried to record in his notebooks. At one point, he noted in his journals, he had remained behind to complete some sketches when suddenly he became "alarmed at my unprotected situation" in what was still hostile enemy territory. He raced to catch up with his colleagues, whose "eager curiosity had led them to a large temple near the village of Medinet Habu."

SKETCHES OF
AN ANCIENT
STRUGGLE

The Temple of Medinet Habu was by far the most impressive monument on the western side of Thebes. A high fortified gateway opened onto a broad courtyard beyond which rose the facade of the inner temple structure, still preserved to its original height of ninety feet. Carved on both sides of the entrance portal were colossal scenes of an ancient Egyptian king smiting groups of frightened captives, whom he grasped by the hair and threatened with a mace. Denon assumed that this was a memorial to some great victory. His supposition was confirmed when he examined the reliefs on the inner colonnades of the temple, also decorated with depictions of the same martial theme.

While Denon recognized the carvings as important historical records, he was unable to read the hieroglyphic inscriptions identifying the events and personalities depicted. Relying on Herodotus, therefore, he assumed that he had found confirmation of the historian's reports of the victories of the Egyptian king Sesostris in India. (As scholars later learned, Sesostris, who reigned during the Middle Kingdom, c.2050–1786 B.C., never waged war so far afield.) Denon carefully recorded the vivid scenes showing the Egyptians fighting hand to hand with their enemies; the bound captives marching in procession; and a chaotic naval scene filled with tangled ships and drowning sailors, all serenely watched from the shore by the oversized figure of a king. Denon was percipient enough to note that among the physical types shown on the walls of the Medinet Habut temple were certain figures that "have not the least resemblance to known forms of Egyptian heads."

These strange figures were always depicted as enemies or captives, and their characteristic costumes and facial features were unique (plate 2). Unlike the bareheaded Egyptian soliders, they had distinctive "feathered" headdresses, secured with straps under their chins (plate 3). They wore short, kiltlike garments with prominent tassels, and some of the warriors also wore close-fitting ribbed corselets on their upper torsos.

Medinet Habu mortuary temple of Ramesses III, Thebes.

15

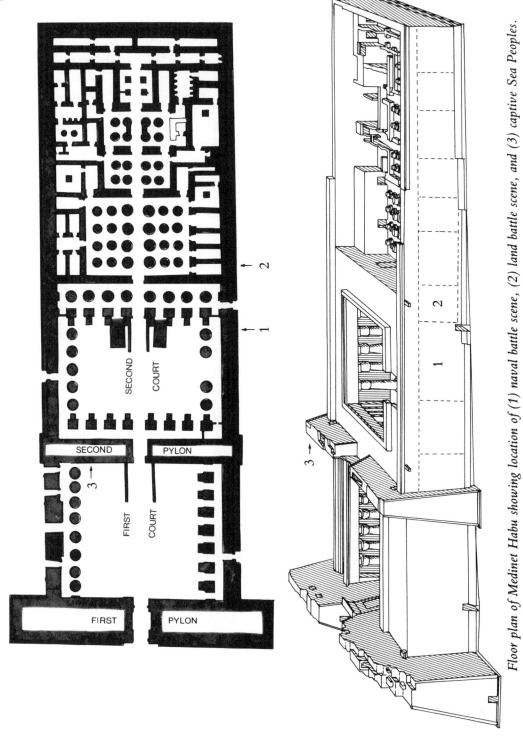

Floor plan of Medinet Habu showing location of (1) naval battle scene, (2) land battle scene, and (3) captive Sea Peoples.

SECOND COURT

SECOND PYLON

FIRST COURT

FIRST PYLON

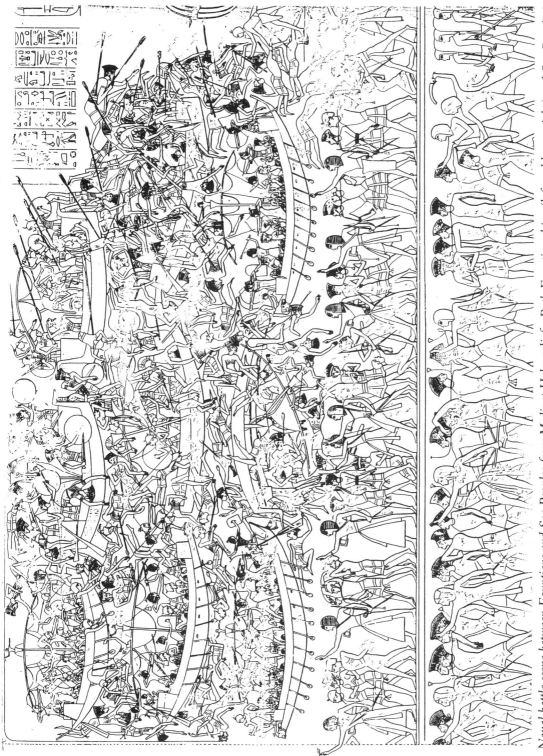

Naval battle scene between Egyptians and Sea Peoples from Medinet Habu reliefs. Both Egyptian ships (left and lower right) and Sea Peoples' (center and upper right) have sails, here furled, a single mast with crow's nest, identical rigging, and brails, devices for shortening a sail, which appear here for the first time in history. The Egyptian oars are rectangular; those of the Sea Peoples are stowed, as if they had been caught by surprise. Egyptian shields are rectangular, those of the Sea Peoples rounded. The Sherden (center) wear horned headdresses, whereas the Philistines and other Sea Peoples wear characteristic feathered headdresses, apparently attached to a metal band. The Egyptians use bows, the Sea Peoples long spears.

The inscription identifies three groups of Sea Peoples—the Philistines, the Tjekker, and the Denyen. The captives are manacled and stripped of weapons. The prisoners may have been stripped of their corselets, for they seem to be wearing only a plain shirt or jerkin, or possibly a smooth, one-piece breastplate. All wear the characteristic feathered headdresses.

In the few instances where their women were depicted, they were shown with long-flowing hair and clothed in long dresses. Denon logically, if mistakenly, concluded that if the scene was in India, the captives were Hindus. It would take another generation of scholarship to establish their true identity—as Philistines.

Jean François Champollion was only eight years old when Denon was making his sketches, but at the age of thirty-two he was able to provide the linguistic tool by which the archaeological discoveries of Napoleon's savants could be placed in their proper historical context. In 1822 he delivered an epoch-making lecture to members of the French Académie des Inscriptions et Belles Lettres in Paris on his system for deciphering Egyptian hieroglyphics. Six years later Champollion himself led a new French expedition to Egypt, this one without cavalry and artillery. New drawings and transcriptions of the reliefs had to be made if they were to be properly understood and translated.

It was not, however, until the spring of 1829, almost a year after they had arrived in Egypt, that Champollion and his entourage were finally ready to tackle the antiquities of Thebes. While a group of his draftsmen began their work at the Temples of Luxor and Karnak, Champollion crossed over to the western bank and began his own inspection of the Temple of Medinet Habu.

Champollion recognized that the function of the Medinet Habu, like that of several other monuments on the western side of the Nile, was to serve as a funerary temple, memorializing the earthly achievements of an Egyptian king. The cartouches, or royal names and titles carved beside the colossal human figure throughout the temple, showed that the king in question was not the semilegendary Sesostris, but Usermare Meryamun Ramesses, better known to future generations as Ramesses III (plate 1).

It would still take several decades to establish the precise dates of the reign of Ramesses III, now believed to have extended from 1190 to 1165 B.C.* But Champollion was the first modern scholar to recognize that the battle reliefs in the temple were a sequential account of the greatest victories of Ramesses III in a desperate defense of Egypt itself, not a campaign in some far-off country.

In the first scene, according to the deciphered captions, Ramesses was shown mobilizing his forces, distributing weapons, and personally leading the army off to war. In the next scene, the Egyptian forces could be seen inflicting a massacre on the warriors wearing the strange

---

*We feel no need to burden the reader with the problems of high, low, and middle chronologies. Suffice it to say that we are using here the much-debated High Egyptian Chronology. Low chronology would date Ramesses III to about fifteen years later.

Detail of Egyptian ship, with lion-headed prow and undecorated stern.

Detail of Sea Peoples' ship, with bird head at either end.

Land battle scene between Ramesses III and the Sea Peoples, from the Medinet Habu reliefs. The Philistine camp under Egyptian attack is composed of three separate units: the non-combatant civilians, including women and children; the chariotry; and the infantry. Chariots are drawn by two horses and have six-spoked wheels. The infantry fights in small phalanxes of four men, three armed with a long, straight sword and a pair of spears, the fourth with only a sword. All carry round shields and wear the feathered headdress.

"feathered" headdresses and on their women and children, who had for some mysterious reason come along to the battlefield in heavy oxcarts. In the last scene of this series, a second enemy, wearing round helmets with horns, was depicted. The chaotic tangle of ships and sailors, which Denon assumed was a panicked flight into the Indus, was actually a detailed portrayal of a battle at the mouth of the Nile.

Because the events of the reign of Ramesses III were unknown from other sources, the context of this particular war remained a mystery. On his return to Paris, Champollion puzzled over the identity of the various enemies shown in the scene. Since each of them had been carefully labeled with a hieroglyphic inscription, he hoped to match the names with those of ancient tribes and peoples mentioned in Greek and Hebrew texts. Unfortunately, Champollion died in 1832 before he could complete the work, but he did have success with one of the names.

proved to be none other than the biblical Philistines.

DR. GREENE'S UNEXPECTED DISCOVERY

The fact that the reliefs mentioned the Philistines by name and rendered their physical appearance, their costumes, armor, weapons, and even their wagons and ships, provided one of the first solid connections between the Bible and ancient Egyptian history. Yet no battle between the Philistines and the Egyptians was mentioned in the biblical narratives. It was difficult to understand just how the clashes depicted on the Medinet Habu reliefs fit into the stories of the Philistines' wars with the Israelites. Other questions were equally puzzling: Who were the other invading peoples fighting alongside the Philistines? And what had provoked Ramesses III to engage them in war?

While biblical scholars and Egyptologists debated the implications of the Medinet Habu findings, a young Scot named John Baker Greene provided some dramatic new on-the-spot evidence. Wintering in Egypt after his graduation from the Medical School of the University of Dublin, Greene decided that he might be able to make a contribution to the new science of Egyptology by digging in the precincts of the Medinet Habu temple. He ordered his hired laborers, *fellahin*, to start in the huge gateway between the first and second courtyards. His archaeological instinct was uncanny: the workers quickly uncovered twenty-five lines of a long hieroglyphic inscription of which Champollion had never seen more than the first.

Greene could not read the inscription, but on his return to Europe he sought the assistance of the Vicomte Emanuel DeRouge, a senior curator at the Louvre and Champollion's successor to the professorship of Egyptian archaeology at the Collège de France. The study of Egyptian language and history had by now far outstripped the development of archaeological technique, and when DeRouge examined Greene's drawings and photographic plates, he understood that the young doctor had uncovered a vivid narrative explaining the background and outcome of the war between Ramesses III and the Philistines.

The new text provided the precise date of the conflict—the eighth year of the reign of the pharaoh (reckoned by scholars to be 1191 B.C.)—and also explained that the invasion of Egypt by the Philistines and their allies was only the last phase in a wave of destruction that had swept through most of the known world:

> The foreign countries made a conspiracy in their islands. All at once the lands were removed and scattered in the fray. No land could stand before their arms, from Hatti, Kode, Carchemish, Arzawa, Alashiya on, being cut off [at one time]. A camp [was set up] in one place in Amor. They desolated its people, and its land was like that which has never come into being. They were coming forward to Egypt, while the flame was being prepared before them. Their confederation was the Philistines, Tjekker, Sheklesh, Denyen, and Weshesh, lands united. They laid their hands upon lands as far as the circuit of the earth, their hearts confident and trusting, "Our plans will succeed."

In the decades that followed DeRouge's first translation, the precise route of the invasion became a matter of scholarly dispute. But several of the geographical references were commonly accepted: Hatti was the Hittite Empire of central Asia Minor, Kode was farther south on the Asia Minor coast, Alashiya was probably the island of Cyprus, and Amor was somewhere along the coast of the Levant. The general direction of the invasion was, apparently, from the area of the Aegean toward Egypt, though where the Philistines joined it was unclear. In any event there was some advance warning of the impending invasion, for the text went on to reveal the preparations made by Ramesses III:

> I organized my frontier in Djahi, prepared before them: princes, commanders of garrisons, and charioteers. I had the river mouths prepared like a strong wall, with warships, galleys, and coasters [fully equipped], for they were manned completely from bow to stern with valiant warriors carrying their weapons.

DeRouge believed that Djahi was biblical Canaan, which would confirm identification of one of the enemies as the Philistines. The end of the inscription was devoted to the outcome of the invasion and corresponded to the reliefs:

> Those who reached my frontier, their seed is not, their heart and soul are finished forever and ever. Those who came forward on the sea, the full flame was in front of them at the river mouths, while a stockade of lances surrounded them on the shore. They were dragged in, enclosed, and prostrated on the beach, killed and made into heaps from tail to head. Their ships and their goods were as if fallen into the water.

While the tone of the inscription could be dismissed as royal propaganda, DeRouge believed that the account of the war contained far-reaching historical evidence. His translation was privately published by Greene in 1856 in a handsome volume, *Fouilles à Thèbes* (Excavation at Thebes), and the collaboration between the Scotsman and the Frenchman ultimately prompted scholars to make a complete reassessment of the extent of contact between Egypt and the rest of the Mediterranean world.

AN AEGEAN HYPOTHESIS

In 1863 DeRouge made his first expedition to Egypt and undertook his own examination of the other monument of ancient Thebes. He succeeded in finding some previously neglected evidence linking the war of the Philistines to earlier wars and invasions of Egypt, and through them to various population movements mentioned in the legends and traditions of early Greek history.

DeRouge's first clue came when he visited Luxor, which by this time was one of the most famous sites in Egypt and had already provided scholars with information about one of the great victories of Ramesses II (c.1304–1237 B.C.), at Qadesh in northern Syria. DeRouge believed that there might be evidence hidden in the ancient account of this battle that would shed some light, however indirectly, on the origin and early history of the Philistines.

For an expert in hieroglyphics like DeRouge, translating the Luxor inscription was easier than assessing its significance. Beneath the scenes of the battle was a long poem praising Ramesses II's great victory and listing the northern peoples who had joined the enemy cause. The list seemed to be arranged geographically, and the section that described the peoples of western Asia Minor was of particular interest. It was there, according to Greek mythology, that the Trojan War had taken place. Much to his amazement, DeRouge found the names of several peoples that seemed remarkably similar to the peoples mentioned in the *Iliad* as Troy's allies. Among them were the Masa, the Lukka, and the Derden, whom DeRouge identified, respectively, with the Mysians, Priam's faithful recruits; the Apollo-worshiping Lycians; and—most dramatically—the Dardanians, the race of the Trojans themselves.

This turned out not to be the only case of correspondence between Egyptian and Greek records. At the Temple of Karnak in the northern part of the ancient city, DeRouge identified and translated a later inscription concerning a victory by Merneptah, Ramesses II's son and successor, which contained what he believed to be even more convincing proof of early Aegean-Egyptian contact. It described an invasion of Egypt in about 1232 B.C. by a hostile confederation that included a number of previously unmentioned peoples coming from the "countries of the sea."

There were the Tursha, whom DeRouge identified with Aeneas and the Etruscans, and the Akaiwasha, whom he took to be none other than the common name of the Greeks in the *Iliad*, King Agamemnon's Achaeans.

On his return to France, DeRouge wrote an article for the *Revue Archéologique* (1867) in which he laid out the conclusions he had drawn from his research at Luxor, Karnak, and Medinet Habu. The article, entitled "Attacks Directed Against Egypt by the Peoples of the Mediterranean," suggested that the Trojan War had caused great disturbances and movements of population throughout the eastern Mediterranean. Furthermore, wrote DeRouge, the invasion of Egypt by the Philistines and their allies was the last and greatest of these attacks.

DeRouge's hypothesis was greeted by cries of outrage from both biblical and classical scholars, who resented his attempt to confirm hazy legendary traditions on the basis of archaeological finds. This was still a few years before Heinrich Schliemann's excavations at Troy, and little credence was given to the historical reliability of Homer. As for the participation of the Philistines in an Aegean confederacy, there seemed to be a serious gap in the evidence.

If the Philistines were settled on the southern coast of Canaan, hundreds of miles from the Aegean, what could explain their joining a group of seaborne raiders who had been involved in the Trojan War? Fortunately, the Medinet Habu reliefs, which had been so carefully copied by the members of Napoleon's commission, offered additional evidence. Two of DeRouge's students, François Chabas and Gaston Maspero, proposed that the Philistines themselves had come from the Aegean.

Chabas, a middle-aged Bordeaux wine merchant who had taken up Egyptology in his retirement, was intrigued by the scene in the reliefs which showed the Philistines accompanied by their women and children in unwieldy oxcarts. These carts could certainly not have been used in a lightning raid across the border. To Chabas they suggested, rather, a long migration in search of new territory, in which the prospective settlers traveled with their families and all their household effects. As to the starting point of this hypothesized migration, there was evidence from Herodotus and the historian Strabo, writing four hundred years later, that sailors along the Aegean coasts of Asia Minor were long known for their "feathered crests." Following Champollion's attempts to link the peoples of the earlier invasions with various Greek ethnic groups, Chabas now suggested that the Philistines' allies, the Tjekker, might be the followers of the Greek hero Teucer, the Teucrians, and the Denyen, the Danaans of Argolis.

Maspero, who was later to succeed to DeRouge's professorship at the Collège de France and, ultimately, to the directorship of the Egyptian Antiquities Service, took this idea a step further. Chabas's theories

Detail of land battle. A spokeless-wheeled wagon harnessed to a team of four oxen is caught up in battle while carrying women and children to settle in territories conquered by Sea People warriors. The carts are built of crossed bars of wood or woven weeds. Similar carts are used today in parts of the Middle East.

of Philistine migration from the Aegean, he believed, could be fitted into the scheme of biblical history. Since the Bible notes that the Philistines were migrants to Canaan from "the coastline of Caphtor," tentatively identified with Crete, the Medinet Habu reliefs actually showed them at the time of their arrival in the eastern Mediterranean. Maspero further suggested, on the basis of what he believed was conclusive new evidence, that the Philistines' defeat by Ramesses III was the *reason* for their eventual settlement along the Canaanite coast.

This new evidence was a huge papyrus acquired by the British Museum in the 1870s from the collection of an antiquities dealer, Anthony Harris. Composed soon after the death of Ramesses III, the document reported that while exterminating or enslaving many of the invaders, Ramesses also thought it expedient to settle some of them in mercenary garrisons in his lands:

> I extended the frontiers of Egypt and overthrew those who had attacked them from their lands. I slew the Denyen in their islands, while the Tjekker and Philistines were made ashes. The Sherden and the Weshesh of the sea were made non-existent, captured all together and brought in captivity to Egypt like the sands of the shore. Their military classes were as numerous as hundred-thousands. I assigned portions for them all with clothing and provisions from the treasuries and granaries every year.

This passage suddenly bridged the gap between the reliefs of Medinet Habu and the stories in Judges and Samuel. For if Maspero was right, the long-standing war between the Israelites and the Philistines, including the rampages of Samson and the battle between David and Goliath, was just a lingering aftereffect of Ramesses III's desperate attempts to save his crumbling empire. Biblical scholars had previously had no larger political and military context to explain Philistine possession of their coastal enclave. But now the background was clearer. The Philistines, Maspero explained, had migrated from the Aegean at the beginning of the twelfth century B.C., and, after an unsuccessful attempt to stop them, Ramesses III settled a significant number as vassals in the Egyptian-ruled cities of the Canaanite coast. It was inevitable that the newly hired guardians of the old order would come into conflict with the Israelites and the other subject peoples of Canaan.

This deft reconstruction of accumulated evidence was the crowning achievement of nearly a century of exploration, discovery, and research. What had previously been surmised from the Bible and Greek legend was now found written on parchment and chiseled in stone. Maspero had demonstrated that the Philistines were part of a great migration from the Aegean to the eastern Mediterranean, and in identifying the various invaders, as did DeRouge and Chabas, with peoples mentioned in Greek history and legend, he coined a term that has been used to describe them ever since: *Les Peuples de la Mer*, the Peoples of the Sea.

The story, of course, was not yet complete. What had happened in the Aegean homelands to produce the Philistine invasion of Egypt could not be inferred from the Medinet Habu reliefs. These broader historical issues would soon emerge from the digging at sites hardly less shrouded in legend than those of Egypt: the cities of the Homeric epics on the mainland of Greece.

CHAPTER 3

The Clue
of the Potsherds

Heinrich Schliemann began his preliminary excavations of Troy in 1870. Until then, the legends of the Greek heroic age, preserved so vividly in the *Iliad* and the *Odyssey*, had never been confirmed by archaeological evidence. Homer had described the great cities and people that had flourished there in remote times until the fall of Troy, the date of which, according to Thucydides (fifth century B.C.), was the equivalent of 1184 B.C. This date, it should be recalled, is strikingly close to the eighth year of the reign of the pharaoh, reckoned by later scholars to be 1191 B.C.—that is, the date of the battle depicted in the reliefs of Medinet Habu.

While scholars largely discounted Schliemann's claims to having found the "Treasure of Priam" at Troy and the "Tomb of Agamemnon" at Mycenae, even the most cautious of them had to admit that the remains of the Bronze Age civilization found at sites prominently described in the Homeric epics might represent a previously unrecognized chapter of early Greek history and validate sources that had been dismissed as mythical.

Before Schliemann, every schoolchild was taught that the history of Greek civilization began with the celebration of the First Olympiad in 776 B.C. The heroic struggle between the Achaeans and the Trojans beneath the walls of Troy was attributed to poetic imagination. Schliemann's discovery of burial offerings, pottery, weapons, fortifications, and palaces that closely corresponded to Homer's descriptions tangibly confirmed the early foundations of Greek civilization.

Schliemann called this newfound culture Mycenaean, after the citadel of Mycenae on the Greek mainland, the traditional site of Agamemnon's capital. Before long, numerous expeditions from the museums and universities of Europe were intently digging for Homeric history at Mycenaean sites. The excavations on the mainland and on the islands, which showed the striking uniformity of Mycenaean culture, tended to substantiate the legends describing Agamemnon's power and wealth. With the scholarly work of two other German archaeologists, Adolf Furtwängler and Georg Loeschcke, it soon became evident how Mycenaean culture had slowly developed over the span of centuries and how far its influence had ultimately spread.

While most attention was predictably drawn to the spectacular finds—massive fortification systems, bronze armor and weapons, precious grave offerings—Furtwängler and Loeschcke concentrated on the thousands of fragments of characteristic Mycenaean painted pottery found at every level, recognizing that these fragments could provide a continuous view of the development of the culture. By classifying all known examples of Mycenaean pottery from excavations, museums, and private collections, they were able to distinguish four successive stages of artistic development. Beginning with naturalistic floral representations in the First and Second styles, the Mycenaean potters' art gradually became more abstract and stylized. By the Third Style, it had reached a level of uniformity that suggested a central place of production, perhaps Mycenae itself, for the entire Aegean world. The final, Fourth Style, they believed, coincided with the end of Mycenaean culture, and indicated a sudden breakdown of artistic uniformity and the appearance of regional divergence. This last development, which may have reflected political disintegration, seemed to have occurred close to the time of the Sea Peoples' migrations in the twelfth century B.C.

There was little question that the uniform Third Style represented Mycenaean culture at its highest. Nearly identical vessels were found as far from the Greek mainland as Sicily, Rhodes, Cyprus, and even Egypt. In 1889 the British archaeologist William Matthew Flinders Petrie was excavating New Kingdom tombs in the Fayum district of Middle Egypt when he came upon plentiful deposits of Mycenaean pottery, datable by the royal Egyptian scarabs found with them. They ranged in time from Pharaoh Thutmosis III in the fifteenth century B.C., through the time of Amenhotep III in the fourteenth, and down to the reign of Ramesses III in the twelfth. They showed that Egypt's contact with Aegean culture was not restricted to isolated waves of invasion but was apparently the result of cultural and, perhaps, even commercial contact.

Petrie was of the opinion that the presence of Mycenaean pottery in Egypt signified the physical presence of groups of migrants and settlers from the Aegean. He was convinced, therefore, that the discovery of additional examples of such pottery in the eastern Mediterranean might provide evidence of the settlement of the Sea Peoples themselves. In an article entitled "The Egyptian Bases of Greek History," published in 1890 in the *Journal of Hellenic Studies*, Petrie went even further and suggested that the Sea Peoples' invasion of Egypt was part of a long and intimate series of cultural interactions between the Aegean and eastern Mediterranean worlds.

That same year Petrie went to Palestine for the Palestine Exploration Fund (P.E.F.), to excavate the ancient Judean city mound of Tell el-Hesy. The P.E.F. had been founded in 1865 by a group of British churchmen, philanthropists, and biblical scholars who hoped, somewhat paradoxically, that the science of archaeology would help restore faith in the accuracy of biblical tradition, much of which was being eroded by Darwinism. At Tell el-Hesy, Petrie was able to distinguish characteristic archaeological artifacts of the Canaanite and Israelite cultures, previously known primarily from scriptural references. And some years later it was Petrie who selected Tell el-Safi, the site of ancient Philistine Gath, for the P.E.F., now interested in verifying the historical nature of the biblical Philistines.

What Schliemann had done at Agamemnon's Mycenae, the P.E.F. now hoped to do at Goliath's Gath. In 1899 two young explorers, Frederick Bliss, who had worked with Petrie in Egypt and at Tell el-Hesy, and Robert A. S. Macalister, who had done work on ancient settlements and cemeteries in the British Isles, were entrusted with the mission and set up their tents at the site, twelve miles inland from the Mediterranean. Their scientific method was based on the principles that Schliemann had introduced and that Petrie had refined—namely, that superimposed layers of ancient settlements and changing styles of pottery offered more important clues to a civilization than literary references or historical theories.

After a few weeks of digging, the two men were able to distinguish a clear cultural sequence for Tell el-Safi's history, identifying four superimposed strata of occupation that extended, they believed, from around 1700 B.C. to the time of the construction of the Crusader fortress of Blanche Garde in the twelfth century A.D.

They had dug a series of trial pits down to the bedrock at several points across the surface, all of whose results were identical. Immediately beneath the modern ground level came a layer containing medieval pottery sherds that could be connected with the Crusader settlement. Farther down was a layer whose artifacts included jar handles bearing Hebrew stamp impressions that could be connected with the Israelite monarchy. At the bottom of the debris were two layers containing pottery that Petrie had defined as "pre-Israelite." Bliss and Macalister subsequently instructed their workers to open a large excavation area in which the structural remains they uncovered confirmed the historical divisions revealed by the pottery. And from the earth around the tangle of mudbrick and stone structures of the "late pre-Israelite period," they collected thousands of sherds of distinctive local pottery, some of them elaborately decorated. But more important, they found a handful of Mycenaean sherds of the Third Style, identical to those found by Petrie in Egypt.

MYCENAEAN STYLES AND THE PHILISTINES

Although somewhat disappointing in quantity, the Mycenaean sherds were the first recognizable evidence of Aegean culture at a Philistine site. Because the study of Mycenaean pottery styles had, by now, become a field for specialists, the P.E.F. called in F. B. Welch, a scholar from the British School of Archaeology in Athens. Welch had been the pottery expert at the British excavations at Phylakopi on the island of Melos, and on his way to Palestine he conducted his own excavations at some tombs in Cyprus. After examining the Tell el-Safi/Gath sherds, Welch could make only a cautious statement. Since the Third Style Mycenaean finds were fewer than might have been expected had they been the Philistines' distinctive class of pottery, their appearance, he wrote, was "suggestive, in light of the probable northwestern origin of the Philistines."

This was the first formal attempt to link the Philistines with Mycenaean culture, but it was obviously not very substantial. If the Philistines had occupied the city for several centuries, they must have left more impressive archaeological traces. This, at least, was the opinion of Dr. Hermann Thiersch, a member of the Imperial German Archaeological Institute, who had come to Palestine to scout locations for a projected German excavation and was interested in the findings of his British colleagues. He agreed with Bliss and Macalister that Tell el-Safi was the site of Philistine Gath, but when he examined their drawings of the local pottery, published in their reports, his interest was immediately drawn not to the Mycenaean vessels, but to a distinctive class of local pottery from the late pre-Israelite level, unique in its decoration and shape.

The best-preserved example was a nearly complete jug, about eleven inches high, with an unusual "strainer spout" on its shoulder, and an

Philistine strainer-spout jug
found at Tell el-Safi.

elaborate zone of red and black decoration featuring a highly stylized
bird on its upper half. All were made from the local light reddish clay
covered with a thin white wash, and had surprisingly uniform decorative motifs in red and black—either the stylized bird, or checkerboard
patterns or spirals filled with Maltese crosses. Welch had ascribed this
developed artistic tradition to a late and debased continuation of the
Mycenaean tradition. Macalister admitted that he had found "no very
close analogues in the parallel art of contemporary races." Thiersch,
however, was of a different opinion. A student of Adolf Furtwängler,
the pioneer in the study of Mycenaean pottery, he recognized that the
shapes of the Tell el-Safi vessels—the deep kraters, the small bowls
with horizontal handles, the strainer jugs, and the stirrup jars—were,
despite their relatively crude clay finish, faithful reproductions of My-

Monochrome bowl found at
Tell el-Safi (the Philistine city
of Gath).

33

cenaean prototypes. Their closest stylistic parallels came from Furt-wängler's Fourth Style, when the centers of production had disintegrated. Whether the cause was the aftereffects of the Trojan War, the invasion of the Dorians, or a historical circumstance as yet unknown, the appearance of a unique continuation of the Mycenaean tradition at Tell el-Safi, at precisely the same time that the Sea Peoples were known to have arrived in the eastern Mediterranean, was too much of a concidence to be accidental. And although it would be several years before Thiersch's theory would become generally accepted, the historical and cultural significance of the black and red painted vessels would eventually lead to other discoveries. Archaeology was beginning to retrieve another ancient people from the haze of legend and fragmentary textual references.

THE CRETAN CONNECTION AGAIN

This was an important archaeological breakthrough, yet it only pushed the ultimate question about the Philistines' origin and character one step further back. There were as yet no known reasons for the sudden collapse of Aegean civilization. It took the excavations of Arthur Evans at Knossos on Crete to reveal that the Mycenaean culture described in Homer represented only the *concluding* chapter of Bronze Age Aegean history.

Evans was determined to show that legends of the Cretan king Minos and his vast maritime empire were no less trustworthy than the Homeric accounts of Agamemnon. In the spring of 1900, Evans and his chief assistant, Dr. Duncan Mackenzie of the British School of Archaeology at Athens, directed a large team of workmen to dig into the mound of Kephala just outside Heraklion, a site traditionally identified as Knossos, Minos's capital. Just beneath the surface, the workers uncovered a succession of lavish palaces, storerooms, and administrative centers whose distinctive culture, which Evans called "Minoan," reached back centuries before the earlier Mycenaean finds. And in the southwestern corridor of one of the palaces they found a "Cupbearer Fresco," with a slim, kilted figure carrying his offering.

Ever since Calmet's speculation, almost two hundred years ealier, that Crete was the biblical island of Caphtor and, therefore, the homeland of the Philistines, certain evidence to the contrary had, literally, surfaced. In the New Kingdom tombs on the western side of Thebes, connected with Thutmosis III (c.1503–1450 B.C.), reliefs of slim, kilted figures bearing precious offerings to the pharaoh were identified as "ambassadors from Kephtiu." The connection of Kephtiu with Caphtor was not only phonetic: geographical documents were uncovered indicating that Kephtiu lay across the "Great Green" or the Mediterranean; and, after Schliemann, the shapes of the vases carried by the ambassadors were recognized by some scholars as Mycenaean. Caphtor/Kephtiu was assumed to be an ancient designation for the Greek mainland. Now, at Knossos, the tide turned again and Calmet appeared to be vindicated.

More than merely establishing the likely Cretan origin of the ambassadors from Kephtiu, Evans's discoveries—among them Egyptian artifacts—offered a new interpretation of the whole range of ancient connections between the Aegean and the Near East. By studying the pottery, Mackenzie came to the conclusion that the Mycenaean pottery found on the mainland was not more than a late and degenerate expression of the much earlier Minoan styles. And by dating several of the levels at Knossos by the Egyptian artifacts and their inscriptions, he was able to subdivide the impressive range of Minoan history into Early, Middle, and Late periods, extending from approximately 2500 to 1050 B.C. The final flowering of Minoan culture, according to Mackenzie, was represented by the richly decorated vessels of Knossian "Palace Ware" of the Late Minoan II period, that is, 1450–1400 B.C., or precisely when the ambassadors from Kephtiu appeared in the Egyptian tomb paintings of the XVIIIth Dynasty.

Both Evans and Mackenzie believed, then, that the so-called Mycenaean culture was simply a colonial offshoot of Minoan civilization, and that the common Mycenaean vessels, even if they were produced on the mainland, were really products of the Late Minoan III period on Crete (c.1400–1050 B.C.). This was the period, according to Evans, after the last palace at Knossos had been destroyed by an invasion of former colonial subjects from the mainland, who took over Minoan civilization for themselves. The rise of the Mycenaean king Agamemnon, the Trojan War, and the impressive citadels on the mainland could thus all be seen as indications of the breakdown of Minoan power. Furthermore, Evans and Mackenzie asserted, this political development had driven a stream of refugees from Crete toward their former trading grounds in the Near East.

This reconstruction of Aegean history would subsequently undergo many revisions, but Evans's excavations at Knossos had made one thing clear: the interaction between Aegean and Near Eastern cultures had to be viewed over a period of centuries and not simply at the moment of the Sea Peoples' invasions.

An additional piece of evidence relating to the Philistines was found by Italian excavators in 1908, digging at the Minoan palace near Phaistos, near the southern coast of the island. It was a clay disc stamped with pictographic symbols, among which were a warrior's head crowned with what seemed to be a "feathered headdress," ships, and weapons. It was dated from the Middle Minoan III period (c.1600 B.C.),

Clay disc with pictographic symbols found at Phaistos, Crete, in 1908.

and its significance became a matter of intense scholarly interest since it was suggestive of the Philistines and the other Sea Peoples. But the inscription and even its language are puzzling to scholars. Evans suggested that it was not produced on Crete but merely deposited there by sailors or traders from the Aegean coast of Asia Minor. Nevertheless, it did indicate the continued involvement of the Sea Peoples in the rise and fall of Minoan sea trade.

TO THE TEMPLE OF THE SUN

During the first decade of the twentieth century there was a certain amount of archaeological "cross-fertilization." While Evans and his staff revealed the splendor of the ancient palaces of Knossos, excavations at Philistine sites in Palestine continued. The connections between the two were to grow. In 1904, Duncan Mackenzie traveled to Palestine to visit the excavations of Macalister, who had by now moved on to Gezer, another biblical Philistine settlement. Mackenzie surprised and delighted Macalister by identifying a sherd of pottery found in an earlier level as an example of the most characteristic type of Knossian "Palace Ware." He also pointed out the foundations of a structure at Gezer that he believed might have been a Minoan-style palace. Both of his identifications proved to be mistaken, but they did have the effect of persuading the P.E.F. that the future of Philistine studies lay in the direction of Crete.

In 1910, after the completion of the Gezer excavations, the P.E.F. began to look for a new project, one that could expand on the Minoan connection. Macalister had decided to accept a professorship at the National University of Ireland in the meantime, but before he left he agreed to travel through the country to select a promising spot for the next excavation. The site he eventually recommended was a mound about sixteen miles west of Jerusalem, identified with the ancient city of Beth Shemesh, "House of the Sun" or "Temple of the Sun" in Hebrew. In modern Arabic it had survived as Ain Shems, "Fountain of the Sun." In biblical times, the town had been on the border of the territory of the tribe of Judah, and was a focal point in the wars between the Israelites and the Philistines. It was to Beth Shemesh that the Philistines had returned the Israelites' Holy Ark after it had caused a plague in their midst [1 Samuel 6]. Beth Shemesh offered not only a view of Philistine culture from an Israelite perspective. Its name hinted at sun worship, which was, in the opinion of Arthur Evans, now a member of the executive of the P.E.F., an important characteristic of Minoan civilization.

Mackenzie was chosen to direct the Beth Shemesh excavations because of his extensive experience in the Aegean and Crete, and his reputation as an international authority on Minoan pottery styles. The

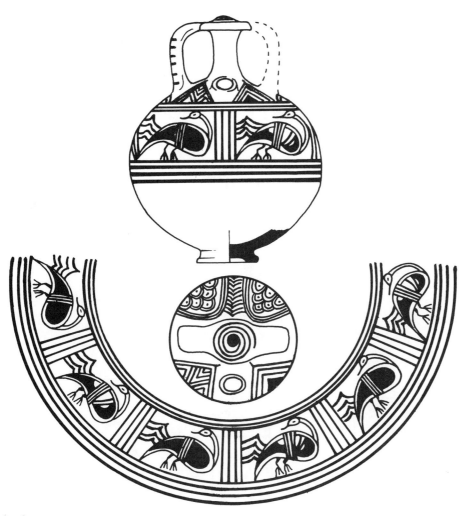

*Stirrup jar found by Macalister
expedition at Gezer.*

biblical connections of Beth Shemesh were less important to him than
the light they could shed on the ancient city's cultural contacts. The
position of Beth Shemesh on the border between the hill country and
the coastal plain seemed to substantiate its importance as a natural
stopping place on overland routes in international trade.

Mackenzie arrived at the site in April 1911 with an architect from
the British School of Archaeology at Athens, Francis Newton, and
began to probe for evidence of Beth Shemesh's ancient trading links.
On the eastern edge of the tell, overlooking a road still used by modern
caravans, he recognized the ruins of a Byzantine monastery which he
suspected might have been erected to commemorate the Return of the
Ark. He instructed his crew of local workmen to search for the line of

37

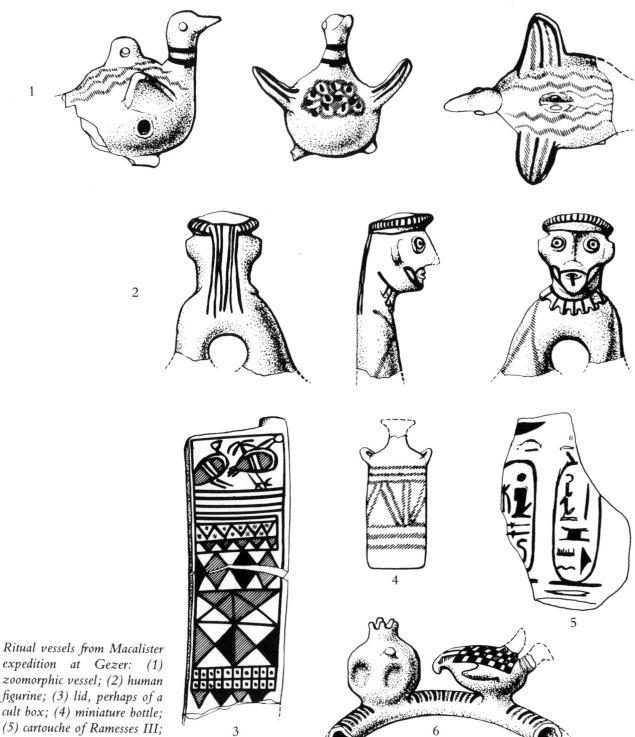

Ritual vessels from Macalister expedition at Gezer: (1) zoomorphic vessel; (2) human figurine; (3) lid, perhaps of a cult box; (4) miniature bottle; (5) cartouche of Ramesses III; (6) ring kernos.

the city's fortifications slightly lower down the slope, and they quickly uncovered a long stretch of massively built stone wall. Then they discovered in a natural cave beneath the fortifications, apparently used in the Bronze Age as a burial chamber, an impressive variety of imported Aegean and Cypriot pottery. More important, the cave seemed to be connected with the construction of the fortifications, which made Mackenzie think that there was more than a casual connection with the rise of the city here. He recognized the pottery types as being from the Late Minoan III period, contemporary with the XVIIIth Dynasty of Egypt and the "ambassadors from Kephtiu." If the initial finds from Beth Shemesh were any indication, the Kephtiu had exerted their influence on Canaan during this same period. It seemed clear, for the moment, that the Philistines were part of a centuries-long connection between the Aegean and the Near East, in which their settlement at the time of Ramesses III was simply the final stage.

The picture began to take on quite a different aspect, however, when Mackenzie began the excavation within the area of the Byzantine monastery on the summit of the tell. After clearing the monastery levels, which were drawn and mapped by Newton, the workmen began immediately (and, in fact, against Mackenzie's specific orders) to dig into the earlier levels. There they discovered a characteristic Philistine vessel whose style and date had little to do with either the Kephtiu in Egypt or the peaceful Minoan thalassocracy.

The jug itself was almost identical with the example first found by Bliss and Macalister at Tell el-Safi. It was painted with elaborate black and red decoration with a stylized bird, and it bore a strainer spout. The careful division of the decoration in panels, or metopes, was an important chronological indication that appeared at Knossos only after the final destruction of the settlement around 1200 B.C. Mackenzie could now see that the Philistine vessel belonged to one of the few ceramic types that could be identified as products of mainland Greece, not Crete.

Before joining Evans at Knossos, Mackenzie had excavated a site called Phylakopi on the island of Melos. It was there that he had first become interested in the complete change of culture that had suddenly occurred throughout the Aegean at the end of the Late Bronze Age. With the subsequent discovery of the Minoan civilization, the cause for this change appeared to be connected with the invasion of the region by northern Greek tribes. Among them were the Achaeans, who, moving southward, established the later Hellenic culture on the ashes of the Minoan and Mycenaean civilizations. The metope decoration was characteristic of the northern Achaean invaders, especially on large kraters with horizontal handles.

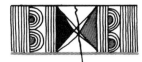

Strainer-spout jugs from Beth Shemesh.

39

When he returned to Beth Shemesh for another season of digging in 1912 and began to uncover the Philistine levels, Mackenzie found vessels of this type to be most common. The relative abundance of this type of krater, especially at a site that the Bible identified as an Israelite town, was puzzling, to say the least.

In his final report on the excavations, Mackenzie wrote:

> From the area I have excavated, I have calculated that a vase of this type must have been present in every house. One is inclined to ask whether they were valued for the strange exotic character of their spiral or panel decoration, or whether they originally came to Beth Shemesh filled with the rare products of Ashkelon and Gaza that were once the specialty of the Aegean and Crete.

In other words, whatever the biblical narrative may have reported about the hostility between Israelites and Philistines, there was certainly either economic or artistic intercourse between them, perhaps both. But it was also clear that there was something abrupt or violent in the changeover from early Aegean ware to Philistine pottery.

As Mackenzie began to excavate wide areas of the city, he noticed a clear chronological differentiation between the two types of pottery. In the lower layers there was a wide range of types that showed the connections between Canaan and the Aegean at the time of the New Kingdom and of the appearance in Egypt of the Kephtiu. But not a single sherd of the characteristic Philistine vessels was found there. It was clear that the Philistines had begun their expansion into Judah only after the earlier Aegean trade was destroyed. The temptation to connect the Philistines to the wave of destruction throughout the Mediterranean seemed irresistible. For the first time in the excavations, Mackenzie began to see that the true historical context of the Philistines was not in their connection to sun worship or to the Minoans, but to the Achaeans and to the repercussions of the great economic, social, and political changes that transformed the Bronze Age Aegean world.

This was a radical revision of the hypothesis that had brought Mackenzie to Palestine—namely, that the Philistines were the bearers of Minoan culture. The truth appeared closer to the biblical view of the Philistines as invaders who had brought that culture to an end. But since Beth Shemesh was an inland city, the evidence it provided could not be considered conclusive. The great maritime movements and disruptions at the end of the Late Bronze Age would have to be investigated closer to their source. So at a break in the excavations at Beth Shemesh, Mackenzie and Newton undertook a private excursion across the coastal plain of ancient Philistia down to the Mediterranean coast, to test their new theory at the site of one of the great Philistine cities, the looming tell of Ashkelon.

The fame of Ashkelon rested on its long history as one of the most important ports linking the easternmost shore of the Mediterranean with the rest of the Mediterranean world. Even its final destruction during the Crusader period did not dim its memory. Throughout the later Middle Ages and the Ottoman period, the ruins of Ashkelon, known as Tell el-Khadra, "the mound of the Green One," for the Muslim shrine that stood at its summit, remained an attraction for pilgrims and travelers.

Arriving at the tell at sunset, Mackenzie first reacted with gloom, but not because the site lacked archaeological value. On the contrary, the site was so enormous that he simply despaired of being able to come to any quick conclusions about the nature of the Philistine occupation there. The perimeter of the site was ringed with the massive, collapsed remains of the Crusader fortifications.

The following morning, however, the men discovered that their pessimism had been somewhat premature. The most ancient mound of Ashkelon, they soon realized, was a prominent plateau rising on the edge of the cliffs, facing the seashore. Mackenzie was subsequently able to trace the outline of the Philistine city, and to identify the ravine and the tidal inlet to the south of the mound as the protected Philistine anchorage, on the basis of his knowledge of similar ancient harbors along the coasts of Crete.

Making their way down the steep cliffs to the seashore, and then walking along the beach, they found, in Mackenzie's words, "not a bare precipice of virgin rock, but layer upon layer of gradually accumulated debris going up to the surface many feet above our heads." The action of the sea over thousands of years had revealed a clear stratigraphical section, which for an experienced archaeologist could be read in its broad outlines with little difficulty. Without any significant digging, it would be possible to discover the sequence of cultures at Ashkelon and the place of the Philistines in it. Mackenzie's observations, recorded in Newton's pen-and-ink drawing, provided a dramatic confirmation of the theories developed in the excavations at Beth Shemesh.

Immediately above the bedrock, there was evidence of the first inhabitants of the city in a layer containing crude pottery; Mackenzie dated this to around 2000 B.C., just when the first palace civilization was being etablished on Crete. The level above showed Ashkelon's first overseas contacts—imported Cypriot wares and increasing urbanization—and the appearance of the first city walls. In the next layer up, Mackenzie found an alabaster vase fragment that he believed to be characteristic of the Egyptian XVIIIth Dynasty: a period of prosperity and commercial connections with the Aegean, the time of the ambassadors from Kephtiu.

It was in the next layer that the evidence became dramatic. At Beth Shemesh the only evidence of commercial disruption was the end of Aegean and Cypriot imports and their displacement by Philistine vessels. Here at Ashkelon were clear signs of violence. A thick layer of ash, collapsed brick, and charred wood extending all along the section was, according to Mackenzie, "probably significant of some general catastrophe at Ashkelon."

This continuous burnt level marked a turning point in the life of the city, and Mackenzie had already expressed his views as to who the destroyers might be. To check the pottery at the building level that succeeded the destruction, he scrambled up an eroded crevice on the face of the seaside section and dug into the debris with his hands. His find confirmed his suspicions: it was a jug of the characteristic black and red painted Philistine pottery. More such fragments could be seen all along the same level—clear evidence, in Mackenzie's opinion, that the Philistines had conquered and razed the flourishing port city of Ashkelon and built their own city on its ruins.

Mackenzie's discovery had, in a certain sense, provided a fitting culmination to the first decade of archaeological research into the culture of the ancient Philistines. Far from being a purely biblical question, the search for the Philistines would soon become an issue of vital importance in understanding the early history of both the Near Eastern and Aegean worlds.

CHAPTER 4

Back to the Beginning

In the summer of 1920, nine years after Duncan Mackenzie's finds at Ashkelon, the Palestine Exploration Fund began an ambitious plan for the future. Conditions in the country had radically changed for archaeology after the British conquest of Palestine during the First World War; a British Mandatory administration was established and, with it, an efficient Department of Antiquities. Scientific considerations alone would determine the progress of investigation rather than tedious negotiations with the Ottoman bureaucracy, or so it seemed at the time.

In any case, the executive committee of the P.E.F. chose the seaside mound of Ashkelon as their first target. Dr. David Hogarth, chairman of the committee and longtime colleague of Arthur Evans, assured readers in an article he wrote for the *Illustrated London News* that not only would the excavations at Ashkelon attempt to answer the biblical question of "whether it was in virtue of a distinctly higher apparatus of civilization that the Philistines so long terrorized the Hebrews," but also the more general question of "whence that civilization came and whither it went."

The excavation team was headed by the newly appointed director of the British School of Archaeology in Jerusalem, John Garstang, a professor at the University of Liverpool, and William J. Phythian-Adams, a young Anglican cleric and historian who had participated in Garstang's excavations in northern Syria and Egypt before the war. Both were experts in the techniques of stratigraphic excavation and shared the optimistic belief that large-scale clearance of areas of the coastal Philistine city, presumably one of the initial points of arrival of this ancient people, would provide more conclusive evidence than any of the previous finds at Tell el-Safi, Gezer, or Beth Shemesh.

Arriving at the site at the end of August 1920, Garstang and Phythian-Adams pitched camp within the circuit of the Crusader walls and soon discovered how difficult the new excavations at Ashkelon would be. It wasn't that they chose their excavation areas unwisely. They followed Mackenzie's lead and instructed their crew to begin digging two parallel trenches on the side of the mound that faced the ravine, known to the local inhabitants by the suggestive name of Eskale. Here, Mackenzie had theorized, the Philistines had found a protected anchorage, so important for their maritime connections to the Aegean.

The first hint of archaeological trouble came almost immediately. While Mackenzie had believed that the post-Philistine layers of the tell were insubstantial, Garstang and Phythian-Adams discovered that just the opposite was true. First the downward progress of the diggers in one of the trenches was halted by the collapsed walls of a ruined Byzantine church. Then they were further impeded by the massive foundations of public buildings from the Roman and Hellenistic periods. In the second trench it was discovered that construction of the fortifications of the Crusader period had jumbled the lower layers of the tell. It was as if all of the city's history had been mixed up and redeposited at random: Byzantine and Crusader pottery was found together with Mycenaean and Roman ware.

It soon became obvious that the tell of Ashkelon was not a simple layer cake whose stratified deposits could be neatly stripped away to reveal the Philistine city. Indeed, the first digging season necessarily concentrated on the impressive remains of other periods. To get on with the question of the Philistines, the archaeologists would have to wait until they could locate an undisturbed deposit in which a clear Philistine level could be identified.

ATTACKING THE SECTIONS

As Garstang knew from his experience in Syria, a narrow but deep section through the stratigraphical levels, combined with a careful examination of the pottery types, could provide far more reliable information than the discovery of isolated architectural units or artifacts where the levels were disturbed. With this strategy in mind, Phythian-Adams eventually found a suitable place to dig a deep section—on the northern slope of the mound, where erosion had produced an almost vertical scarp between two adjacent vegetable plots.

By cutting a series of carefully measured descending "steps" from the surface of the upper field to the lower, he succeeded in distinguishing three superimposed levels in the accumulation that enabled him to isolate the Philistine culture at Ashkelon for the first time. Then, by clearing the vertical sides of the trench and noting the changes in color and texture of the accumulated debris, he was able to distinguish the major stages in the sequence of accumulation and to see how the pottery styles had changed in each of them.

As it turned out, the fit was perfect. The lowest layer of brown, loamy soil contained fragments of imported Cypriot and Mycenaean vessels, whose date was confirmed by the discovery of an Egyptian alabaster vessel of the thirteenth century B.C. Near the top, in a hard clay level, Phythian-Adams identified pottery from the Hellenistic and Roman periods, beginning in the fourth century B.C. Between them lay a clearly defined layer that would, therefore, represent the building that went on in this part of the city during the centuries when, according to the Bible and other sources, Ashkelon was a Philistine city. This was the first time that Philistine remains had been discovered at a level that was securely dated. Moreover, Phythian-Adams found what he believed to be the first hint of true Philistine architecture: a section of a mudbrick wall built on stone foundations.

In the winter of 1920–21, while Phythian-Adams remained behind in Palestine to complete the scientific report on their first season of digging, Garstang returned to London to confer with the executive committee of the P.E.F. on strategy for the next dig. He also brought with him Philistine pottery fragments to show to those of his colleagues who had made contributions to the search for the Philistines. There was little agreement among them as to the stylistic significance of the sherds. Macalister now suggested that the influence was from Asia Minor; Hogarth opted for Crete; Mackenzie for the Greek mainland. But they were all agreed that the Ashkelon excavations held the key to resolving the mystery, and they urged Garstang to expand the area uncovered in the section on the northern scarp.

When Garstang and Phythian-Adams returned to Ashkelon for a second season, in April 1921, that is exactly what they did. With the evidence of the wall fragment, now optimistically called "The Philistine House," to guide them, and an exact measurement of its depth beneath the surface of the upper terrace, they began to dig through the upper levels of Arab, Byzantine, and Roman remains ("rather ruthlessly," as Garstang later admitted in a report to the P.E.F.), but to no avail. The first section in the northern scarp had been successful because it was so limited in area; any attempt to expand it was frustrated by the very nature of the thick archaeological deposits at the site. After digging down more than eight yards, progressively restricting the area of the excavation to prevent the debris from collapsing, they uncovered only

Bell-shaped bowl from Ash-kelon (top) and Aegean prototype from Sinda, Cyprus (bottom).

a tiny surface area near the wall of the Philistine period. And what they did uncover turned out to have been so badly disturbed by later building that it provided no additional information about the Philistines.

With the passing months and evaporating funds, Garstang and Phythian-Adams came under pressure to turn up something definite. Their only hope seemed to be in excavating another deep stratigraphical section, this time on a larger scale. The portion of the seaside cliff that Mackenzie had examined in 1911 seemed the best option. Phythian-Adams laid out an area approximately twelve yards square at the edge of the tell and dug down through the superimposed layers, using the same technique of detailed stratigraphical analysis that he had the year before. By the end of the excavation of this section, he had confirmed Mackenzie's assumptions about the massive destruction that preceded Philistine settlement in Ashkelon and, to boot, had collected examples of a wide range of Philistine pottery forms.

LIFESTYLES AND ORIGINS

Beneath the thick blanket of black earth mixed with ashes, Phythian-Adams found the pottery styles that represented Ashkelon's culture before the Philistines' arrival. The imported Mycenaean and Cypriot vessels indicated to him that "the finer arts of the Late Bronze Age were imposed on the Canaanites from the outside." At the time when the Mycenaean palaces in Greece were thriving, that is c.1400–1200 B.C., Ashkelon had been overwhelmed by Mycenaean influence. The quantity and function of the imported wares, according to Phythian-Adams, represented the results not only of considerable trading but of a significant cultural orientation as well—a widespread acceptance of the feasting rituals of the Minoan-Mycenaean world. The fact that the Philistine pottery *above* the destruction level contained strikingly different types of drinking vessels denoted "not merely a difference in technique: it is much more a difference in style of living."

In place of the high-stemmed Mycenaean *kylixes* and the sharp-profiled Cypriot base ring bowls come the heavy Philistine kraters and cups with horizontal handles which Mackenzie had attributed to the Philistines' northern Achaean origins. In Greece, such bowls had continued to be manufactured for centuries, and if any vessel could have been considered "naturally Greek" in inspiration, Phythian-Adams agreed, this was one. The most famous example of this type was the "Warrior Vase" uncovered by Schliemann in Mycenae: its portrayal of armed marchers had long been used to illustrate the cultural contrast between the Indo-Aryan Achaeans and the earlier, unarmed Minoan-Mycenaean princes and priestesses. Although Mackenzie had suggested connecting the Philistines' arrival in Canaan to the wave of northern invasions that had destroyed the Minoan-Mycenaean civilization, he

Soldiers in full battle dress decorate an early-twelfth-century B.C. *vase uncovered by Schliemann in Mycenae. Their bronze helmets and leg guards, coats of mail, and spears are all similar to Goliath's armor and weaponry as described in the Bible. These well-known elements of warfare, shared by the Mycenaean warriors and Goliath, show the transfer of Aegean tradition to Philistia.*

had not been able to provide conclusive proof. Now Phythian-Adams was ready to make the connection explicit. He reported to the P.E.F. that "we may dare to think once more of the 'Achaean' armor of Goliath, and reexamine with greater confidence the problem of Philistine origins."

Unfortunately, despite the importance of the finds from the Philistine period, however meager, they were not enough to attract the public contributions necessary to defray the expenses incurred by the dig. Even the wholehearted support of the Mandate authorities had not enabled the excavators to uncover any impressive Philistine palaces, temples, or citadels at Ashkelon. In May 1922, after just two seasons of digging, the P.E.F. had to admit that the site itself proved too much of an impediment. Considering the Arab, Crusader, Roman, and Hellenistic remains thickly overlaying the area, it was clear, according to Dr. Hogarth, "that no one except a government or a very rich society can hope properly to excavate the site down to the Philistine level." With the few hundred pounds left in the fund's treasury, they directed Phythian-Adams to undertake a less ambitious project: to determine if the same cultural transformations he had recognized at Ashkelon would apply to the other cities of Philistia as well.

Phythian-Adams decided to begin with Tell Haruba at Gaza, the most famous of Philistine cities and the site briefly and inconclusively explored by the Chevalier D'Arvieux in 1659. Here, too, tons of earth had to be removed before the Philistine levels could be reached. More troubling, the site was located in the midst of the modern town of Gaza, and endless acrimonious negotiations with the local landowners caused constant delays in the work. In the end, Phythian-Adams gave up and moved to the unoccupied mound of Tell Jemmeh, about ten miles south of Gaza, on the border between Canaan and Sinai. Here again, despite promising beginnings, he was forced to give up: continual clashes between bedouin smugglers and the British Mandatory police began to threaten the very physical safety of the excavators.

Even with all his setbacks, Phythian-Adams had managed to collect plentiful and well-stratified samples of Philistine pottery, and was confident that of all the types within the Philistine ceramic repertoire, the "northern" forms were the most significant for determining their geographical origins. But he realized that he would have to correlate these findings with other kinds of information.

In the 1923 volume of the *Bulletin of the British School of Archaeology in Jerusalem*, he published an article entitled "Philistine Origins in Light of Palestinian Archaeology," in which he made such correlations by deftly interweaving his initial pottery analysis with other archaeological, historical, and linguistic evidence.

A TRAIL TO THE PHILISTINES' HOMELAND

Ever since the late nineteenth century, he wrote, many scholars had recognized the similarity between the names of the various Sea Peoples mentioned in the ancient Egyptian records and the lists of combatants in the Trojan War preserved in the *Iliad*. Most conspicuous had been the correspondence between the Ekwesh and the Achaeans, which had led Mackenzie to suggest that the Philistines and the other Sea Peoples were related to the northern Achaean invaders. Consequently, Phythian-Adams believed that any solution to the mystery of the Philistines had to come from an examination of the homeland of the Achaeans themselves. Since the Achaeans had moved southward to the Peloponnese and the Philistines had moved southeastward toward Canaan, the original joint homeland of the two peoples might be somewhere to the north of the Balkan Peninsula, where the land routes to their later destinations naturally diverged.

Modern archaeological excavation had barely begun in the newly established nation of Yugoslavia, he noted. But what had been found there seemed to validate this idea. Excavations at the Early Iron Age cemetery at Glasinatz near Sarajevo had uncovered the tomb of a warrior buried with a helmet, greaves, shield, and spear that were strikingly similar to descriptions of the armor of both the Philistine champion

Goliath and the Homeric heroes. To make the connection even more persuasive, Phythian-Adams pointed out, the other grave offering in Glasinatz included numerous kraters and bowls similar to those he had identified in the Philistine layers of Ashkelon.

BACK TO THE BEGINNING

He further focused his attention on the physical geography of the Balkans. To the north of the mainland routes leading south, he found several ancient place-names, such as Dardania and Sardica, which suggested the names of the Derden and the Sherden, the latter of which had been an ally of the Philistines. Even more important, he had found in Roman geography mention of a tribe called the Pirvstae, living on the Illyrian coast of the Balkan Peninsula, a name linguistically similar to the Egyptian name for the Philistines, *P-r/l-s-t*. Here, he concluded, was the original homeland of the Philistines. It was not, he admitted, a final answer, but it did provide "a working basis for future researches in this field."

Phythian-Adams's assembled evidence led to a single conclusion: the Philistines and the Sea Peoples fit into early Aegean history as the destroyers of the Minoan-Mycenaean culture and the heralds of the new Hellenic age. In this sense the Philistines could be seen as the first Europeans in biblical history. Yet, in another sense, they remained as before: historical villains, the destroyers of an ancient civilization. But however pat the idea, Phythian-Adams's Balkan theory would soon be challenged as the result of an increasingly bitter debate between two factions of Aegean archaeologists.

Walter Abel Heurtley, a graduate of Oxford, where he had specialized in preclassical art, certainly wasn't thinking of the Philistines when he arrived in Athens in the summer of 1920 to take up his new post as assistant director and librarian at the British School of Archaeology. The British School had been at the forefront of developments in Aegean archaeology since its establishment in the 1880s, and in the four decades that had passed, the study of Bronze Age archaeology had become a full-fledged academic discipline.

THE RISE OF A COUNTERTHEORY

The timing of Heurtley's arrival was especially fortunate: the director of the school, Alan Wace, had received permission from the Greek government to undertake new excavations at Mycenae, and in the course of his work on that project Heurtley was to make a discovery that would undermine some of the most basic historical assumptions regarding the origin and early history of the Philistines.

Wace had a theory that he wanted to test at Mycenae. In his previous archaeological surveys and excavations in Greece, he had come to the conclusion, in collaboration with Carl Blegen of the American School of Classical Studies in Athens—later famous for his new excavations at Troy and his discovery of Pylos—that the Greek mainland had always possessed its own distinctive culture, which they called Helladic to distinguish it from the Minoan. If an Indo-European migration could be distinguished in the archaeological record, it had not occurred at the end of the Mycenaean period but early in the second millennium B.C.— that is, almost a thousand years before the end of Mycenaean civilization. This was entirely different from the predominant view of most scholars, who, influenced by Evans's excavations at Knossos, viewed mainland Greek culture as a late and derivative extension of the Minoan culture of Crete.

One of Mycenae's most famous landmarks was the "Lion's Gate," with its impressive carved lintel. Despite Schliemann's thoroughgoing clearance of the site, the new British excavators discovered a relatively untouched area of accumulation just inside the western wing, where they looked for and found reliable stratigraphical evidence for determining the date and circumstances of Mycenaean final destruction. The most dramatic finds in this area came from a structure attached to the city wall that Wace called "The Granary," after the storejars filled with carbonized wheat found intact on the building's basement floor. The Granary had been destroyed in an intense conflagration that had apparently marked the end of the occupation of the site. If Evans's theories were correct, it would have been reasonable to look for the characteristic "northern" panel-style bowls and kraters—assumed to be the clearest evidence of the arrival of the Achaean invaders—*above* the destruction debris. Yet Wace and Heurtley found a different picture altogether: the so-called northern types were already present at Mycenae long before the citadel was conquered and burned, and were not, therefore, intrusive; they were a product of Mycenaean culture itself. Furthermore, although they appeared fairly late in the sequence of accumulation, they were the latest ceramic development. By the time of Mycenae's destruction, the panel-style vessels had already been entirely superseded by a more simply decorated style of pottery, which came to be called "Granary Ware."

The popularity of the panel-style prototypes of Philistine pottery at Mycenae and their disappearance before its destruction was a blow to the accepted view of the Philistines' involvement in a sudden wave of invasions. But for Heurtley it was only the first stage in the development of an entirely new theory about the Philistines. As he went on to make the first thorough archaeological survey of Macedonia, the northeastern region of the Greek mainland, he found further evidence for questioning the accepted sequence of events.

Since Macedonia was even closer to the suggested Balkan homeland, it should have provided even greater archaeological indications of the northern invasion, but it did not. In fact, the evidence uncovered by Heurtley made the connection of the Philistines and the other Sea Peoples to the Balkans seem quite unlikely. At several sites he found unmistakable signs of the destruction of the Late Mycenaean settlements. But as at Mycenae itself, the destruction occurred, in every case, only *after* the appearance of the "Granary Ware." So that even if there had been an invasion from the north which ended the Mycenaean period, it would have had to take place long after the Philistine pottery had lost vogue. The origins of the Philistines would have to be sought within Mycenaean civilization.

In 1932 Heurtley accepted a position with the Palestine Department of Antiquities, which gave him a chance to examine pottery finds from the cities of Philistia. It also gave him an opportunity to attack the archaeological mystery of the Philistines head-on. His firsthand experience in Aegean archaeology had led him to recognize that while general Mycenaean pottery styles had spread throughout the entire eastern Mediterranean world in the Late Bronze Age, there were several clear-cut regional variants. By examining the entire range of excavated materials from these areas, he could determine if a particular regional variant could be identified as *the* artistic source.

But his analysis turned up a complex and confusing series of interconnections. Each region of the Mycenaean world, it seemed, had contributed something to Philistine ware. From Pylos in the southwestern Peloponnese came the use of concentric loops in rows and masses, the filling of decorative motifs with black paint, and the characteristic bent bird wing. From the Ionian island of Cephalonia came panel-style kraters with spirals and lozenges. From Crete in the south came more birds and such distinctive shapes as the stirrup jar. From Rhodes in the east came painted birds so close to the Philistine examples that they seemed to be the prototype. Closest of all to the Philistine ware was the pottery of Cyprus, with birds, concentric loops, and even the unusual form of jug with the strainer spout.

In fact, as Heurtley's analysis demonstrated, far from being invaders from the outside, the Philistine potters appeared to have had an intimate and surprisingly eclectic familiarity with artistic trends from all over the Late Mycenaean world. What made this familiarity even more striking was that only in Philistia did the Late Mycenaean style continue. The twelfth-century B.C. potters of the mainland, of the Ionian islands, of Crete, Rhodes, and Cyprus had all abandoned Mycenaean traditions in favor of the newer Granary style, a style completely absent from Philistine ware. The Philistines appear to have been cut off from the

Mycenaean IIIC:1b stirrup jar from Rhodes (left) and strainer-spout jug prototype from Kouklia, Cyprus (right).

rest of the Aegean world for some still unexplained reason, maintaining Mycenaean styles long after they had disappeared from the Aegean itself.

KEEPERS OF
THE TRADITION

Heurtley remained extremely cautious in assessing the implications of his findings. "The most we can say," he wrote in 1936 in the *Quarterly of the Department of Antiquities in Palestine*, "is that [the Philistine pottery] may have been made to satisfy a demand by the newcomers for something which had a Mycenaean look, and infer from its composite character that they were familiar with the whole Aegean." The Philistines were *part* of the Mycenaean world, not its destroyers. This Heurtley maintained, and in his insistence he defined the future lines of the Philistine debate.

The first four decades of archaeological research into the material culture of the Philistines had transformed the nature of the historical debate about them while leaving their geographical origins, the character of their civilization, and their proper place in history still shrouded in mystery. It was possible to agree that they had arrived in the country during the reign of Ramesses III, but there were still two schools of

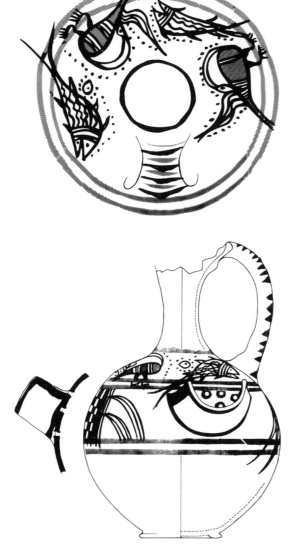

*Philistine strainer-spout jug
from Tell Aitun.*

53

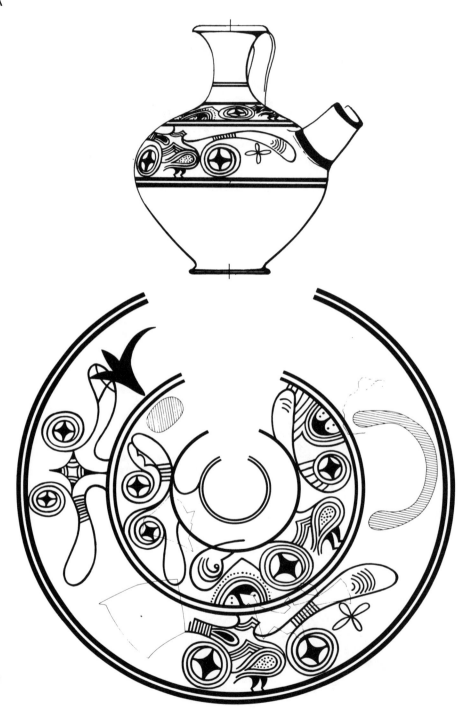

*Strainer-spout jug prototype
from Sinda, Cyprus.*

thought regarding the interpretation of the evidence of the pottery vis-à-vis the other questions. One set of scholars still clung to the theory of their northern origin, attributing to them the warlike behavior and martial values that typified the biblical view. The other, with Heurtley, maintained that their pottery and culture had developed from *within* Mycenaean tradition and that the Philistines were a civilizing force, bringing a high level of culture to Canaan after the destruction of Mycenaean cities at the end of the Late Bronze Age.

CHAPTER 5

Coffins
and Controversy

Scholarly disagreement may have been bitter over the question of the exact origin of the Philistines, but there was, nevertheless, more or less general agreement on one crucial issue. The sudden appearance of the black and red painted pottery in the coastal regions and adjoining hill country which the Bible ascribes to the Philistines clearly indicated that they had settled in Canaan during the Early Iron Age, at the time of the breakdown of Mycenaean civilization. The extent of their settlement in Canaan and the precise nature of their culture were some of the questions that had yet to be clearly answered. As it turned out, the next decade or so of archaeological inquiry in Palestine, while yielding an impressive variety of artifacts, was not quite as impressive in yielding unambiguous answers. If anything, controversy grew, beginning with the totally unexpected finds at Beth Shean.

In 1921 the University Museum in Philadelphia began a massive archaeological project, its first full-scale excavation of a tell in Palestine, at Tell el-Hosn, "the mound of the fortress." The site was located about twelve miles south of the Sea of Galilee, at the junction of the Esdraelon and Jordan valleys, both well-traveled routes of commerce and war in ancient times. The nearby Arab village of Beisan preserved the biblical name of the place, Beth Shean, known from ancient Egyptian records as a royal garrison town and administrative center that controlled trade and transportation passing through Canaan to the north. The circum-

stances and date of the end of Egyptian rule at Beth Shean were unclear from the records, and there was no precise information regarding the garrison's later fate. It became a settlement, and though far from the coast was, according to the descriptions of battles in the Bible, connected with the Philistines.

The first director of the dig, Dr. Clarence Fisher, had adopted an ambitious and rather one-track excavation strategy. He himself was particularly interested in Egyptian archaeological remains. He had recently completed an excavation at Memphis in Egypt, during which he uncovered the palace of Merneptah (c. 1237–1223 B.C.), the last great pharaoh of the XIXth Dynasty. One of Fisher's first major discoveries at Beth Shean was an inscribed stele, erected by Merneptah's grandfather, Seti I (c. 1318–1304 B.C.), a find that encouraged him to anticipate a rich yield of Egyptian remains. In light of the dig's substantial funding, he intended to peel away each of the successive city layers until he reached the levels in which he was interested. Compared to Ashkelon, the medieval, Byzantine, Roman, and Hellenistic periods at Beth Shean were relatively insubstantial and the crew dug through them quickly to the remains they hoped would prove more significant, those of the Israelite monarchy and the preceding centuries of Egyptian rule.

In 1923, after three seasons of digging, the team had removed more than thirty feet of accumulation from the upper surface of the mound and found a complex of Egyptian-style buildings, temples, and storerooms near its southern edge, substantiating the assumption that Beth Shean was an Egyptian garrison town. Two large structures, later identified as barracks and administrative centers, were built with characteristic Egyptian doorjambs and lintels, some of which bore fragmentary hieroglyphic inscriptions. The entire complex had been rebuilt a number of times over the centuries, but its last reconstruction proved to be the most significant of all. Its date was surprising: several of the inscribed lintels bore the name of Ramesses-Weser-Khephesh, commander of the garrison at Beth Shean, whose titles were accompanied by royal cartouches of Ramesses III. Until then it had been assumed that the reign of Ramesses III—during which the Philistines and their allies had settled in Philistia and other former Egyptian provinces in Canaan—had been a period of dramatic decline in Egyptian power. Here, at Beth Shean, the evidence seemed to indicate that the Egyptian presence in Canaan had been strengthened with the arrival of the Philistines and their allies.

COFFINS AND MERCENARIES

To the north of the tell, on the northern bank of Wadi Jalud, "Goliath's Brook," the American expedition discovered the ancient cemetery of the city, the largest ever discovered in Palestine. It appeared to have been in continuous use for more than three thousand years, from the Early Bronze Age to the Byzantine period. What particularly riveted the excavators' attention was the discovery in eleven funeral deposits of fragments of fifty human-shaped clay coffins, known in archaeological terminology as "anthropoid." Only two of them were reconstructed from the fragments, but the presence of the others could be ascertained by the quantity of fragments. It was clear that serious havoc had been wrought—first by time and nature, which had crumbled and jumbled the underground chambers, and then by grave robbers, who had repeatedly plundered the tombs after the cemetery went out of use in the seventh century A.D.

The two reassembled coffins were impressive. More than six feet long, they were cylindrical, tapering slightly toward the feet. From the rough interior, it could be seen that they were built of coils of clay, then smoothed on their outside surface. The upper part of each coffin was then cut away from the insertion of the body, and each of these detachable lids was ornamented with a distinctive face mask, in apparent representation of the features or character of the deceased. Fisher and, later, his successor, the British archaeologist Alan Rowe, distinguished two types of coffin lids: the "naturalistic" and the "grotesque."

Fragments of the naturalistic type were most common: they bore a solid, lifelike portrait in clay, framed by a heavy wig. The wigs were decorated with lotus flowers, and the position of the modeled hands, laid horizontally beneath the face, was reminiscent of Egyptian mummy cases. The grotesque coffins were similar in shape, but their exaggerated, stylized features were unlike the Egyptian protoypes. The grim faces, made of separate clay appliqués, were beardless, and in place of the Egyptian-style wigs the heads had elaborate headdresses and headbands (plate 4). In a few cases where the grotesque coffins could be associated with a particular tomb chamber, its square shape—in contrast to the more usual rounded tombs—hinted at this group's foreign origins. The excavators were puzzled: there were both Egyptian and foreign influences in Beth Shean.

In 1 Samuel, the Bible suggests a link between the Philistines and Beth Shean, without mentioning any Egyptian connection. But by that time more than a century and a half had passed since the Philistines' great war with the armies of Ramesses III, and during that time Egypt had for some reason ceased to be a significant factor in Canaanite affairs. According to 1 Samuel 31, the Philistines inflicted a crushing defeat on the Israelite army of King Saul in the vicinity of the city. After the defeat, the Philistine soldiers found Saul's body on the battlefield, cut off his head, stripped off his armor, and "sent messengers throughout the land of the Philistines to carry the good news to the house of their

Anthropoid coffin from Beth Shean. About fifty coffins were discovered, dated to the period ranging from the thirteenth to the eleventh century B.C. Only two could be reconstructed; the others were smashed and scattered all over the area.

idols." Furthermore, they deposited Saul's armor in one of the Beth Shean temples and hung his headless body on the city wall. If the Philistines were so much at home at the eastern end of the Valley of Esdraelon, it was either because they controlled a far wider territory than generally assumed or because they had close connections—religious or other—with Beth Shean's inhabitants.

The question for the Beth Shean excavators at that point was how the coffins fit into the context of the ancient city's history, as recounted by both biblical sources and Egyptian records. Fisher and Rowe had noted that sherds of Mycenaean and Cypriot pottery were found near several of the coffins, as was one thin gold-foil, typically Aegean mouthpiece. So there was obviously a mixture of Egyptian and Aegean cultural influence. But Fisher and Rowe were extremely cautious in their evaluation of the evidence. The anthropoid burials could probably be connected to the presence of foreign mercenaries and their families, attached to the Egyptian army. But the excavators could not necessarily identify the foreign mercenaries with the Philistines, for a very simple, or apparently simple, archaeological reason: not a single sherd of the black and red painted Philistine pottery had yet been found either in the cemetery of Beth Shean or in the tell!

Père Hughes Vincent, the director of the Dominican École Biblique et Archéologique in Jerusalem, reviewed these discoveries and came to the same conclusions for somewhat different reasons. Vincent, by the way, was one of the very few who had never accepted the notion that the red and black painted pottery was the hallmark of the Philistines.

Naturalistic anthropoid coffin lids from Beth Shean. The same patterns of appliquéd horizontal bands, rows of knobs, zigzagging, and vertical fluting are arranged differently on each lid.

AEGEAN PARALLELS

Grotesque coffin lids from Beth Shean. The features are probably the result of intentional stylization rather than artistic ineptitude. The high-ridged nose is applied, the mouth is a horizontal deep groove, and the chin is only faintly indicated. The arms and hands, beginning at the top of the head, are sticklike and bent at the elbows. The hands have outstretched fingers touching below the mouth. Incised grooves near the wrists and above the elbows may represent bracelets.

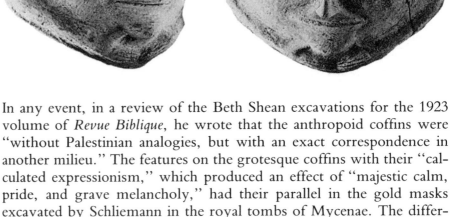

In any event, in a review of the Beth Shean excavations for the 1923 volume of *Revue Biblique*, he wrote that the anthropoid coffins were "without Palestinian analogies, but with an exact correspondence in another milieu." The features on the grotesque coffins with their "calculated expressionism," which produced an effect of "majestic calm, pride, and grave melancholy," had their parallel in the gold masks excavated by Schliemann in the royal tombs of Mycenae. The differences between them, he believed, were due merely to the use of cruder materials.

The only groups of settlers in Canaan who might reasonably have been expected to combine Aegean and Egyptian artistic traditions were the Philistines or one of the other Sea Peoples, and Vincent—like Fisher and Rowe—left open the question of the exact identity of those buried in the Beth Shean coffins. Still, the historical importance of this identification was clear. According to the testimony of Ramesses III in the Papyrus Harris, the pharaoh himself, after the great battles of 1191 B.C., had "settled them in strongholds, bound in my name." This text seemed to match the Beth Shean finds perfectly. The city's garrison had been rebuilt and strengthened under Ramesses III's patronage, and its population began to show clear signs of Aegean cultural influence. Vincent suggested that the Aegean warriors had served for a while at the Egyptian garrison, but with the decline of Egyptian power in Canaan various groups of the Sea Peoples, presumably settled in other strategic garrisons, would have taken control of the Egyptian holdings themselves. The Philistines' migration to Canaan was, therefore, just the opening chapter of their subsequent existence in the area, followed by service in the Egyptian army and their eventual inheritance of control over the most important overland trade routes. The later expansion of the Israelites, at the time of King Saul, had apparently threatened their prosperity.

With Vincent's interpretation, the main direction of the study of Philistine culture perceptibly shifted. Although the pottery question was left unresolved for the time being, the search for the Philistines could no longer be one of merely trying to isolate foreign invaders. It would have to concentrate on the Philistines' interaction with Egyptian power and culture, and on the extent of their expansion throughout Canaan.

With the return to Palestine in 1926 of the founder of modern Near Eastern archaeology, William Matthew Flinders Petrie, the Philistine debate was given a new jolt. As with many great explorers, his astonishing finds easily outweighed the improbability of his historical speculations, which were, to say the least, highly imaginative.

Petrie, now in his seventies, had not excavated outside Egypt for thirty-five years, since his pioneering work in Judea at Tell el-Hesy in 1890. Having excavated more than twenty-five sites in Egypt, from the delta to Upper Egypt, and published more than sixty volumes of reports, catalogs, historical reconstructions, and personal archaeological philosophy, he was, without question, one of the greatest Egyptologists

THE PATRIARCH
RETURNS

and archaeologists of his time. His decision to leave Egypt had to do with the growing unrest in that country, where the demand for independence from the British was producing increasing turmoil.

Petrie hoped to link his vast Egyptian discoveries with a new examination of some ancient city mounds across the border in Palestine. The first of Petrie's renewed Palestinian excavations, in 1926 and 1927, was at Tell Jemmeh, on the southern bank of Wadi Ghazzeh, a site that Phythian-Adams and his crew had been forced to abandon five years earlier in fear of their lives. By the time of Petrie's arrival, order had been restored, and he could later report that there was "not a single raid of the desert tribes, so thorough is the peace ensured by the new police."

One of the main attractions of Tell Jemmeh was that its surface was not burdened with Hellenistic or Roman structures, and it would make the uncovering of Egyptian and Philistine settlements there relatively simple. Phythian-Adams had found a layer of Philistine pottery clearly overlaying the Late Bronze Age levels, but Petrie tended to dismiss the young scholar's evidence. He believed that Tell Jemmeh was the site of the biblical city of Gerar where, according to various verses in Genesis, the Hebrew patriarchs Abraham and Isaac had encounters with "Abimelech, king of the Philistines," centuries before the end of the Late Bronze Age. While most biblical scholars dismissed these stories as anachronisms, Petrie was convinced that there had been a Philistine presence during this period and, with an implicit belief in the accuracy of the Bible, began to build his own theory of early Philistine history.

During six months of work Petrie's large team cleared more than thirty feet of accumulation, uncovering numerous grain silos and a complex of buildings that he attributed to the XVIIIth-Dynasty pharaoh Thutmosis III (c.1503–1450 B.C.). Completely ignoring Phythian-Adams's detailed chronology of Philistine pottery, Petrie assigned this earlier date to the Philistine pottery found there, citing vague stylistic parallels to the contemporary Late Minoan pottery of Crete.

Petrie believed that commercial interests had brought the Philistines to Canaan at the time of the Hebrew patriarchs, around 1700–1600 B.C. That they were never mentioned in the abundant Egyptian records of this period—with which he was intimately familiar—he attributed to the fact that they were "only traders and corn factors." The great invasion of the Philistines depicted at Medinet Habu was a historical fact that had to be accounted for as well. Petrie's explanation was that there was a *second* wave of Philistines, neither peaceful traders nor grain merchants but warlike intruders, as in their biblical image. Petrie intended to substantiate this view through his archaeological finds.

Beginning at the level he assigned to the time of the Philistines' invasion, he discovered a succession of kilns or ovens, which he identified as iron furnaces, some used specifically for the production of swords. There was, however, no evidence of iron slag in any of them. This was intended to accord with the biblical reference to the Philistines' monopoly of metalworking at the time of their wars with the Israelites [1 Samuel 13:19]. Petrie attempted to identify the origin of this technology by suggesting a confusing range of parallels with early iron implements found in Switzerland, Germany, and, even, Siberia. With this reconstruction and its extremely early dating, he had thrown a monkey wrench into previously accepted archaeological chronology, and would continue to do so with the finds at the next dig.

With the completion of the Tell Jemmeh excavations, having, in his own words, "secured a continuous view of Palestine archaeology from 1500 to 500 B.C.," Petrie looked to another site in the vicinity to further his Philistine studies. The site of Tell el-Farah, about eighteen miles south of Gaza, also on the southern bank of Wadi Ghazzeh, was even more imposing than Tell Jemmeh. It was situated on a hill one hundred feet high, with an additional fifty feet of accumulated city levels above. The modern Arabic name means "place of refuge," and Petrie concluded that it was the site of the biblical city of Beth Pelet—and, since one of King David's mercenary bodyguards was called Pelet, his home. Some scholars had suggested that *peletim* (Hebrew for "refugees") was simply a scribal error for *pelishtim*, or Philistines. In this case Petrie chose to acknowledge his colleagues' theories and look for Philistine remains there.

Petrie dug steadily at Tell el-Farah through 1928 and 1929. The surface of the mound was still crisscrossed with trenches dug by the British and Turkish armies in their prolonged battles for this strategic passage between Palestine and Sinai during World War I. This strategic element was also evident in the nature of the archaeological remains at the site, for when Petrie directed the diggers to begin on the southern edge of the tell, they uncovered a structure that he identified as a border fortress. The following year he moved the main scene of the excavations to the northern part of the ancient city, and there the team discovered an even more impressive structure that was, according to Petrie, "doubtless the Egyptian residency for a governor." It was apparent that Tell el-Farah, like Beth Shean, was an important Egyptian garrison city and administrative center. The comparison with Beth Shean was made even more compelling by the discovery of a cemetery to the northwest of the city.

Petrie's discovery of the tombs at the "500" cemetery (all cemeteries were numbered) at Tell el-Farah was the most important evidence of

COFFINS AND
CONTROVERSY

ANOTHER
FORTRESS,
MORE TOMBS

65

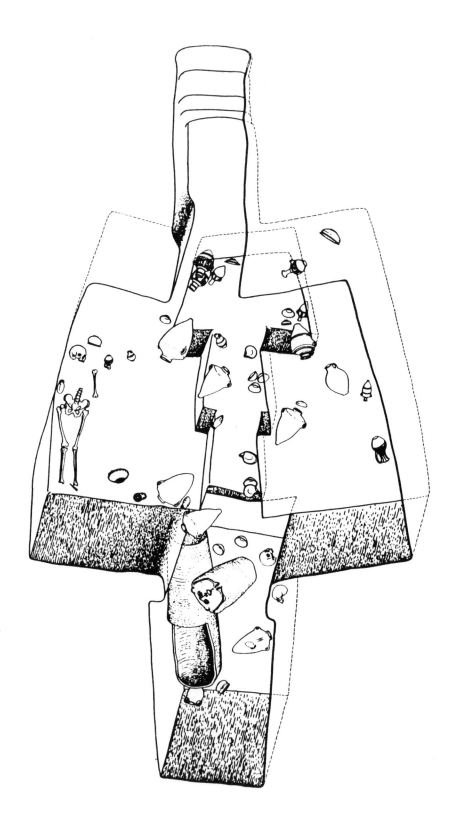

Isometric reconstruction of a tomb from Tell el-Farah.

66

Objects from a Tell el-Farah tomb. In addition to the pottery, typical of local types of the twelfth century B.C., the finds include two daggers, the first with a bronze handle and an iron blade. Three small bronze rings were part of the fittings of the dagger, which was snapped in two in antiquity to prevent its use. The second is a double-edged bronze dagger cast in one piece, with a long fang for a handle.

Early Iron Age burial customs ever found in Palestine. Two tombs contained anthropoid clay coffins. With his unfailing instinct—he was something of an archaeological divining rod—he had set his diggers to work at the edge of the cemetery, where they cleared five large tombs cut into the bedrock. From the similarity of their orientation and shape Petrie recognized that they had been cut in succession. From their size he deduced that they had been the tombs of the most important functionaries in the Egyptian district administration. And because several of the tombs contained Philistine pottery, he identified them as "the tombs of the Philistine lords." For several centuries, it will be remembered, biblical scholars had wrestled with the etymology of the Philistine title *seren*, or "lord," and most had concluded that it was derived from the Greek title *tyrannos*, further proof of the Philistines' Aegean origin. But now Petrie, still in pursuit of substantiation for his own Philistine chronology, suggested that *seren* was derived from the Egyptian word *ser*, the title for district ruler in the Middle Kingdom: the Philistines were for him merely provincial governors in Canaan under the pharaohs of the XVIIIth Dynasty.

Petrie also relied heavily on scarabs—beetle-shaped images held sacred by the ancient Egyptians—for dating the tombs at Tell el-Farah. Since the earliest tomb in the series contained a scarab of the late XVIIIth Dynasty and others contained scarabs dated from Ramesses II (c.1304–1227 B.C.) through Ramesses XI (c.1113–1085 B.C.), he was confident that his proposed chronology had been vindicated. The idea that the scarabs might have remained in circulation as amulets or heirlooms long after the pharaoh named on them had passed over the horizon never troubled Petrie. But while his dating remained open to challenge, his discovery of two anthropoid clay coffins in the Tell el-Farah tombs,

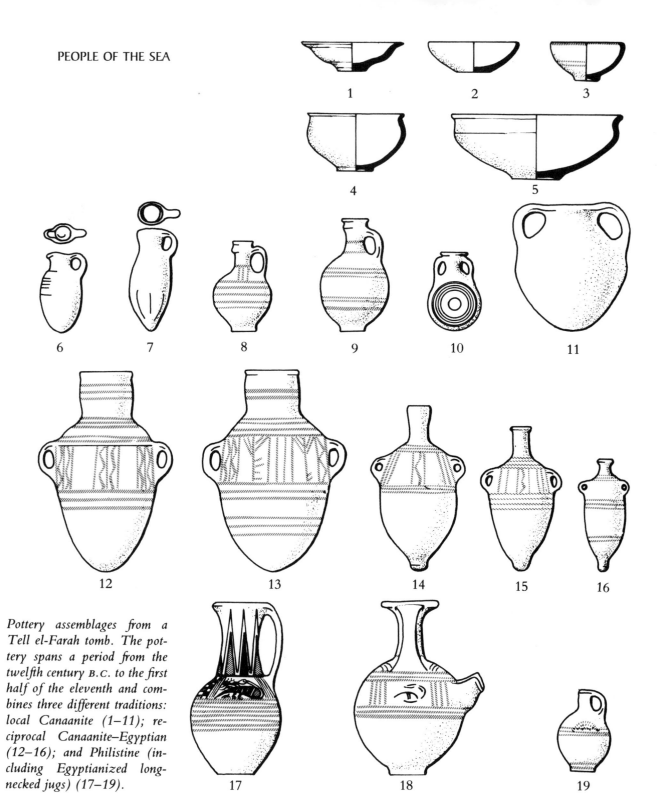

Pottery assemblages from a Tell el-Farah tomb. The pottery spans a period from the twelfth century B.C. to the first half of the eleventh and combines three different traditions: local Canaanite (1–11); reciprocal Canaanite–Egyptian (12–16); and Philistine (including Egyptianized long-necked jugs) (17–19).

together with Philistine pottery, established the connection between the two types of artifacts which had been missing at Beth Shean.

Petrie was apparently not aware that Père Vincent had already noted the resemblance of some of the detachable lids to the gold masks of Mycenae. But while Vincent had been forced to admit that there was a long chronological gap between the Mycenaean custom and the appearance of the clay coffins in Canaan, Petrie had no such problem. On the contrary, he assumed a close chronological connection. He further dismissed the idea that the faces on the two coffin lids were stylized; referring to the naturalistic mask on one of them, he wrote that "the special interest of the pottery mask of a lord of the Philistines lies in the fact that no portraits of these *seren* have been known hitherto. Rough as the work is, the main type is evident, with a large aquiline nose, a short beard on the lower lip, and plaited locks down the sides of the face." Petrie judiciously failed to mention the grotesque mask on the second coffin lid, whose features were more animal than human. He preferred to leave no room for doubt. "We obtain from this series," he asserted, "a full and clear view of the burial customs during the age of the Philistine lords under the suzerainty of the Egyptians."

If Petrie's extremely early dating were accurate, the study of Philistine history would have to start again, virtually from scratch. There were soon, however, some serious doubts about how full and clear a picture Petrie had really drawn. Dr. William F. Albright, director of the American School of Oriental Research in Jerusalem and one of the rising figures in the world of Near Eastern archaeology, was ready to challenge the implications of Petrie's assertions, despite the latter's almost legendary standing in the field.

EGYPTIAN IMPACT— ON WHOM?

Albright had been deeply impressed by the work of Garstang and Phythian-Adams at Ashkelon and was convinced that the generally accepted dating of the time of the Philistines' arrival in Canaan was correct. On the basis of his own work at the inland site of Tell Beit Mirsim from 1926 to 1932, Albright had found stratigraphic confirmation for the appearance of Philistine pottery only in the levels that began in the twelfth century B.C., shortly after the war with Ramesses III. In 1932 he published an article in the *American Journal of Archaeology* in which he convincingly restored Philistine pottery to its proper chronological place. But at the same time he also sidestepped the "Philistine-anthropoid coffin connection."

In reviewing Petrie's finds from the "Tombs of the Philistine Lords," he quickly came to the conclusion that while the sequence that Petrie had established was reliable, his dating of the tombs was wrong. For example, the earliest tomb, dated by Petrie to 1320 B.C., had contained

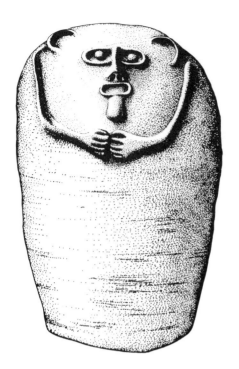

Anthropoid coffin lids from Tell el-Farah. Left: The ears are placed high on the head and are more animal-like than human. The sticklike arms, with clenched fists meeting below the stylized Osiris beard, frame the crude features of the face. Ineptly modeled on the grotesque style, it is far removed from the deliberate exaggeration of the Beth Shean grotesque lids. Right: This lid shows a debased version of a wig made in a combination of appliqué and deep incisions, with oval ears incorporated. The sticklike arms with overlapping hands follow the curving line of the wig and frame the face. An unusual feature is the round indentation at the base of the Osiris beard.

no Mycenaean pottery, as might have been expected. It had only the characteristic Philistine and local forms that appeared in the twelfth century B.C. Similarly, a tomb containing a scarab of Ramesses II from the thirteenth century B.C., a time when Mycenaean trade with Canaan was flourishing, had been dated to that period when, in fact, it belonged to a later period: it, too, contained only Philistine and other local Early Iron Age forms. The whole series, Albright contended, should be placed, like the pottery itself, in the period following the historically attested-to Philistine invasion around 1190 B.C. In 1885, Petrie himself had substantiated that dating when excavating a site with anthropoid clay coffins called Tell Nebesheh in the northwestern Nile delta. It had contained pottery similiar to the finds at Tell el-Farah. In 1887 two other Egyptologists, the Swiss Edouard Naville and the British Francis Griffith, had discovered anthropoid coffins and twelfth–century B.C. pottery at another delta site, Tell el-Yahudiyeh.

As for the Philistine connection to the clay coffins, Albright argued that since all of the clay anthropoid coffins in Egypt and in Canaan had been found at sites of strategic or commercial importance, he was inclined to attribute their appearance not to a specific group of invaders, but to the existence of Egyptian military garrisons at those sites. Mummy cases were among the most characteristic of Egyptian artifacts, and if there were any historical conclusions to be drawn from their

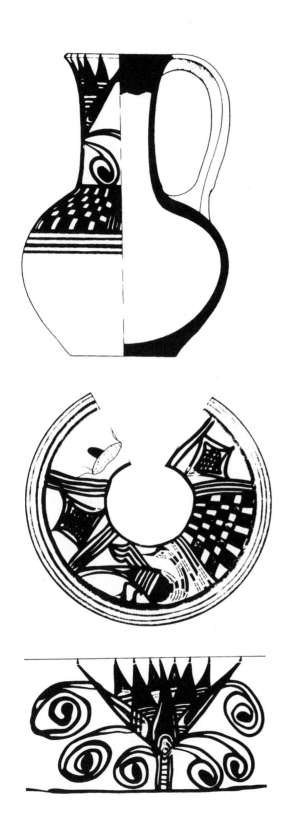

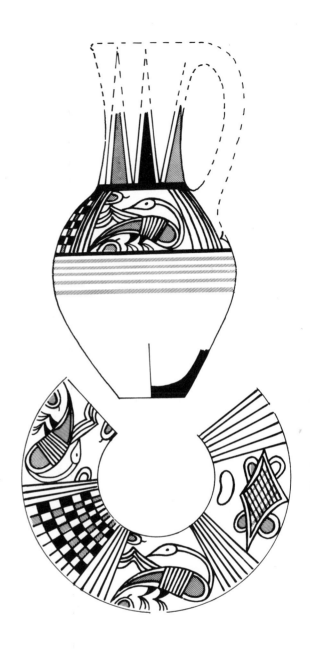

Two Philistine jugs in the Egyptian tradition, with long necks and lotus motifs that are stylized (right) and naturalistic (left).

discovery, they would be more relevant to Egyptian history than to that of the Philistines.

Burial in anthropoid coffins had been the official mode of interment for Egyptian royalty for more than seven centuries before the Philistines' arrival. The custom, reserved originally for kings, queens, and other high court officials, became popular and more widespread within Egyptian society as traditional class distinctions began to break down. Cheaper materials, such as wood and clay, were used to imitate the earlier coffins of granite and gold. That most Egyptologists had concentrated on the earlier and more elaborate coffins did not in any way indicate that clay coffins were uncommon in ancient times. Quite the contrary, according to Albright: the progressive development of the styles of the clay coffins (the wood coffins did not survive) demonstrated the spread of the influence of the culture of the Egyptian aristocracy. In the examples from Canaan, the progression could be seen clearly.

Albright pointed to a distinction that had never been noticed before: the "naturalistic" coffins from Beth Shean, with their heavy Egyptian-style wigs and lotus decorations, were associated with the imported Mycenaean pottery and were clearly the earliest in the series, from the thirteenth century B.C. On the other hand, the "grotesque" coffins from Beth Shean and Tell el-Farah, found together with later Philistine and local pottery bore Egyptian attributes such as the Osiris beard and hands resting on the chest, attributes that had clearly lost their original significance. These coffins, he asserted, were simply further away in time from the original Egyptian styles.

From Albright's review of the evidence of the anthropoid coffins, it was plain that the impact of Egyptian culture on Canaan had continued long after the breakdown of Egypt's political power, and was being felt long after the arrival and settlement of the Philistines. Nonetheless, in the matter of the Philistines, their presence at Beth Shean at the time of King Saul's death, or their connection to the "Tombs of the Philistine Lords" at Tell el-Farah, Albright was reluctant to make any definite commitment. Although the anthropoid coffins were obvious imitations of Egyptian protoypes, "who the imitators were and whether they belonged to one race or to many races escapes us completely. The problem seems at present insoluble."

Until the end of the thirties, various expeditions continued digging in Palestine, corroborating evidence for the Early Iron Age dating of Philistine pottery. From 1928 to 1933 an American expedition from Haverford College had resumed digging at Beth Shean, and from 1925 to 1939 an expedition from the Oriental Institute of the University of Chicago uncovered evidence of a Philistine presence at the great biblical city of Megiddo in the north of the country. But with the outbreak of

World War II and the continuing disturbances in Palestine that led to the Israeli War of Independence, almost all archaeological fieldwork in the country came to a halt. The "golden age" of Palestinian archaeology under the aegis of the British Mandatory administration was over. The only hope for significant progress on the question of Philistine culture, as with other apsects of biblical archaeology, would have to come, at least for the foreseeable future, from the students and scholars of the Hebrew University of Jerusalem, the only institution of higher learning in the humanities in the country at the time.

Until now our intellectual curiosity about the Philistines was stimulated by the amazing achievements—and even the instructive misconceptions—of generations of archaeological pioneers before us. From now on, we ourselves would be brought face-to-face, pick and shovel in hand, with the remains of some of the mysterious protagonists of our own ancient history.

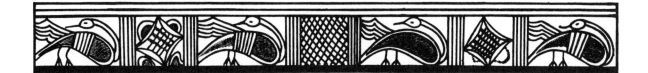

PART II

OUR OWN
SEARCH BEGINS

Trude Dothan

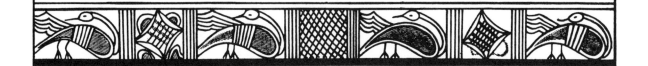

CHAPTER 6

Through Layers
of History

Archaeology had long held an attraction for the Palestinian Jewish community. From the time of the founding of the Hebrew University of Jerusalem in 1925, it had been recognized as a means of providing a tangible connection between the ancient Land of Israel, called *Eretz Yisrael* in Hebrew, and the Jewish people now returning to its borders. With the discovery in 1928 of a spectacular mosaic pavement at the site of an ancient synagogue in Kibbutz Beth Alpha, not far from Beth Shean, public interest soared. Scholars and amateurs alike would often undertake casual explorations of sites much as one went to a picnic or down to the beach. My own interest in archaeology was fired by the trips around the country I took with my father while I was still a Jerusalem schoolgirl.

I was brought to Jerusalem before I was two years old by my mother, who was a painter. My father, an architect and artist, had come from Vienna a year earlier to pave the way for us. I was an adventuresome girl, attracted apparently to wide horizons, because my first love was astronomy. But when, in 1941, I registered at the Hebrew University, I changed directions: from up and out to down and back. I enrolled in the Archaeology Department, where a formal program of study had been established in 1934 by Professor Eliezer Sukenik.

The course of study was, theoretically, a five-year master's program, but I received my degree only in 1950, after the establishment of the

State of Israel. All of those years in between are irrevocably tied in my memory not only to libraries, examinations, and academic interests but also to the war in Europe, especially with the German advances in Africa, and the subsequent unrest in Palestine. It was the rule, not the exception, for the Palestinian Jewish student, male or female, to become involved in the day-to-day struggle for independence, and I was no different. Between one exam and the next I was in the army, in intelligence, drawing maps from aerial photographs. It was in the intelligence, by the way, that I met Moshe, although we probably were acquainted from the lecture hall at the university.

Moshe's road to archaeology was somewhat different from mine. He had come to Jerusalem in October 1938 from his hometown, Cracow, Poland. Getting a student's visa to study at the Hebrew University was one of the few ways open to young Jews to reach Palestine just before the war. Moshe spent a year as a student of literature and philosophy until 1940, when he joined a kibbutz near Haifa. From the kibbutz he would often take the horse and wagon for jaunts to nearby Beth She'arim, where a Jewish necropolis from the Roman period had been excavated. Moshe joined the British army at the end of 1942 and caught a glimpse of the Pyramids while in uniform in Egypt. But it wasn't until he found himself in 1944, still in uniform, face-to-face with the great monuments of Rome, that he made up his mind where his future lay. When he was released from military service in 1945 and returned to Palestine, he again registered at the university, this time as a student of archaeology.

It took Moshe somewhat longer to get his M.A. because, like everyone else, he was caught up in the struggle for Israeli independence and, in the middle of his studies, donned an army uniform for the second time. If our university studies had been interwoven with army service, both our army "careers" were just as certainly interwoven with archaeology, whether through surveying or mapping or actually digging. In all events, I was still in uniform when, in the autumn of 1948, a half a year after Israel's Declaration of Independence, I was recruited by my professor, Dr. Benjamin Mazar, for the dig at Tell Qasile, on the northern outskirts of Tel Aviv. And it was at Tell Qasile that my lifelong curiosity about the Philistines was kindled.

Mazar was one of the country's prominent archaeologists and biblical historians and, no less important, a formative influence on successive generations of Israeli archaeologists. Born in Russia and educated in ancient history and languages at the universities of Giessen and Berlin, he came to Palestine in the late twenties with an interest in combining the evidence of written history with physical geography and archaeology. Traveling through the country and collecting pottery samples,

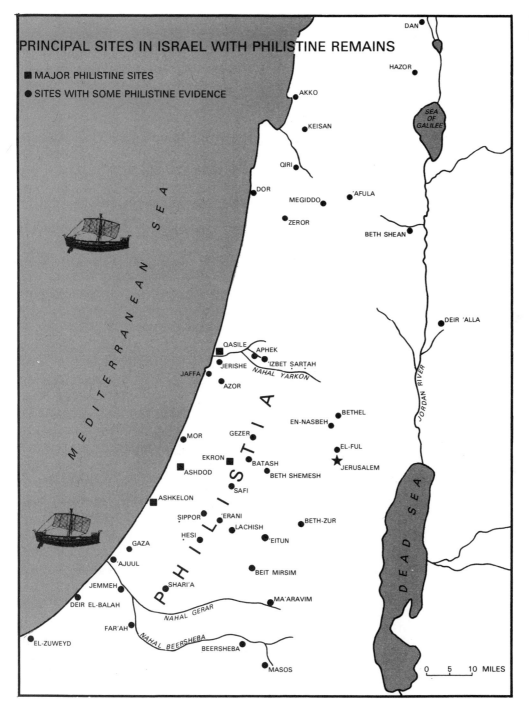

PRINCIPAL SITES IN ISRAEL WITH PHILISTINE REMAINS

■ MAJOR PHILISTINE SITES
● SITES WITH SOME PHILISTINE EVIDENCE

MEDITERRANEAN SEA

DAN

HAZOR

AKKO

KEISAN

SEA OF GALILEE

QIRI

DOR

MEGIDDO

'AFULA

ZEROR

BETH SHEAN

JORDAN RIVER

DEIR 'ALLA

QASILE

APHEK

JERISHE

'IZBET SARTAH

NAHAL YARKON

JAFFA

AZOR

BETHEL

EN-NASBEH

MOR

GEZER

EL-FUL

EKRON

BATASH

JERUSALEM

ASHDOD

BETH SHEMESH

SAFI

ASHKELON

SIPPOR

'ERANI

BETH-ZUR

LACHISH

HESI

'EITUN

GAZA

'AJUUL

BEIT MIRSIM

JEMMEH

SHARI'A

DEIR EL-BALAH

MA'ARAVIM

NAHAL GERAR

FAR'AH

NAHAL BEERSHEBA

EL-ZUWEYD

BEERSHEBA

MASOS

PHILISTIA

DEAD SEA

0 5 10 MILES

he was able to establish the location of dozens of biblical places. He realized that it might be possible to use this method to reconstruct changes in settlement patterns and commercial and cultural connections over the millennia. Mazar's interest was not restricted to the biblical period. During the thirties he conducted pioneering work at Beth She'arim, and during the forties at the Early Bronze Age city of Beth Yerah on the southern shore of the Sea of Galilee.

"FOR THE KING . . ." In 1945 Tel Aviv engineer and archaeologist Jacob Kaplan and his wife, Haya, were exploring the summit of the mound of Tell Qasile when they happened to pick up a fragment of an ancient bowl with Hebrew letters incised on its base. What made this chance discovery especially intriguing was the inscription, a short but complete text relating to royal commerce or taxation during the period of the Israelite monarchy. Written in cursive Hebrew letters characteristic of the ninth or eighth century B.C., it read: "For the King, one thousand and one hundred [measures of] oil." It was signed by Hiyahu, a typical Israelite name. The following year a second Hebrew inscription was found at Tell Qasile recording the shipment of thirty shekels, or about eleven ounces, of the "Gold of Ophir," a precious commodity mentioned in the biblical accounts of King Solomon's overseas trades.

When the Kaplans brought these two *ostraca*, or inscribed sherds, to Mazar's attention, he became convinced that Tell Qasile and the surrounding area might be of great archaeological significance. Mazar believed that the Yarkon River, on whose northern bank Tell Qasile was located, played a large role in the settlement's history as a convenient means of transport between the coastal plain and the Mediterranean. In the biblical description of the negotiations between Solomon and King Hiram of Tyre over building materials for the temple in Jerusalem, Hiram is quoted as saying [2 Chronicles 2:16] that "we will cut whatever timber you need from Lebanon, and bring it to you in rafts by sea to Jaffa so that you may take it up to Jerusalem." The precise route of that shipment had long puzzled scholars. The rocky and windswept harbor of Jaffa seemed an unwise place to unload the fragile and valuable cedar logs, and since the Hebrew speaks not of the "sea of Jaffa" but of the "Jaffa sea," Mazar realized that the Yarkon River, only six miles north of Jaffa, could have provided the sheltered anchorage needed. Although there were several other ancient sites along the river's banks, the receipts found at Tell Qasile suggested that excavations there might uncover the remains of a royal Israelite port city.

With a pledge of financial assistance from Israel Rokach, the mayor of Tel Aviv, Mazar began to assemble a staff from among Israeli stu-

dents and specialists who had worked with him before. By this time
the fiercest fighting was over and people were eager to get back to
work. Among those who joined the project were Immanuel Dunayevsky, an experienced engineer and architect who had worked with
Mazar at Beth She'arim and Beth Yerah and who would become a
prominent figure in Israeli archaeology; Jacob Kaplan; and another
experienced excavator, Pesach Bar Adon. Mazar arranged leave for me
from the army, and together with a fellow student, Miriam Tadmor,
we worked as registrars of the excavation finds. The dig at Tell Qasile
is noteworthy—aside from archaeological reasons—for reasons of sen-
timent. First of all, it received Excavation License #1 from the newly
established Israel Department of Antiquities. Second and more personally, although Moshe was still on active duty when we started the dig,
he joined us a year later after completing his studies, and, not long
after, we were married.

When I first arrived from Jerusalem before the start of the excavations,
I was frankly disappointed by Tell Qasile's four-acre summit. It was
just a low hill covered with thistles and a single mulberry tree. There
were no signs of ancient buildings or fortifications on the surface, just
a few small stones and a scattering of pottery sherds here and there.
Aside from a pumphouse at the foot of the southern slope and a mudbrick storehouse that would become our headquarters, the tell itself
seemed ominously desolate. But soon Dunayevsky and Kaplan had
surveyed the entire mound, drawn a topographical map, and established
a grid. Mazar chose to begin the excavations in two twenty-meter
squares on the southern slope, where the most important buildings of
the assumed port should have been located, and from that point on it
didn't take long before I came to share Mazar's enthusiasm.

As soon as we had cleared the surface soil from the initial excavation
area, it became clear that Tell Qasile had supported a series of thriving
settlements, the last of which had been abandoned only in the Middle
Ages. The latest remains had eroded and were fragmentary, but beneath
a thin layer of soil filled with fragments of pottery characteristic of the
period of Egyptian Mamluk rule in Palestine (till the fifteenth century
A.D.) we began to uncover the superimposed levels of more fully preserved towns from Byzantine, Roman, Hellenistic, and Persian times.
In addition to the everyday pottery typical of these periods, each of the
compressed levels provided evocative glimpses of the changing culture
at the site. At a depth of only one yard below the surface of the tell,
we found the remains of a well-built royal Israelite town. The existence
of "casemate walls"—a double row of fortifications separated by a row
of chambers—pointed to the period of King Solomon, since such walls

had been found at Gezer and Megiddo, two other excavated royal cities of this period.

For the most part, the remains of the Israelite level consisted of open courtyards, dwellings, silos, and hearths, but in the south an impressive structure had apparently dominated that part of the city for at least a hundred years. The building, almost twenty yards long and twelve yards wide, was built of mudbrick. Its outer walls were almost a meter thick. It was clearly a public building of some sort, for the main portion of the basement contained four long storerooms, similar to those at the "governor's residence" at Megiddo. Furthermore, while there was little domestic pottery in the rooms, two official seals and a bronze spearhead were found.

Mazar's initial theory that Tell Qasile functioned as a royal Israelite port and store city seemed to have been confirmed. But that was not the end of the story: beneath a thick layer of destruction and burnt debris on which the Israelite city was founded, we uncovered the even richer and more unexpected levels of three Philistine cities.

PHILISTINE FARMERS AND CRAFTSMEN

As students of archaeology we had learned the basic facts of Philistine history and culture as they had been pieced together over the previous decades. But the finds from Tell Qasile suddenly threw a blanket of doubt over some of our accepted notions. First of all, Tell Qasile was not easily identifiable with any Philistine city known from the Bible. It is more than twenty-four miles north of Ashdod, the northernmost of the Philistine capitals, which indicates a far wider area of initial settlement than previously thought. But more significant, it was believed that the Philistines had arrived in Canaan as hostile invaders, either destroying the Canaanite cities that lay in their path and settling on their ruins or, in some cases, finding employment as mercenaries in Egyptian-controlled garrison towns. Based in large measure on the Medinet Habu reliefs and inscriptions, it was generally believed that, whatever their specific Aegean origin, the Philistines had indeed brought only ruin and upheaval to Canaan at the end of the Late Bronze Age. The finds at Tell el-Safi, Beth Shemesh, Ashkelon, Gezer, Beth Shean, and Megiddo had all seemed to validate this hypothesis. Philistine society was assumed to be predatory, based on the exploitation of the country's natural riches by an aristocratic or military ruling class. When we got down to the earliest levels at Tell Qasile, it was clear that this site, at least, would not support the idea of violent Philistine settlements. No earlier settlement preceded the Philistines. This city had actually been *founded* by them.

Although the lowest level was severely damaged by erosion, it appeared to have been a sparsely populated village of farmers. The Philistine pottery was as elaborate as any found at other sites in the country, and Mazar dated it to about the middle of the twelfth century B.C., soon after their battles with Ramesses III. The Philistines of Tell Qasile had chosen to live on a previously unoccupied ridge overlooking a fertile valley. This level produced no signs of weapons or fortifications, only flint sickle blades for harvesting grain, underground silos for storing it, and millstones for grinding it into flour.

This peaceful Philistine settlement also respresented only the first stage in their untroubled and steadily prospering development. Overlaying the lowest stratum and slightly to the north were structures and artifacts indicating a gradual yet dramatic change in the inhabitants' way of life. Within about two generations of their arrival, the people of Tell Qasile were no longer only farmers. They were now craftsmen and apparently merchants as well. Around the tell a thick mudbrick fortification appeared. The inhabitants rebuilt and expanded one of the mudbrick buildings of the earlier stratum, installing two large furnaces, similar to those discovered by Petrie at Tell Jemmeh. Petrie had claimed his furnaces as conclusive evidence for the Philistines' biblically reported monopoly on iron. The furnaces of Tell Qasile revealed only copper and bronze smelting, shown by traces still adhering to the insides of pottery crucibles.

Crucible from Tell Qasile.

The metal workshop was just one part of the large complex. To the east was a granary with a subterranean silo, and beyond it a room paved with fieldstone on which we discovered evidence of other trades. We found pottery and stone vessels and rectangular blocks of clay pierced at the top for hanging. This was a class of artifacts that earlier archaeologists had identified as loomweights. Somewhat more enigmatic were the bowls found on this level with handles strangely positioned inside, similar to other such bowls found at other sites in Canaan and Egypt. Various theories had been proposed about their possible function, but the most significant clue was the grooves worn in the bottom of their handles, evidence of the continuous friction of threads. That the bowls were found in the same building with the loomweights suggested to us that we had uncovered an area for textile production. They were, in fact, "spinning bowls," used to hold balls of yarn as they were twisted into thread. The process, I later discovered, was clearly depicted in Egyptian tomb reliefs.

The latest Philistine level was by far the richest, for all over the digging areas we found signs of intensified reconstruction and the final development of a symmetrical city plan. As we expanded the area of the digging northward, toward the center of the tell, we uncovered two blocks of buildings separated by a clearly defined street. The southern

Storejars in situ *in Tell Qasile storerooms.*

block of buildings was just a reconstruction of the industrial quarter of the preceding period, for we found more evidence of the specialization of crafts and trades. The blast furnaces had been repaired and continued to be used for metalworking, and the underground silo in the adjoining room continued to be maintained. If in the previous stratum we had found evidence of spinning and weaving, here we found a vat with two connected basins that may have been used for dyeing. Another structure had been built either as a public storeroom or granary for the use of the entire community.

All the structures here were aligned on a rectangular grid, divided by parallel and intersecting streets. The private dwellings were of an architectural unity: each was entered directly from the street and consisted of an inner courtyard around which were kitchens with ovens, living quarters, and storerooms. While the earlier levels had provided evidence of local craftsmen serving the immediate area and surroundings, a storeroom here, filled with rows of heavy storejars, seemed to indicate the city's widening horizons—the first evidence of overseas contact since the cutoff of trade with Cyprus and the Aegean at the end of the Late Bronze Age more than a century before.

The rows of storejars carefully arranged in this building represented what must have been a lively bulk trade in wine or oil. The most common form had a capacity of more than five gallons and resembled those found at other sites in the country which dated to the eleventh century B.C. Among the other large vessels were two jars with high, vertical necks of distinctly Egyptian form. We knew little of international commerce at this period, but it seemed that Tell Qasile on the coast had become a focus of agricultural trade. Several flasks of a type known from Cyprus and Phoenicia indicated a possible route for the trade. One of the most commonly held misconceptions about the source of the Philistines' power—namely, their monopoly on ironworking—seemed to be conclusively disproved by our finds. There had been no trace of iron in the earlier strata, and even in this, the latest and richest community, iron was still rare. The only iron objects found were two fragmentary knives and a single sword blade.

It was at this point that violent destruction swept the city. Overlaying all the structures of this stratum was a thick layer of ash and collapsed debris. The city had been burned and leveled; charred beams from the ceilings of some of the houses, storerooms, and workshops had collapsed and smashed the pottery vessels on the lower floors. The fire had been so intense that it baked the mudbricks and filled them with a thick layer of rubble from the walls. The date of this destruction, determined by the various pottery types under the debris, was about

1000 B.C. The date, by the way, provided a suggestive correspondence to some of the most famous historical events of this period: King David's victorious campaigns against the Philistines.

TRADITION AND ASSIMILATION

Most earlier scholars of Philistine pottery had interpreted it as a homogeneous archaeological phenomenon, representing the establishment and expansion of Philistine culture for the nearly two centuries between their arrival in the country in the twelfth century B.C. and their defeat by the Israelites. Certainly, their pottery was at first distinct from the other ceramic traditions in Canaan, but none of the early excavations at Philistine sites had succeeded in tracing its subsequent development. The only attempt to divide Philistine pottery into stylistic stages had been undertaken by Arne Furumark, a Swedish archaeologist and art historian, who, in 1944, had published an encyclopedic corpus of Mycenaean decorations and forms. Following the method of comparative analysis that Walter Heurtley had begun in the thirties, Furumark viewed Philistine pottery as a regional variation of the Late Mycenaean tradition, in which he distinguished a progressive deterioration in the quality of the Aegean motifs. Because it was based on rather subjective stylistic criteria and was supported only by the questionable stratigraphy of the earlier Philistine digs, his chronological scheme was not considered definitive. The excavations at Tell Qasile, however, confirmed and elaborated upon Furumark's hypotheses.

We found, for example, that the elaborate decoration so characteristic of the first settlement became more schematic and was less carefully executed by the potters of the succeeding city, as if the memories of their Aegean origin were slowly fading away. The clearest example of this was the gradual simplification and ultimate disappearance of the "Philistine bird," which had been so common in the local potters' repertoire.

In fact, in the third Philistine city of the end of the eleventh century B.C., it was difficult for us to distinguish more than a few vestiges of the Mycenaean tradition in the pottery. The everyday bowls, jugs, and jars were similar to those found at inland sites: in place of the thick white slip, or clay coating, that covered the distinctive Philistine vessels of the earlier periods, in apparent imitation of the light finely levigated Mycenaean clays, the dominant fashion now favored a reddish surface, often given a shiny finish by burnishing or rubbing the clay surface of the vessels before they were baked. The frequent decoration of red and brown bands recalled the styles that were, by the end of the eleventh century B.C., becoming popular throughout the eastern Mediterranean. The most distinctive vessel type of this stratum was a heavy, thick krater whose only artistic connection to the earlier Aegean styles was the use of heavy crude spirals painted on the reddish surface in dark brown paint. By the time of the destruction of this city, the Philistines' culture had become largely indistinguishable from that of their Israelite foes. In other words, assimilation into the surrounding cultural environment had, over the years, beset them. Tell Qasile offered the first indication of the Philistines' gradual cultural transformation from an Aegean people to a Near Eastern one.

As the excavations continued for three more seasons, our discoveries naturally aroused the interest of other scholars involved in the study of the development of Philistine culture. And through Mazar's talent for conveying the excitement of these discoveries to the general public as well, the ancient settlements of Tell Qasile—Philistine and Israelite— became a source of considerable interest.

One rather amusing offshoot of this interest was the visit of a reporter from *Ha'aretz*, Israel's most sober and serious daily newspaper. He came in search of a compelling story of archaeologists, buried cities, and the mystery of the Philistines, and Mazar accompanied him over the various digging areas, patiently explaining to him the significance of the three strata, the labyrinthine structural components, and the pottery finds. Mazar related, among other things, the difficulties of unraveling the mystery of the Philistines' exact Aegean origin, pointing out that there seemed to be evidence, however inconclusive, that they were connected with the Minoan culture of Crete.

The reporter nodded politely the whole time, thanked Mazar for his patience, and left. A week later headlines in the paper announced to an expectant world: KING MINOS FOUND! The article barely mentioned the three cities or the gradual development of Philistine pottery. It was devoted instead to a description of the palaces of Knossos, the legend of King Minos and the Labyrinth, and their intimate connection to the northern outskirts of Tel Aviv. On his way home from Tell Qasile, the reporter had probably been struck by the rich connotations hidden in the name of the neighboring Arab village of Sheikh Munnis, which he had to pass. He developed his own etymology and ludicrously linked the possible Cretan origin of the Philistines with the name of the village. It may not have been accurate archaeological reporting, but it was certainly dramatic!

Eventually, of course, the public came to understand and appreciate our findings in their proper context, just as I came to understand that my own interest in the mystery of the Philistines was not a passing fancy.

CHAPTER 7

Piecing Together a Civilization

By the early 1950s, archaeological understanding of Philistine culture was undergoing a dramatic transformation, due not only to the recent discoveries in Israel, but to those in other parts of the eastern Mediterranean as well. Excavations in Greece, Cyprus, and throughout the Aegean were beginning to uncover evidence of the extent of the social upheavals and movements of population that took place throughout the entire region at the end of the Late Bronze Age.

The migration, settlement, and expansion of the Philistines in Canaan has, therefore, to be viewed in that wider perspective, as one of the many consequences of the breakdown of Mycenaean civilization. Yet as the research continued, it gradually became clear that the peculiarities of the Philistines' material culture—their settlement patterns, pottery tradition, and burial customs—offered evidence of the unique way in which they had adapted themselves in this period of widespread cultural change.

From the excavations at Tell Qasile, we had learned the main outlines of their economic and cultural development. From an apparent agricultural basis, the settlers had gradually turned to crafts and commerce, transforming their city into a regional center of trade.

The process of Philistine settlement and expansion was obviously much more complex than had been previously imagined, but generalizations were still somewhat premature. What we needed was evidence

for the economic and cultural development of the great cities of the Philistine heartland, and as I worked on the finds from Tell Qasile, I realized that such evidence was already available. Although their potential had never been exploited fully, the pottery and other artifacts uncovered during the excavations of the much larger Philistine settlements during the twenties and thirties could perhaps serve as the basis for a far-reaching reassessment of their role in the transitional period from the Late Bronze Age to the Early Iron Age.

In 1951, while Moshe was undertaking a survey of the lower Sorek Valley and beginning to work with the Department of Antiquities, I began to consider attempting such a reassessment myself. I had reached a point in my graduate studies at which I had to select a subject for my doctoral dissertation. I was fascinated by the aesthetic qualities of Philistine pottery and hoped to concentrate on the relations between art, archaeology, and cultural interconnections. The wealth of finds from the earlier excavations at Tell el-Safi, Beth Shemesh, Ashkelon, Tell Jemmeh, and Tell el-Farah, among others, had yet to be fully analyzed. Just as the Medinet Habu reliefs and inscriptions offered us information from the Egyptian perspective and the biblical accounts offered information from the Israelite, the excavated Philistine settlements offered us the unwritten historical records of the Philistines themselves. It might be possible, I hoped, to "read" this record.

Direct access to the finds themselves was, of course, essential. The excavated Philistine artifacts had to be handled and studied directly, for the quality of the materials used and the techniques of the ancient artisans were the best indications of their origins and development. Yet as I began to consider the practical challenge of examining the earlier finds, I realized that the vast majority were stored at the Palestine Archaeological Museum, the headquarters of the Department of Antiquities during the British Mandate, now in territory controlled by the Hashemite Kingdom of Jordan. A barrier of barbed wire, land mines, and bunkers lay between me and the materials I wanted to study. There was an alternative, however, since the Department of Antiquities had routinely allowed a representative sample of finds from every excavation to be taken out of the country for study and analysis by the foreign institutions that sponsored the digs. And so I began to compile a list of the most important foreign collections of finds from Philistine sites.

Many of the most characteristic finds from Petrie's excavations at Tell Jemmeh and Tell el-Farah were at the Institute of Archaeology at the University of London; many complete vessels from Beth Shemesh were at Haverford College near Philadelphia; and a significant collection of finds from Beth Shean, including some of the anthropoid coffins, were at the University Museum in Philadelphia. Much of the material from Megiddo, a site that provided a continuous sequence of the country's ancient cultural development, was available for study at the University of Chicago's Oriental Institute.

At the initiative of Professor Mazar, who had been visiting professor at the Oriental Institute at the end of 1951, I was able to undertake a year of study abroad. I spent eight months in Chicago, where I was privileged to work under Professor Helene J. Kantor, author of the seminal study *The Aegean and the Orient in the Second Millennium*. Helene was, without question, the great formative influence on the direction of my work. That year I met many prominent archaeologists and, while acquiring academic disciplines, was exposed to broad and stimulating intellectual vistas. I visited the collections at Haverford, Philadelphia, New York, and Boston and was able to examine excavation notes, photographs, drawings, and the finds themselves. Later, in London where Moshe was also at work, I spent months going through the enormous and complex assemblages of Petrie's finds from the relevant sites in Palestine and Egypt, stored in the basement of the Institute of Archaeology. From my examinations of two major elements of the Philistines' material culture—their pottery and the anthropoid coffins—I began to sense the essential character of Philistine society itself.

Fifteen years had passed since Walter Heurtley attempted to trace the geographical origins and character of the Philistines through their pottery traditions. His main conclusion—that it was simply a nostalgic survival of the Late Bronze Age Mycenaean tradition, made "to satisfy a demand by the newcomers for something which had a Mycenaean look"—was no longer tenable. The later classification by Arne Furumark in 1941 showed that many Philistine shapes and decorations were exact reproductions of the contemporary styles of the early twelfth century B.C., the so-called Mycenaean IIIC period (c.1225–1050 B.C.). The similarities were apparently based on active contacts and not on wistful memories. But in searching for the Philistines' precise point of origin, Furumark had been no more successful than Heurtley. The close stylistic similarities of Philistine pottery to the shapes and decorative elements of such disparate regions as Crete, the Greek mainland, Rhodes, and Cyprus were difficult to explain in terms of a single geographical point of origin.

I decided on a different approach. Instead of looking for a single source of cultural influence, I wanted, first of all, to establish the full range of Philistine vessel types and decorative patterns (plate 5). The *mixture* of traditions was, perhaps, no less significant than the preservation of a single tradition, and my basic work of classification con-

89

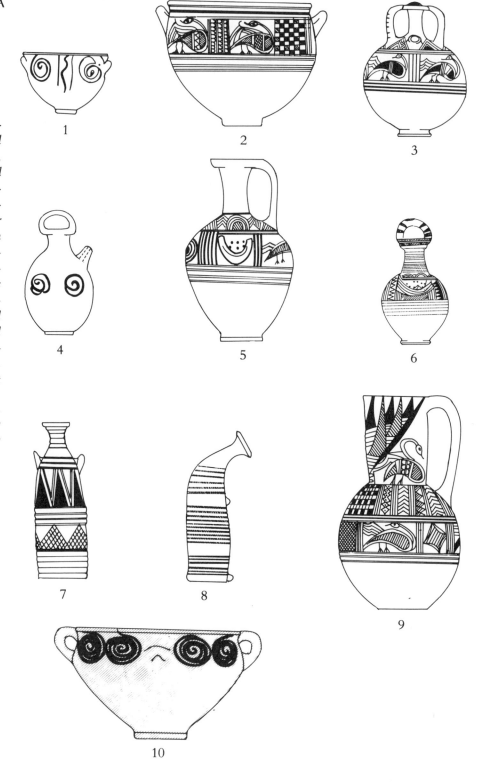

Main types of Philistine pottery. 1. The bell-shaped bowl with horizontal loop handles, usually decorated with looped spirals. 2. The krater with horizontal handles, usually decorated elaborately. 3. Stirrup or false-necked jar with spout on the shoulder, elaborately decorated. 4. Jug with basket handle and spout, known as "feeding bottle." 5. Most common, elaborately decorated strainer-spout jug, so-called Philistine beer bottle. Nos. 1–5 are derived from Mycenaean prototypes. 6. Strainer-spout jug with basket handle. 7. Elongated cylindrical bottle with horizontal loop or pierced lug handles. 8. Horn-shaped vessel, twin to the cylindrical bottle. Nos. 7 and 8 relate to Cypriot types. 9. Jug with high bulging neck, Egyptian in shape and neck decoration, Aegean in the decorative motifs on the main band. 10. A krater, a striking example of latter-period debased hybrid Philistine pottery. Nos. 1–7 are predominantly with white slip and bichrome red-and-black decoration. No. 10 is red slip with black decoration. The decorative motifs on all are based predominantly on the Aegean repertoire.

firmed this assumption. I was eventually able to isolate eighteen distinct vessel types and four separate artistic influences that composed the standard Philistine repertoire. The Mycenaean connections, though obviously close and by far the most important, were not the whole story. Egyptian, Cypriot, and Canaanite influences were evident in Philistine tradition as well. The most revealing characteristic of Philistine pottery was not, in my opinion—as both Heurtley and Furumark had suggested—its conservative character, but rather its surprising innovativeness.

It seems apparent, for example, that at least some Philistine potters had firsthand knowledge of Mycenaean techniques. Their exact reproduction of the intricate filling motifs of Mycenaean IIIC pottery seemed too close to be the result of coincidence or haphazard mimicry. Yet the ways in which they diverged from the Mycenaean tradition were no less significant. Standard Aegean motifs were arranged in new compositions or combined to create new motifs. This innovative transformation of Mycenaean tradition was not the traditional style of any particular homeland but the crystallization of influences that suddenly came together during the period of population movements and social dislocations at the end of the Late Bronze Age and were picked up by the Philistines during migrations that took them gradually from the Aegean to the Near East.

The presence of at least some groups of the Sea Peoples on Cyprus had long been suspected by dint of both archaeological and textual evidence: the sudden flood of Mycenaean IIIC pottery on the island, the Greek legends of heroes of the Trojan War, and the identification of Cyprus as Alashiya, one of the places captured by the Sea Peoples according to the Medinet Habu inscriptions. And while the motifs that appeared on Philistine pottery were especially close to those of the Mycenaean pottery of Cyprus, I found that native Cypriot influences had also been assimilated. The specific historical connection between the Philistine and the Early Iron Age settlers of Cyprus would become an increasingly important issue with further excavations in the coming years.

As for Egyptian influence, we knew from the Medinet Habu reliefs and inscriptions that the Philistines came into close contact with the Egyptians, first as enemies locked in battle and later as mercenaries in Egyptian garrison towns. Yet despite this close historical contact, the Egyptian culture was never before recognized as a component of the Philistines' eclectic artistic tradition. As I went over the material excavated by Petrie at Tell el-Farah, the extent of Egyptian influence was too pervasive to be missed. The adoption of Egyptian forms and decorations on certain types of Philistine artifacts had implications for understanding the character of Philistine society as a whole.

Among the regional offshoots of the Mycenaean tradition that developed throughout the eastern Mediterranean during the twelfth century B.C., the Philistine pottery was distinctive. While most styles clung to the progressively fading memories of the Mycenaean heritage, the Philistines alone rejuvenated the Mycenaean core with new elements. One aspect of this innovation was that required by technical considerations. The local sandy clays of the Canaanite coast required extensive improvisation in order to simulate the appearance of the smooth, fine-grained clay of the Mycenaean pottery of the Aegean. So the Philistines covered their vessels with a thick white slip—a veneer of more finely levigated clay. Yet technical considerations did not explain the mixture of styles or even the use of black and red decoration in place of the less lively Mycenaean monochrome.

Whatever the reason, the innovative Philistine tradition seemed to have already come together by the time of its first appearance in the archaeological record. One of the goals of my systematic study of the Philistine pottery was to place the examples from each site in a chronological series of development, and I found that the main outlines of progression we had distinguished at Tell Qasile proved valid for the other Philistine sites as well. The greatest periods of innovation and mixing of tradition apparently occurred at the time of the Philistines' initial settlement in the early twelfth century B.C. Then, as if the original spirit were fading, the repertoire of shapes and decorations gradually became standardized and simplified, eventually losing its uniqueness to become indistinguishable from the common Iron Age repertoire of the rest of the country at the end of the eleventh century B.C. Although the last phase of Philistine pottery had yet to be delineated more clearly, the main lines of the ceramic developments were already evident. Philistine pottery represented more than just the sum of its components: it seemed to reflect a complex and otherwise unparelleled cultural process that took place in Canaan during the Early Iron Age.

A NEW ANSWER
FOR THE COFFINS

No study of the excavated Philistine artifacts would be complete without at least an attempt to solve the question of the origin and identity of the anthropoid coffins: burial customs were sensitive indicators of the character of ancient societies. The question had been left at a scholarly deadlock. Vincent and Petrie had ascribed all the coffins to the Philistines, whereas Albright denied that they had anything at all to do with the Philistines. Meanwhile, two more coffins were discovered at the Judean site of Lachish. This site was apparently occupied at the time of the Philistines' initial settlement, but its character was unknown and it contained no Philistine pottery. In any case, toward the end of my year abroad, I attempted to deal with the problem of the coffins as I had dealt with that of the pottery—disentangling the various cultural elements they contained to see what scheme of historical development they revealed.

At first glance the Egyptian context was overwhelming. The lid fragments and reconstructed examples from Beth Shean at Philadelphia and those from Tell el-Farah and Lachish at the Institute of Archaeology in London reflected the impact of Egyptian culture at those sites. Leaving Lachish aside, both Tell el-Farah and Beth Shean were Egyptian garrison towns under the direct control of the royal administration. But in Tell el-Farah I found the same *mixture* of influences in the rich assemblage of pottery from the tombs as I had discerned in the tradition of Philistine pottery. They included Egyptian vessels, Canaanite forms, and the elaborately decorated, hybrid Philistine wares.

All scholars who had previously dealt with the coffins had emphasized the distinction between "naturalistic" and "grotesque," a distinction especially pronounced at Beth Shean. Albright had originally suggested that the difference lay in the progressive deterioration of the Egyptian tradition and concluded that the grotesque coffins were just later, debased copies of the naturalistic prototypes. My own opinion was that, while there was a clear progression away from the Egyptian tradition, of equal importance was the evidence of innovation as well.

Earlier scholars had failed to recognize that the mixing of traditions in Early Iron Age Canaan had created completely new forms. Albright had seen only the Egyptian, Vincent and Petrie only the Mycenaean. To my mind, both sides were valid and incomplete. Both Egyptian and Mycenean traditions were brought together in the burial offerings in the coffins. Furthermore, another element in the grotesque coffins was noteworthy.

In contrast to the Egyptian-style wigs on the naturalistic coffins, the grotesque types bore elaborate headdresses or diadems. This transformation was obviously not mere deterioration but a conscious attempt to depict something new. It was only after I returned to Israel and began to classify and study the specific examples that I realized that the varying combinations of bands, knobs, and triangles closely paralleled the combinations of ornaments on the Sea Peoples' headdresses as they were depicted in the Medinet Habu reliefs. And although the so-called feathered headdresses could be found in a variety of representations in ancient Middle Eastern art, the total context of these objects suggested a clear Philistine connection—namely, their date, the biblical association of the Philistines with Beth Shean, and the discovery of other anthropoid coffins with some fragments of Philistine pottery.

Grotesque coffin lids with elaborate headdresses or diadems (above) and parallels from Medinet Habu reliefs (below).

I later learned that the German scholar Hermann Ranke had made a similar suggestion in the thirties, identifying the grotesque coffins with Philistine mercenaries. But since the dominant view of Philistine culture at the time was that of a dutiful imitation of the Mycenaean, his suggestion had been ignored. Now it seemed, in light of the trends evident in the pottery, that Philistine culture was the result of a complex transformation and integration of various influences.

THE INTEGRATION OF INFLUENCES

This was the final link in the cultural chain that I sought to reconstruct in my initial study of the excavated artifacts of the Philistines' material culture. And although my work would continue in the succeeding years with a more detailed assembling of evidence for the Philistines' cultic practices, architecture, and daily life, a single dominating theme was already evident. The massive population movements and social changes

94

These two depictions of warriors with headgear found at Enkomi, Cyprus, and dated to the early twelfth century B.C., are very similar to the Medinet Habu representations. Left: Warrior of the Sea Peoples with knobbed feathered headdress, carved in relief on an ivory game box. Right: Warrior with knobbed feathered headdress engraved on a conical stone seal.

that accompanied the end of the Mycenaean Age gave birth to the culture of the Philistines. Piece by piece, elements of the shattered traditions of Late Bronze Age Greece, Cyprus, Egypt, and Canaan were reassembled to create a new and innovative culture. Who the Philistines were and where precisely they came from remained unanswered questions. But what they *did* was becoming increasingly clear. The roots of the economic and political developments that characterized Philistine settlement in Canaan at the beginning of the Iron Age lay in their unique cultural synthesis.

It was on the background of this cultural pluralism, so to speak, that much of my future work would evolve. The Philistines and other Sea Peoples were a dynamic entity who absorbed and radiated a variety of influences, and to understand them one had to understand the transition from Late Bronze to Early Iron Age culture in the Mediterranean in all of its ramifications.

Back in Israel, the noted Israeli archaeologist Yigael Yadin was about to undertake the first large-scale Israeli dig, in the ancient Galilean city-state of Hazor, which, according to Joshua 11:10, "formerly was the head of all those [Canaanite] kingdoms." The site had been cursorily excavated by John Garstang following his work at Ashkelon in the twenties, and its identification with biblical Hazor, en route from Canaan to Syria and Mesopotamia, was accepted by most scholars.

Moshe had already "done" Hazor briefly for the Israel Department of Antiquities. The National Water Authority of Israel, Mekorot, was beginning a massive project of piping fresh water from the sources of the Jordan River in the far north of the country to irrigate the fields of the semiarid regions of the south. The engineers planning the pipeline proposed that it pass along the eastern edge of Tell Waqqas, one of the largest and most prominent ancient mounds in the country, and this gave Moshe an opportunity to determine if there was any suggestion at Hazor of the cultural changes that were taking place in other parts of the country at the time of the Philistines. The rise of Hazor's importance and its international trading connections throughout the Middle and Late Bronze ages were clear from the many fragments of imported Cypriot and Mycenaean pottery found there. But Moshe also found two characteristic Philistine sherds. True, two sherds out of hundreds were not much, but their very presence was provocative: Hazor was, after all, 165 miles from the core of Philistine settlement.

Now it was my luck to be appointed one of the four area supervisors for Yadin's big dig. In terms of fieldwork, it was the first time I took part in an excavation of such a broad scope and with so many colleagues and students who were later to take their places in the forefront of Israeli archaeology. Second, in terms of my particular interest, the site was from the end, the problematic end, of the Late Bronze Age. Third, as we discovered, this Canaanite city with its international flavor illustrated the merging of several cultural influences. Finally, the wealth of material uncovered here was an amazing assemblage of architectural and artistic artifacts. In every way it was the perfect *in situ* corollary to my recent theoretical studies.

For the next ten years I was to divide my time, more or less, between Hazor in the summers and the Hebrew University during the rest of the year, meanwhile working on my dissertation, and—together with Moshe—having and raising our two sons, Dani and Uri.

PART III

IN THE FOOTSTEPS OF THE PHILISTINES

Moshe Dothan

CHAPTER 8

Along the Trade Routes

My particular interest at the university had been the archaeology of the protohistoric periods in Canaan—that is, the development of settled life, agriculture, and commerce during the Chalcolithic period of the fourth millennium B.C. When I came to join the dig at Tell Qasile, however, during the second season, I became fascinated with the surprising culture of the Philistines and their part in the development of civilization in this country. Professor Mazar, always eager to involve his students in expanding the scope of their research, urged me to look into the question of how the Philistines of the twelfth and eleventh centuries B.C. had influenced the country's coastal development and how they had used the routes of overland trade. I was enormously impressed by the way in which Mazar had been able to reconstruct Tell Qasile's gradual transition from an agricultural village to a flourishing commercial center on the basis of the surrounding topography, as well as from the specific finds. Even before the start of the excavations, Mazar had pointed out the formative influence of the Yarkon River as a dependable highway between the hinterland and the coast, providing a sheltered anchorage for boats plying Mediterranean ports. And the dig had shown that the expansion of this Philistine community had been accompanied by the intensified production and distribution of specialized crafts and industries such as metalworking, textiles, and, of course, pottery. The Yarkon River certainly appeared to have been the crucial factor in the expansion of the Philistine settlement at Tell Qasile.

Farther south on the coast of Israel were several more tidal rivers

within the traditional territory of the Philistines, each of which must have had a similar economic potential. In 1913, it will be remembered, Duncan Mackenzie had theorized that the Wadi Eskale, the tidal river to the south of the Ashkelon tell, had probably played an important role in the city's economic life. Only the difficulties in excavating the site had prevented Garstang and Phythian-Adams from uncovering the Philistine remains in this part of the city. That such remains were there seems to have been confirmed by the fact that the two other great Philistine cities were located on or near the banks of tidal rivers as well. To the north, near Ashdod, the outlet of the Lachish River (Wadi Sukreir in Arabic) could have served as a possible anchorage and a convenient highway inland toward the southern Judean hills. And to the south, near Gaza, the Besor Valley (Wadi Ghazzeh in Arabic) offered a similar link between the ancient cities of Tell el-Farah and Tell Jemmeh and the Mediterranean.

A NATURAL HIGHWAY

Previous exploration studies had concentrated on the individual sites and neglected the possible connection *between* them. As a result, no coherent picture had emerged of the economic development and expansion of Philistia as a whole. The Bible describes the gradual conquest by the Philistines or their allies of the inland areas of the country, reaching eventually to Beth Shean at the eastern end of the Valley of Esdraelon. But only the sites of the major Philistine cities had been explored thoroughly. I realized that it might be useful to undertake a detailed archaeological survey of ancient settlement patterns between the major cities along a section of the Philistine coast.

At the time political and military considerations restricted my choice of possible regions for such a survey. Although the War of Independence was over, the 1949 cease-fire lines had placed the Gaza Strip under Egyptian control, and the coast on our side of the border as far as Ashdod was still a military zone. So, with the major portion of ancient Philistia closed to archaeological investigation for the time being, I opted for an area halfway between Ashdod and the Yarkon, the Sorek Valley, to begin my survey. I was looking for geographical links between the northernmost Philistine capital at Ashdod and their settlement at Tell Qasile. The preliminary indications from the Sorek Valley survey suggested that while we suppposed the Philistines to be one of the Sea Peoples with strong maritime leanings, their vital interests and activities lay firmly on dry land.

The Sorek Valley had held little attraction for archaeologists because of the forbidding nature of its terrain. Ancient descriptions painted it as a fertile area, but it was now covered with high, drifting sand dunes, a serious impediment to digging. The geologists who had studied this

area were not in complete agreement as to the precise natural causes of
the massive drifting. Some argued for the cumulative effect of the
prevailing southwest winds and coastwise currents; others opted for a
profound climatic change. From the Middle Ages to the twentieth
century, the area supported only a few scattered villages and a meager
agricultural population. But as we began our survey in the spring of
1949, we discovered that a very different level of existence had prevailed
here during the millennia that preceded the coming of the dunes.

Leaving the Philistines aside for the moment, our first objective was
to reconstruct the basic framework of the area's archaeological history
as a whole. This meant a systematic exploration of the area on foot,
recording the precise location of every sign of ancient settlement and
collecting representative samples of pottery or other artifacts. Gradually, we came to understand the importance of the Sorek River in ancient
times. Along both banks were archaeological sites of varying size and
function which, taken together, provided a striking picture of the commerce and prosperity of the area in the centuries that *preceded* the arrival
of the Philistines.

The focal point of the region was the large mound of Tell el-Sultan,
on the southern bank of the river, about three miles from the sea. The
tell was not large by the standards of the great cities of Canaan—its
top surface covered only about two and a half acres—but it had obviously controlled the once-fertile agricultural land of the valley. From
the evidence of some of the characteristic pottery fragments scattered
on its slope and surface, it appeared that Tell el-Sultan was among the
earliest of the Canaanite coastal cities, founded in the Early Bronze
Age, around 2500 B.C.

Pottery finds from other sites in the vicinity expanded the picture of
increasing trade connections and highlighted the fact that Tell el-Sultan's
prosperity was not based on agriculture alone. At the small seaside
mound of Yavne Yam (Minet Rubin in Arabic), just south of the outlet
of the river, we found evidence that it might have served as a sheltered
anchorage at the beginning of the Middle Bronze Age, around 2000
B.C. Furthermore, it was near the main north-south highway, which
came to be called the Via Maris, the biblical *derech hayam*, or sea route,
and, even in modern times, passed only a mile and a half to the east.
It was the most heavily traveled route between Egypt and Mesopotamia, and the cities along its course were gradually transformed into
commercial and manufacturing centers, themselves producing for an
expanding international trade.

Some earlier chance discoveries in the vicinity had already hinted at
the extent and duration of the area's prosperity. Four Middle Bronze
Age tombs with burial offerings of scarabs, alabaster vessels, bronze

weapons, and carved bone inlays were uncovered by the Palestine Department of Antiquities in 1940 and indicated strong Egyptian influence. Closer to the shore, a Late Bronze Age cemetery containing sixty-three burials with impressive quantities of imported Cypriot and Mycenaean pottery was later discovered. Our survey now put these finds into a clear archaeological context as a thriving commerical settlement in the centuries before the arrival of the Philistines. But it already revealed a so far unsuspected end to that prosperity after the twelfth century B.C. In searching for evidence of the post–Late Bronze, Philistine period, we could not identify even a single sherd of Philistine pottery; when later explorations did find some, their quantity was smaller than at inland sites.

This posed an unexpected problem. From the excavations at Tell Qasile it was assumed that the Early Iron Age was a period of dramatic expansion along the coast, an assumption that was confirmed by the abundance of Philistine pottery at Ashdod. But here at the Sorek Valley, Early Iron Age occupation was sparse; it appeared that the population had descended to a lower form of organization, supporting themselves by agriculture alone during the Philistine period. It occurred to me that the reason had to lie in the sudden diversion of the trade routes.

Tell el-Sultan was, after all, only about ten miles north of Ashdod, and after the rise of Philistine power it apparently became just a minor settlement in the shadow of Ashdod's extensive domain, without an independent economic existence. This suggested a Philistine monopoly on trade and overland commerce, but it was a hypothesis that could not be sustained by a survey of the lower Sorek Valley alone. If the trade routes were the key to understanding Philistine power, we would have to look into other regions of the country where their influence had been felt. Our next step, therefore, was to determine the changing patterns of Early Iron Age settlement and trade along another section of the Via Maris.

A FARMHOUSE IN AFULA

As sometimes happens, the best-laid schemes of archaeological noviatiates do not always proceed in a direct line. Trude and I were married that year, and since she was intent on pursuing her studies further I decided to combine my interests with a steady job. I joined the staff of the Israel Department of Antiquities, whose main function was to preserve the country's archaeological remains and undertake emergency digs in the face of a burgeoning population and the need for massive housing and road building. The records of the ancient past were in danger of being severely "damaged by improvement." My own particular interests were shelved for the time being. Yet in the autumn of 1951 my official responsibilities unexpectedly came smack up against the Philistines in, of all places, Afula, an oft-maligned one-horse town in the Valley of Esdraelon.

Modern Afula was built on the remains of an ancient city, identified by some scholars with a place mentioned in the lists of conquests of Pharaoh Thutmosis III in the fifteenth century B.C. The name was apparently derived from the Semitic root עפל, or *o-ph-l*, "citadel," an appropriate designation for the town's strategic position on one of the richest and most fertile stretches of land along the ancient caravan route. The topography of the country forced the Via Maris to turn inland as it neared the Carmel range, running northeastward through the narrow passes and continuing eastward through the Valley of Esdraelon as it made its way toward the Jordan Valley and points farther to the north. Pottery finds from the excavations at Afula in the twenties and thirties had revealed an affinity with the styles of pottery common in Egypt during the rule of the Hyksos, in the Middle Bronze Age. Its situation in the Early Iron Age had not yet been determined, and this was a point of considerable importance in understanding the nature of the Philistines' northward expansion.

The Bible describes the Philistines' presence and activity in their coastal enclave and the adjoining hill country. But their deadly military encounter with King Saul near Beth Shean was never fully explained. Some scholars had speculated that their zealous control of overland commerce had brought them into conflict with the Israelites in this region, but there had, so far, been little archaeological evidence. It will be remembered that almost no Philistine pottery sherds had been found at Beth Shean.

The northernmost site at which Philistine pottery had been found up to this time was Megiddo, at the western end of the Valley of Esdraelon. The excavators from the University of Chicago expedition in the thirties had found that at the time of the Philistines' arrival in Canaan, Megiddo was an Egyptian vassal city on the international trade route. But by the end of the twelfth century B.C., the old city plan was abandoned and new buildings—one of which was identified as a "governor's residence"—were constructed at the site. The sudden appearance of Philistine pottery at the Early Iron Age levels suggested that Megiddo had come under the direct rule of the Philistines—presumably by military conquest—during the period of their expansion northward along the Via Maris.

Our excavation team, called in to give the green light to a road-building project in Afula, had dug down about three feet through the fragmentary remains of the medieval and Roman periods when we uncovered a meager complex of structures built of sun-dried mudbrick on foundations of stone. In contrast to Afula's urban commercial char-

Fragment of lion-headed Philistine drinking vessel with typical bichrome decoration, from Megiddo.

acter in the Middle Bronze Age when international trade along the Via Maris was vigorous, the Early Iron Age occupation here was agricultural. In the twelfth and eleventh centuries B.C. it was apparently a farming settlement, bordered by open courtyards for keeping livestock, with silos dug throughout the entire area. Additional evidence came from several unbroken storejars, some of which contained carbonized husks of bitter vetch, a common fodder for livestock. The other jars held the remains of broad beans, chick-peas, and olives, all for human consumption—and all still cultivated today in the fertile Valley of Esdraelon.

The architecture of the settlement was simple, but its style provided a link with a place far beyond the neighboring city of Megiddo. The main building we excavated at Iron Age Afula had much in common with the early Philistine layers of Tell Qasile. Its central area was divided by a row of pillars separating the roofed living quarters from the adjoining kitchen with its oven and silo. The pottery on the floor of this building, on the surface of the surrounding courtyards, and in the nearby tombs also pointed to a southerly orientation. And in addition to fragments of undecorated storejars, bowls, cooking pots, and juglets were dozens of fragments of elaborately decorated Philistine pottery.

CANAANITES TO PHILISTINES

From the standpoint of simple geographical distribution, the discovery of Philistine pottery at Afula was an advance in the archaeological knowledge of the extent of the Philistines' expansion from the coast, moving its outer boundary a few miles to the east. But of greater significance was the possibility that, in contrast to the situation at Megiddo, the coming of the Philistines to Afula might not necessarily have been the result of a military campaign.

In carefully peeling away the thin layers of accumulation that contained Philistine pottery, I realized that this farming community had an earlier stage of existence during the period immediately preceding the Philistines. Beneath the beaten earth floor of the central building we discovered an earlier floor whose pottery included fragments of vessels imported from Cyprus at the very end of the Late Bronze Age. So, contrary to the accepted view that the economy of the country had been completely disrupted with the cutoff of international trade and the settlement of the Philistines along the coast, the evidence here pointed to a peaceful transition. The farmers of Afula had apparently adapted themselves to the changing economic conditions with little alteration in the patterns of their daily life.

While the occupants of the farming community had modernized the structure of their dwellings with rows of pillars, in accordance with the popular architectural fashions of the time, their everyday pottery vessels—cooking pots, jugs, and storejars—continued the Late Bronze Age traditions. The painted Philistine vessels had apparently taken the place only of the now unavailable imported Cypriot and Mycenaean ware. The gradual, evolutionary nature of this transition was further attested to by an unusual male pottery figurine found on the surface of one of the courtyards. No figurine like it had ever been found in excavations in Israel. Checking later, I discovered that it closely corresponded to a clay figure found at the citadel of Mycenae some years before by the noted Greek archaeologist George Mylonas. He had placed great significance on the fact that the figure was *male*, since female figurines were the most common religious representations in Mycenaean times. Resurrecting the old hypothesis of a northern "Achaean" invasion, he believed that it represented the arrival of a new, more martial influence at the end of the thirteenth century B.C. The appearance of a similar artifact in Afula seemed further evidence that Philistine influence had been a gradual filtering through of a new complex of styles and ideas much farther north than previously believed. Just how far north their influence extended became clear to me soon after, when I was called out on another emergency excavation, at Hazor, sometime before Trude was to join Yigael Yadin's major dig there. It was there, as already noted, that we found two Philistine sherds.

In my two years of work for the Israel Department of Antiquities, my interest in the Philistines, stimulated originally by Professor Mazar's interest in their trade connections, grew. Partly by intention and partly

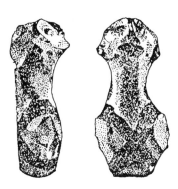

Male figurine from Afula.

by accidental finds, the larger picture of their settlement was taking shape. It was becoming evident to me that the Bible relates only the events of Philistine history that directly concerned the Israelites and the kingdom of Judah. There certainly appeared to be a great deal more to their settlement and expansion in Canaan than religious antagonism and military campaigns. The true nature of Philistine history, it now appeared, would have to be understood as a function of their interaction with the trade routes and resources of the country as a whole, not in maritime but in agricultural and commercial activity. True, at this stage there were many more questions than there was evidence for answers, but the challenge was enormous.

CHAPTER 9

The Tombs of Azor

In 1956 I became director of the Excavation and Survey Branch of the Israel Department of Antiquities. It was a promotion that entailed a general administrative responsibility for the discovery and protection of all of the country's archaeological remains. The funding and organization of the department had improved since its establishment, but this went hand in hand with a tremendous increase in the work load. To begin with, all over Israel, from the Upper Galilee to the southern Negev, construction crews were at work on new apartment houses, schools, roads, and industrial areas. This meant that almost daily they were uncovering—and endangering—valuable archaeological evidence. Development was essential to Israel's economic future, and considering the ambitious scale on which it was moving forward, the task of preserving every accidentally discovered vestige of former times was practically impossible. The department, however, had to do what it could to make sure that at least some archaeological information was obtained from every chance discovery. But there was a second, less appetizing facet to our increased work load.

Many Israelis had quickly learned that quite apart fom tradition and links to the past, there was money to be made from ancient artifacts. Private antiquities dealers and collectors from all over the world were willing to pay high prices for unique or especially attractive pieces from Israel, with no questions asked about how they had been obtained. Since the regional inspectors and staff archaeologists were kept constantly busy with emergency excavations on building sites, I was often called away from my administrative duties by the second type of emer-

gency. The case of Azor, early in 1958, was an example, but it led, indirectly and almost by accident, to the next major clue in our search for the Philistines.

Azor is a small town on the old Tel Aviv–Jerusalem road, and though at the time no systematic excavations had ever been conducted there, its historical importance was a matter of common knowledge. Mentioned first in the Septuagint version of Joshua [19:45] as a town in the territory of the tribe of Dan, it stood at a strategic junction on the Via Maris, at a point where a secondary route—now a modern highway—branched off inland. It was conquered and destroyed by the Assyrian king Sennacherib in his campaign against Philistia in the eighth century B.C. The ruins of the Crusader fortress, Château des Plains, still stood on the summit of the ancient mound in the center of present-day Azor. But the current threat to the site's antiquities was not there. It was rather at a low sandstone hill, about two hundred yards to the east, on the side of the road. There the nightly flicker of the flashlights and lanterns of "amateur" excavators had aroused the local inspector's suspicions.

Every morning he found fresh mounds of discarded earth beside pits all over the hill's surface. It was evidence of an ongoing, illegal, and apparently very successful treasure hunt because Tel Aviv's known antiquities shops had received a flood of new merchandise. Dozens of complete pottery vessels had suddenly appeared and just as suddenly vanished off the dealers' shelves, as they made their way into private collections in Israel and abroad. Once in private hands they were no longer available for archaeological study. What made the plunder of Azor especially disturbing was, first of all, the extent to which the site had become a "free-for-all," and, second, the nature of the finds. The pottery and other artifacts seemed to be burial offerings, and their quantity and quality suggested that the ancient cemetery of Azor was one of the richest ever found in Israel.

After a cursory examination of the site, the Department of Antiquities contacted a number of antiquities dealers in order to examine what had already been unearthed. Apart from any aesthetic value, I discovered, the finds revealed that the cemetery had been used continually for thousands of years. Among the illegally excavated artifacts were many of house-shaped clay ossuaries, or bone containers, of the Chalcolithic period, which provided a unique glimpse of the burial customs of the country in the fourth millennium B.C. There were also Egyptian scarabs, Bronze Age storejars, imported Cypriot and Mycenaean vessels, and—of particular interest to both Trude and me—quite a large quantity of elaborately decorated Philistine pottery.

From the Assyrian account of Sennacherib's conquest, Azor was identified as a vassalage of the great Philistine city of Ashkelon. Here again was evidence of the Philistines' expansion along the coastal trade route. When I showed Trude photographs of some of the Philistine vessels taken from the cemetery, she pointed out how intense Philistine influence must have been. One jug in particular was the most elaborate example of Philistine art that had ever been found: it clearly displayed the mixture of Mycenaean, Egyptian, and Canaanite influences that typified the first stage of the Philistines' cultural development, with a characteristic Egyptian lotus flanked by two well-executed Philistine birds.

Back in Jerusalem pondering our severely overextended manpower problem, I came to the conclusion that the best possible solution would be to propose a joint expedition with a foreign institution. The one I had in mind was the French Center for Scientific Research in Jerusalem, whose director, Dr. Jean Perrot, had excavated two important Chalcolithic sites near Beersheba just at the time I was excavating a Chalcolithic site at Horvat Betar nearby. I knew that the Chalcolithic tombs at Azor would be of interest to him, and I could then concentrate my efforts at the top of the hill.

The only Philistine burials identified so far were those from Beth Shean, Tell el-Farah, and Lachish, and not all scholars even accepted the accuracy of the identification. Trude, it will be remembered, suggested that the "headdresses" of some of the Beth Shean coffins closely resembled the headgear of the Sea Peoples depicted in the Medinet Habu reliefs, although she refrained from launching into far-reaching generalizations. But even if there were no doubt about the identity of the people interred in the anthropoid coffins, so far this form of burial had been found only at sites of probable Egyptian mercenary garrisons and could not be regarded as representative of Philistine funerary practices as a whole. Here at Azor, though, there was a reasonable possibility that—assuming the plundering had not been total—other types of Philistine burials might be discovered. Azor was, after all, a city on the coastal sea route and presumably occupied by a civilian population. In any case, in May 1958 I arrived with a team of thirty hired workers and some students from the Hebrew University to begin excavation of the Philistine cemetery.

The presence of the French and Israeli teams at the site and the constant surveillance that resulted put at least a temporary halt to illegal digging, but I must admit that the destruction already wrought gave us our initial digging strategy. While the illegal pits were scattered all over the surface of the ancient cemetery, they were most numerous on the eastern edge. It seemed reasonable to assume that the digging had been most

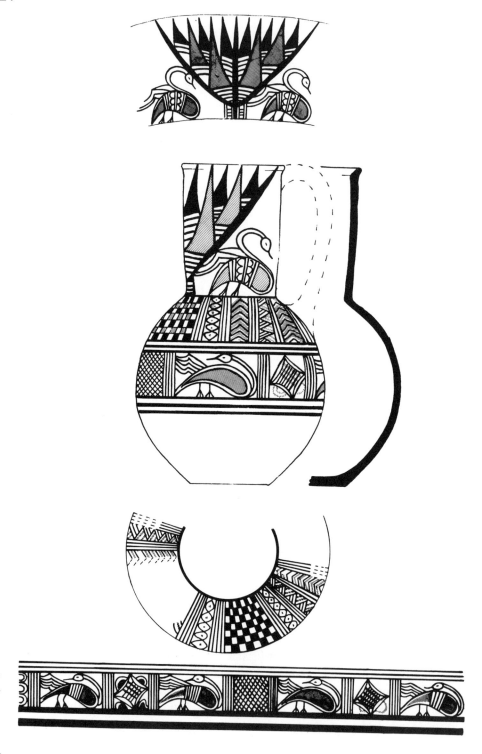

Jug found at Azor showing Egyptian-style lotus flower decoration flanked by Philistine birds.

intense where the finds had been the richest, so I decided we would begin there. We marked off two five-yard squares in this area. This relatively small probe was intended to determine the depth beneath the modern surface of the burials of the various periods.

After clearing the weeds and topsoil we noticed the presence of carefully laid rows of stone, and soon after discovered a series of simple graves, each containing a few offerings and a single skeleton, evidence of the early Islamic and Crusader use of the cemetery from the eighth through the fifteenth centuries A.D.

Digging through another five feet of sandy soil, we discovered a uniform level of simple graves, each of which, like those of the Middle Ages, contained only a single skeleton. The pottery and offerings, however, indicated a far earlier date: They were unmistakably Philistine in shape and decoration. And though they were far simpler than the elaborate examples the illegal diggers had found, they could be dated to the time of the Philistines' first great period of territorial expansion, around 1100 B.C.

As we expanded the excavation area within the two squares, we eventually uncovered more than twenty-five graves. All the bodies were interred in an identical manner, with the arms laid stiffly along the sides and the heads all oriented to the east. In sharp contrast to the rock-cut communal tombs of Tell el-Farah and Beth Shean, these individual burials revealed an unknown Philistine funerary custom—and presumably a different conception of the afterlife of the deceased. In the communal tombs common in Canaan throughout the preceding Late Bronze Age, the bones of one generation were haphazardly pushed aside to make room for the bones of the next, suggesting that it was not the sanctity of the individual bodies which was important but rather their gradual mixture with the remains of the community's ancestors. Strangely enough, the custom of single burial, evident here, had also occurred throughout the Aegean world precisely at the time when Philistine pottery emerged.

Throughout the Late Bronze Age, in both the Aegean and the eastern Mediterranean, burial in communal tombs was the accepted practice. The great beehive-shaped monuments, called *tholoi*, so characteristic of the last phase of Mycenaean culture, were only the most elaborate examples. Most scholars regarded their continued use over a number of generations as evidence of the social stability of the period. At the time of the breakdown of the Mycenaean trading network and the palace system it supported, communal burial began to die out. In the twelfth century B.C. individual burial became the accepted rite in the Aegean world.

This was dramatically different from the local customs of Early Iron

Age Canaan: ancient cemeteries excavated at sites beyond the traditional boundaries of Philistia contained only family tombs. Seen in this context, the Philistine burials at Azor in the twelfth century B.C. reflected the emergence of the new social and religious practices that were beginning then to transform Aegean civilization.

A QUESTION OF RACE

Although our pottery finds were meager compared with those of the illegal diggers, there was another angle that offered us the possibility of making some progress with regard to the question of Philistine identity. The plentiful and "worthless" bones in the graves had been carelessly discarded by our industrious looters and we were able to amass a good quantity of skeletal material. From a scientific viewpoint, this proved extremely valuable for subsequent anthropological analysis.

Only one anthropological study of Philistine skeletons had ever been attempted and its scientific value had been questioned from the start. This was when R.A.S. Macalister excavated at Gezer at the turn of the century, several years before the identity of Philistine pottery had been established. He uncovered a series of tombs containing silver vessels, pottery, and iron that he confidently ascribed to the Philistines. He carefully measured the skeletons in these graves and found them to be individuals "of fairly tall stature," comparable to human remains of the Minoan period that had been discovered on Crete. Other scholars quickly pointed out that Macalister had seriously misdated the pottery found in the tombs and that they actually represented late Phoenician burials of the fifth century B.C.

The disordered condition of later skeletal finds at Tell el-Farah and Beth Shean made anthropological analysis impossible, and the question of their ethnic affinities had to be analyzed through the cultural connections of the tomb offerings. Trude's efforts to trace the origin of the Philistines through the various elements of their cultural traditions had shown how difficult it was to pinpoint a specific provenance. The relatively well preserved skeletons of Azor seemed to me, therefore, a possible way of attacking the problem. Since the bodies buried at Azor could reasonably be regarded as Philistine, they just might take us a little closer to home.

The technique of physical anthropology had advanced considerably since Macalister's time. While it was now clearly recognized that the physical proportions of individual members of every human racial grouping may vary considerably, the averages nonetheless remain fairly distinct. The strong Mycenaean influence on the Philistines' pottery and burial customs suggested an origin on the Greek mainland or in the Aegean, and earlier anthropological studies of skeletons from that area provided some significant data against which the Azor material could be compared.

The most important of these studies had been undertaken in the late thirties by the American anthropologist J. Lawrence Angel. He had found that in a sample of sixty-seven skulls excavated at various sites of the late Mycenaean period throughout the Greek mainland, the predominant physical characteristic of the population was the "Mediterranean" subtype, distinguished by the rather narrow shape of the skull. While other characteristics were present in some of the examples, the preponderance of Mediterranean types made it reasonable to assume that if the Philistines were immigrants from one of the centers of Mycenaean culture, the examples from Azor would be dolichocephalic, or "long-headed."

Among the finds from Azor, five of the skulls were well enough preserved to permit anthropological analysis. Fortunately, there was an expert close at hand. Dr. Denise Ferembach, a member of the French expedition working with Perrot on the Chalcolithic burials, was attempting to analyze the ethnic backgrounds of the various peoples of the ancient Middle East. Back in Jerusalem at the end of the first season of digging, I gave her the skeletal material in order to determine the age and sex of each and, if possible, their racial or geographical affinity. Her answers were, to say the least, disappointing.

There wasn't a single pure Mediterranean type at Azor! The salient feature of the tiny sample population was its surprising diversity. Two of the five showed clear characteristics of the brachycephalic, or "short-headed," Armenoid or Dinaric classes, probably of Balkan or Asian Minor origin. One was a "short-headed" Alpine type of central Europe. One jaw pointed to another short-headed type of an indeterminate subgroup. And the last was a skull that contained mixed Mediterranean and short-headed characteristics.

Of course, the limited number of the examples precluded any sweeping generalizations about the ethnic makeup of the Philistines. At the same time, the analysis comfirmed to a certain degree what Trude had already observed about the nature of Philistine pottery. Whatever their origins, the Philistines were *not* a homogeneous group. Their culture and even their physical characteristics indicated a surprising mixture of influences that had suddenly joined together in Canaan at the early phase of the Iron Age.

With the end of the digging season of 1958, tomb robbing at Azor began again with renewed vigor. This was clear from the upsurge of business on the antiquities market. I had been of the opinion, in the light of our unimpressive pottery finds, that the richest burials in the cemetery had already been plundered. I was wrong. There were still Philistine burials to be uncovered on the hill at Azor. But it wasn't until the autumn of 1960 that I was able to return to the site with another team of workers and students.

Again we followed the lead of the illegal diggers, who had continued to concentrate on the eastern edge of the hill, only this time we extended the work to cover as much of the area as possible, more then doubling the extent of the dig. Once again we found a layer of medieval graves just below the surface, and about five feet farther down more Philistine burials. The first, a simple grave dug directly into the soil, resembled those we had found two years before. Its contents, however, were intriguing. It contained a single skeleton laid on its back, its head facing east; but it was a child's skeleton, and it was covered with several Philistine vessels, among them a shallow plate decorated with a stylized Egyptian lotus design. As we removed the pottery we discovered further evidence of Egyptian influence. Resting on the child's throat, as the apparent pendant of a necklace, was an intricately carved scarab bearing the image of Hapy, the Egyptian God of the Nile. No similar scarab had been found in Israel before, but its shape and style, known from finds in Egypt, matched the chronology of the pottery: early Philistine settlement in the twelfth century B.C. We also found an iron bracelet that was one of the earliest examples of ironwork ever found in the country.

As we expanded the area of the excavation we discovered that single graves were not the only kind at Azor, although they were the most common. For example, we found two storejars fitted together which contained a skeleton—a type of burial found once before, farther north, at the western approach to the Valley of Esdraelon. This form of burial resembled the Hittite mode, discovered at Alishar Huyak, in the highlands of Asia Minor. Even more intriguing were several tombs lined and covered with mudbrick in a manner unmistakably similar to the tombs of Tell el-Yahudiyeh in the Nile delta, a site at which anthropoid coffins had been found.

But the most surprising discovery we made in the middle of the area of single graves was under a square stone structure, more than three feet in height, containing a large pithos, or earthenware jar, surrounded by smaller vessels. Inside the pithos were additional offerings: a bronze bowl, a small clay flask, and a thin oval-shaped piece of gold foil. I immediately recognized this as a funerary mouthpiece, common in the Aegean, and similar to the finds at Beth Shean. And underneath this layer of grave offerings we found the charred bones of an adult and a child.

*Storage-jar burial from Azor.
Two storage jars were cut at the
shoulders, joined mouth to
mouth; the body was interred
inside. This type of burial is
rare in Israel.*

RITES OF
CREMATION

The custom of cremation was a troublesome subject in Mediterranean
archaeology, since its origins, distribution, and religious meaning were
hard to fathom. This method of disposing of the dead had long been
considered "heroic" and is described in detail in the *Iliad*, in the funerals
of Hector and Patroclus. Their bodies were burned on pyres, doused
with libations of wine, and then the ashes were collected by their
comrades for burial in jars. European scholars of the eighteenth and
nineteenth centuries suggested that it was a distinctly Indo-Aryan rite,
practiced by cultures from India to northern Europe. Both Duncan
Mackenzie and William Phythian-Adams had unhesitatingly identified
the Philistines as Indo-Aryans and believed that at least some of the
painted Philistine kraters had been used as cremation urns.

But the discovery of Philistine inhumations in the tombs of Tell el-
Farah and Beth Shean provided evidence of different burial customs.
Excavations in Greece had showed that cremation was alien to the
Mycenaean tradition that had exercised such a profound influence on
the Philistines. The custom, therefore, originated apparently not in the
Indo-Aryan invasions, but in the adoption of new religious ideas from
Asia Minor, where a number of cremation burials from the Late Bronze
Age had been found. In fact, excavations eventually showed that cre-
mation became popular in Greece only *after* the destruction of the
Mycenaean palaces. Even then, its popularity was restricted to certain
areas, and it was still not the only burial method. Cremation could
thus be understood as a reflection of religious developments that
emerged no earlier than the eleventh century B.C., more than a hundred

Cremation burial and tomb from Azor, dated to second half of eleventh century B.C. The storage jar containing the charred bones of an adult and child, covered with votive vessels, is the earliest example of cremation found in Israel.

years after the Philistines' migration. It was the connection to this relatively late development, rather than to an Indo-Aryan ethnic association, that appeared significant for our understanding of the Philistines.

The date of the Azor cremation burial more or less matched the appearance of the custom in Greece. The pithos in which the charred bones were deposited was similar to examples from Tell Qasile at the end of the eleventh century B.C. And suddenly I was reminded of an intriguing parallel in the western Mediterranean. Similar pithoi had been excavated in the cemetery of Dessueri on the southern coast of Sicily, which—like Azor—had been used in the eleventh century B.C. The identity of the people buried there was uncertain, but a number of scholars had suggested that they were Sikels, a group often connected with one of the Sea Peoples who, like the Philistines, had been uprooted from their Aegean homelands at the end of the Late Bronze Age. The close correspondence of this pottery form and method of burial in regions so distant suggested the possibility that the Philistines might have shared at least some aspects of their culture with other Sea Peoples,

specifically the Dannuna. There have been suggestions to the effect that
there is a close connection—perhaps, even identity—between the Dannuna and the Danites, since the tribe of Dan was partly settled in the
territory north of Philistia proper, up to Dor. According to the Bible,
the Danites, or at least a part of them, were engaged in maritime crafts
[Judges 5:17]. In any case, the fact that these cultural contacts were still
active in the eleventh century B.C.—a time of supposed regional isolation—hinted at extensive and long-term communications between
the various peoples uprooted during the great upheavals at the end of
the Mycenaean Age.

The dig at Azor made it clear that our understanding of Philistine
funerary customs was still fragmentary, as was our understanding of
Philistine culture as a whole. Their architectural tradition and religious
practices were still terra incognita for the most part. Trude's study and
classification of Philistine pottery had suggested a chronological and
cultural framework, but it remained only a framework and had yet to
be filled in. Further systematic excavations were essential to fill these
gaps. Perhaps the time had come for a serious dig at the site of one of
the Philistine capitals. No such excavation had been undertaken since
the twenties, and our archaeological sophistication and excavation techniques had made great strides forward since then.

As in Afula a few years earlier, it was the development needs of
modern Israel that provided me with the golden opportunity to excavate
a Philistine capital. A new port city on the dunes of ancient Ashdod
was in the making; as a result I spent the next ten years excavating one
of the great cities of the Philistine pentapolis.

CHAPTER 10

An Elusive Invasion

Hopes for excavating one of the great Philistine capitals had lain dormant since the great disappointments of the twenties. At all major Philistine sites so far excavated, the physical difficulties of digging through thick layers of accumulation had prevented wide exposure of Philistine remains. The only alternative that remained for the new generation of archaeologists was the use of a combination of more limited methods: surveys, digs at small sites, and a reexamination of the already excavated finds.

This is not to say that great progress had not been made since then. The results of Mazar's excavations at Tell Qasile, Trude's study of the background and connections of Philistine culture, and my own surveys and rescue operations had already proved themselves. But the new discoveries were still just fragmentary clues that needed a single, continuous context that only the excavation of a large Philistine city could provide.

Strangely enough, Ashdod, the more promising of the Philistine cities from an archaeological standpoint, had never been seriously considered for extensive excavation. Early Western travelers had no difficulty in pinpointing its location—just a few dozen yards west of the modern village of Esdud. When Duncan Mackenzie visited the site in 1911 he was the first to recognize its value for archaeology and urged the Palestine Exploration Fund to consider it for detailed examination. The leaders of the P.E.F., however, chose the more complicated site of Ashkelon, and their subsequent frustrations have already been recorded here.

Soon after the end of Israel's War of Independence, in the spring of 1949, Professor Mazar had taken a group of us on an exploratory tour of Ashdod. Sherds of Philistine pottery could be found scattered over the surface, and it appeared that perhaps in some places the process of erosion had brought the Philistine levels tantalizingly close to the present surface. At the time, however, excavation was not even a remote possibility. But during the next decade, in the wake of Israel's rapid development, the situation changed radically.

Ever since the destruction of the ports of this region by the Mamluk rulers of Egypt in the fourteenth century A.D., the maritime contacts of southern Palestine had been almost entirely cut off. The few harbors that remained during the later Middle Ages became little more than fishing villages, unimportant in comparison with Jaffa, Haifa, and Sidon, farther up the coast. The situation began to change in the nineteenth century with the construction of the Suez Canal and the increase in maritime trade and traffic, and by the time of the establishment of Israel, the harbors of Jaffa and Haifa were unable to handle the country's increasing exports. With new settlements and dramatically increased population in the south, there was a need for a modern harbor in the south to serve Israel's growing international trade.

In the summer of 1957 the directors of a joint Israeli-American development company announced plans for the construction of a new harbor and city on a tract of about ten thousand acres of sand dunes on the site of the ancient city of Ashdod. Within seven years, they hoped, it would include an artificial breakwater and complete port facilities, planned neighborhoods, a commercial center, and an industrial area.

It was clear from ancient sources that Ashdod's territory was extensive, and while the mound of Ashdod itself lay safely beyond the area of the projected development, a number of small ancient sites were directly endangered by the construction work. We in the Israel Department of Antiquities were concerned about them. Thus, with financial support from the Ashdod Development Company, we carried out a preliminary survey of the archaeological remains in the area, mapping and collecting sherds from Tel Ashdod and the smaller mounds that had once been its subsidiary settlements, and slowly piecing together a tentative picture of the patterns of the ancient settlement. Our work on Ashdod's past went on, for the most part, in isolation from the work on the future city, but at an early stage in the construction of the new harbor our divergent interests suddenly clashed.

PAST AND FUTURE IN CONFLICT

Since easy access to the proposed harbor was a first requirement of the development plan and the main road was almost a mile away, work

crews were brought in to pave an access road. Using the resources at
hand, they began to quarry *kurkar* sandstone from the eastern slope of
a nearby mound. A member of the neighboring Kibbutz Yavne, David
Yair, a longtime volunteer inspector for the Department of Antiquities,
was the first to recognize the seriousness of the situation: the mound
they were rapidly destroying was Tel Mor (Tell Murra in Arabic), the
most likely candidate for the ancient harbor town that had served the
inland metropolis of Ashdod.

When his attempts to persuade the crew to stop failed he called us
in, and I immediately saw why he was so concerned. The upper surface
of the mound covered only about a quarter of an acre: its original
area had been considerably reduced over the centuries by erosion, which
had shaped the mound into the form of a flattened cone. The quarrying
had already removed much of the eastern side of the ancient settlement;
if the destruction continued, the entire site would be lost forever. It
was crucial for us at this moment to step in to save it and establish a
useful precedent with the Ashdod development authorities.

Although the modern topography was far different from the ancient
landscape of this region, the physical connection between Tel Mor and
Ashdod was clear. Tel Mor was situated on the northern bank of the
Lachish River, which wound its way eastward and then southward,
branching off in the vicinity of Tel Ashdod. Yair told us that as late as
the thirties, the river had provided the region's inhabitants with a vital
link to the sea. Despite the silting caused by the sand dunes, small boats
had still been able to navigate the six-mile distance from the kibbutz
to the coastline. Before the coming of the dunes, they surmised, the
river might have provided an even easier connection between the inland
city of Ashdod and Tel Mor, only about half a mile from the sea.

We knew from the Medinet Habu reliefs that the Philistines had been
a maritime people. My own attempts to find significant evidence of
Early Iron Age maritime commerce farther up the coast had failed. I
hoped that excavations at Tel Mor would provide some indications of
the extent of the Philistines' maritime activity. Moreover, our initial
visit to the site seemed to confirm the supposition that the ancient
harbor town had been established during the Bronze Age, and we might
therefore be able to trace its development in the period that *preceded* the
arrival of the Philistines. Tell Qasile, founded by the Philistines themselves, contained no evidence of the transition period, and at Ashkelon
it could be distinguished so far only on the evidence of changes in the
pottery and the layer of destruction between the Late Bronze and Early
Iron ages.

Practically and scientifically, intensive archaeological work at Tel
Mor was essential. The quarrying and the road paving would have to

be halted and an archaeological salvage operation immediately undertaken. The development company agreed to finance a rescue operation that would be completed as soon as possible. They, after all, had to get on with their road. Our work got under way in September 1959.

It was our aim to uncover the entire sequence of occupation, both before and after the Philistine period, in order to determine the economic and historical significance of this presumed harbor town. Our excavation strategy was designed to this end. While most of the digging would be concentrated on the summit, we would also probe for the lower levels in a long trench down the damaged eastern slope. There were about thirty feet of accumulated debris between the two areas. By the end of 1960, we had uncovered twelve superimposed city levels that provided us with our first detailed understanding of the nature of maritime commerce along the Philistine coast.

THE RISE AND FALL OF A BRONZE AGE HARBOR

The earliest evidence of permanent occupation, just above the natural bedrock, could be dated to around 1600 B.C., from an Egyptian scarab of the Hyksos period and the base of a commercial storejar with the impression of another Hyksos scarab. We also found a number of fragments of Cypriot "Red on Red" pottery vessels. This meant that at least some of the first settlers at Tel Mor were merchants who had begun trading here at that time.

The origin and identity of the Hyksos rulers of Egypt was itself a major problem of historical research, but there was no question that the cities of Canaan had been a major part of the eastern Mediterranean trade maintained with Egypt and Cyprus. And when we began to excavate a larger area in the level of the fourteenth century B.C.— roughly contemporary with the later XVIIIth Egyptian Dynasty, including the el-Amarna period—there was yet more evidence of the extent of the harbor's international trade. The summit of the mound in this period was dominated by extensive storerooms that had apparently been filled with export merchandise, mainly oil and wine. The many fragments of typical Canaanite storejars gave some indication of the volume of this commerce and the dominant Cypriot connection. The storehouse structure itself was impressive: its four-foot-thick walls were preserved in some places to a height of almost seven feet. In this stratum we also found a stone-built tomb containing a single skeleton, a bronze dagger, and typical Cypriot pottery.

In the next stratum, from the time of the XIXth Dynasty in Egypt, just before the coming of the Sea Peoples, a large part of the summit was occupied by a fortress of several stories similar in plan to fortresses of this period in Canaan as depicted on Egyptian reliefs. It housed the city's garrison, and from the distinctive Egyptian pottery types found

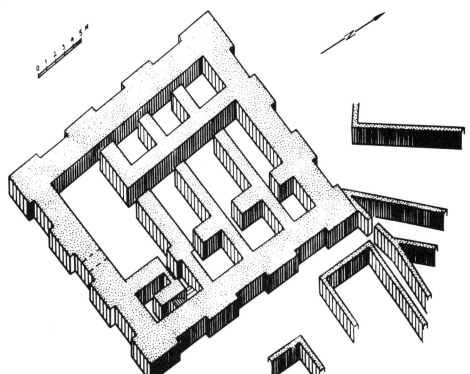

Isometric view of citadel Tel Mor.

on its floors it was apparent that Egyptian forces were stationed there to protect the maritime trade. Tel Mor's international commerce had increased substantially during this period, for there were now wares from the Mycenaean world as well as from Cyprus. This section of the coast that would become Philistine territory within a century was now an important outlet for the Egyptian-controlled Canaanite trade.

The harbor fortress—the most imposing of all the structures we uncovered at Tel Mor—came to a violent end. Over the ruins of its thick walls we found a blanket of ash and collapsed debris, more than three feet thick in some places. The heavy fortifications had clearly not prevented the destruction of the citadel, nor had the fortress guarded the prosperity of the flourishing port.

At every site so far excavated along the coast of Canaan, there seemed to be evidence of a dramatic break in occupation at the end of the Late Bronze Age. As to the role of the Philistines in this wave of destruction, Ashkelon was seen as providing the answer. The thick level of ash first observed in Mackenzie's 1911 seaward section was believed to represent a complete change in the city's culture: beneath it was found typical

A GAP IN THE
EVIDENCE

123

Late Bronze Age Mycenaean and Cypriot imports, and only above the destruction level came the pottery of the Philistines. At Tell Qasile the situation was somewhat different since the site was not occupied in the Late Bronze Age. But the establishment of a settlement on virgin soil, characterized by early Philistine pottery, seemed to provide complementary evidence of the sweeping changes brought about by the arrival of the Philistines.

The connection of the Philistines with the wave of destruction was, in turn, connected with the Great Land and Sea Battles between Egyptians and Philistines in the Medinet Habu reliefs. This link seemed so compelling that the events of Ramesses III's eighth year—in the early twelfth century B.C.—served as a means of dating the end of the Late Bronze Age and the initial settlement of the Philistines. At Tel Mor we were prepared for a slight revision of this chronology, but we had expected to find our general assumptions confirmed in the harbor, so close to their capital city of Ashdod.

The pottery types found in the Egyptian citadel indicated that its end had come sometime in the second half of the thirteenth century B.C.— that is, a full generation before the Philistine invasion depicted at Medinet Habu. This was the period of the first Sea Peoples' invasion of Egypt at the time of Merneptah. But the ancient Egyptian records had described only their attacks on the western Nile delta, never referring to any battles along the Canaanite coast. This was also the first appearance of Israelite settlements in the adjoining hill country, a phenomenon to which many scholars had ascribed the destruction of many Canaanite cities. And although we could not determine the identity of Tel Mor's attackers, the archaeological evidence nevertheless confirmed the turbulent atmosphere of the times. Toward the end of the thirteenth century B.C. the fortress lay in ruins and was temporarily abandoned; above the thick ash layer of destruction, we could distinguish accumulations of wind-drifted sand.

Tel Mor had been reoccupied not long after and another, smaller, fortress constructed. Life continued in a manner similar to what had gone before. It, too, was an Egyptian fortress, now surrounded by houses and workshops containing the remains of furnaces and bellows pipes for the production of bronze. This was a situation unparelleled at any other coastal city of Canaan, where international commerce had ceased with the great destruction at the end of the Late Bronze Age. But at Tel Mor we found evidence for the resumption of international trade, although on a greatly reduced scale. There were no imported Mycenaean vessels in the reoccupied stratum, but there *were* imported Cypriot vessels and local imitation of Cypriot types.

Links with Egypt remained strong, despite conventional theories that

the Philistines had wrested control of the southern coast from a weak- ening Egyptian administration. In an even later renovation of the fortress, which we dated to the time of Ramesses III, the total absence of
even Cypriot imports showed that international trade had finally ended.
There were still Egyptian vessels, scarabs, and local pottery that imitated
Egyptian styles. The most perplexing discovery at Tel Mor was that
at the time of Ramesses III, during whose reign the Philistines were
purported to have laid waste to the Late Bronze Age cities of the
southern coast of Canaan and occupied the nearby metropolis of Ashdod, there was no archaeological evidence of the settlement of a new
group. There was not a single sherd of Philistine pottery at this level.

Only a full century after Ramesses III did the Egyptian presence at
Tel Mor end and the Philistines arrive. Above the ruins of the last
Egyptian outpost we found a few late Philistine fragments scattered
among the silos and baking ovens of a relatively short-lived agricultural
village, abandoned sometime around 1000 B.C. The character of that
late Philistine settlement was itself significant, for throughout their early
history the Philistines there apparently had no direct interest in the sea.
Even at the time of their eventual occupation of Tel Mor they seemed
to be more interested in farming than in maritime trade. I had found
evidence to this effect some years earlier at the Sorek Valley, but had
ascribed it to the alleged concentration of trade at nearby Ashdod. Now
the excavation of the harbor city of Tel Mor turned up no evidence of
trade even there. The harbor had probably long gone out of use by the
time of its settlement by the Philistines.

Frankly, we didn't know what to make of our discoveries: an Egyptian coastal fortress and later a Philistine farming village rather than a
flourishing port city. Had we overestimated the Philistines' character
as seafarers, made on the basis of the Medinet Habu relief? In any case,
the *later* Philistines were just farmers. The identity of the earlier invaders
who destroyed the Egyptian fortress had now to be added to our list
of mysteries.

During our excavations other archaeologists often visited to see our
progress. Among them were Professor David Noel Freedman, then of
the Pittsburgh Theological Seminary, and Dr. James Swauger of Pittsburgh's Carnegie Museum, who had come to choose an excavation site
for themselves. I had known Freedman for several years and we had
often spoken of the possibility of organizing a joint American-Israeli
dig. With the excavations at Tel Mor almost finished and the questions
about the Philistines even further sharpened, it seemed to me that the
ideal site for our joint project might just be at Tel Ashdod itself, four
miles south of Tel Mor. I had traveled with the two men to the north

to seek out some other possible sites, but we kept returning to the idea of Ashdod. As far as I was concerned, if any site could answer our questions the ancient city of Ashdod was high on the list. One of the original of the five Philistine capitals, it was the only one whose mound was not overlaid with thick deposits of later remains. A large excavation of Tel Ashdod would certainly provide evidence about the transition from the Late Bronze Age to the Iron Age. Tel Mor was only a subsidiary settlement and might have had its own unique history. Tel Ashdod, on the other hand, was the Philistine metropolis itself.

The attractions of Ashdod were obvious to us all and the practical conditions seemed ideal. There were convenient accommodations for staff and workers nearby. Financial resources were available on both sides. The excavations at Tel Mor were coming to an end. Our rescue operation there had just been the opening gambit in this new phase in our search for the Philistines.

PART IV

DIGGING UP ASHDOD

Moshe Dothan

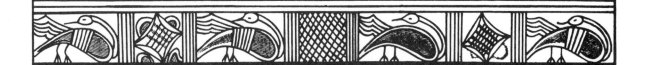

CHAPTER 11

Digging Up Ashdod

From the summit of Tel Ashdod we could see two very different landscapes, each having its own dramatic influence on the history of the city during the previous 3500 years. To the east was the fertile plain of Philistia, a green expanse of fields and orchards extending toward the foothills of Judea beyond the busy north-south highway. To the west, high ridges of rolling sand dunes marked an oncoming wave of desolation advancing from the sea, testimony to the environmental catastrophe that had been plaguing the area since the Middle Ages, gradually blanketing thousands of acres of rich farmland.

During my survey of the coast in 1949, I had visited Tel Ashdod briefly, exploring both the tell and the abandoned mudbrick buildings of the modern village of Esdud, somewhat to the east. Except for a few potsherds and fragments of marble, the tell itself was barren. The oldest buildings still standing in the village were the ruins of a caravanserai and Muslim shrine. The weathered Arab inscriptions affixed to some of the walls provided eloquent testimony to the progressive decline of the city over the last seven hundred years.

Wandering through the ruins, I had mapped the structures and photographed and transcribed the inscriptions as well. In a sense they provided a fragmentary chronicle of the period after which the major historical source left off. The latest mention of Ashdod was in the church records of the fifth century A.D., when the city's bishop participated in the bitter theological debates at the Council of Chalcedon. After the Muslim conquest of Palestine in A.D. 638, Ashdod was mentioned only in passing by Arab geographers and by later European

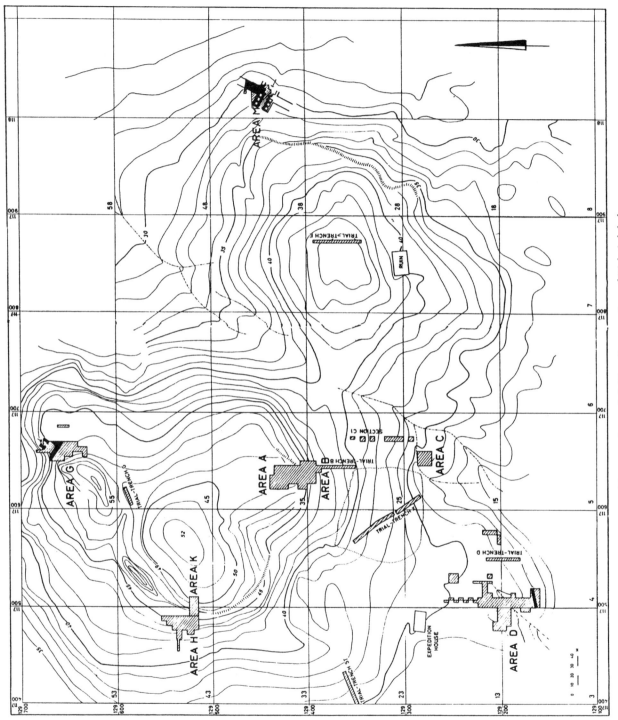

Topography and fields of excavation of Tel Ashdod.

chroniclers of the Crusades. By the Middle Ages, the international maritime trade of this section of the coast had crumbled and Ashdod became an insignificant caravan stop. In the nineteenth century, when a number of European travelers visited Esdud in search of biblical antiquities, the caravanserai itself was being slowly dismantled by the villagers for the stone. Esdud's last note of historical importance came in 1948, when the advance of the Egyptian army was halted by Israeli air strikes and artillery. Indeed, at the time of my initial visit, military trenches still scarred the surface of the tell.

Now, in 1960, as I explored the site with David Freedman and Jim Swauger, the deterioration of the village was almost complete. Local farmers, in search of cheap fertilizer and material for brickmaking, had dug deeply into the mound's southeastern slope, carting away tons of its superimposed layers of sand, clay, and ancient ruins. Ironically, the site's progressive destruction reinforced our determination to dig since the farmers had unintentionally created a vertical section through the superimposed layers that provided a clear indication of the city's long history. At the bottom of the embankment, on the level of the surrounding fields, we picked up dozens of Late Bronze Age pottery fragments, indentical to those we had found at the flourishing harbor town of Tel Mor, with the notable addition of large quantities of typical Philistine ware. Higher up were layers of Hellenistic, Roman, and Byzantine pottery fragments, confirming the site's continuous existence until the sixth century A.D. Taken together, the evidence offered us the possibility of tracing the history of one of the Philistines' most important cities from the time of its founding in the Bronze Age to its medieval decline.

GETTING STARTED

Before starting to dig there was, naturally, a lot of organizing to be done: aside from assuring financial backing in America and Israel, we had to map and mark the places we intended to dig at, and line up the necessary staff of workers and archaeological assistants. By the spring of 1962, we were finally ready.

The most promising excavation areas appeared to be on the damaged southeastern slope of the tell, where we had seen the superimposed layers of occupation so clearly exposed. If we dug on the top surface (Area A) adjoining the section, we could begin with the latest occupation of the city and go down through the thirteen feet of accumulation toward the period of the Philistines. And at the same time, if we dug in the area at the bottom of the section (Area B), we would have the advantage of beginning at the Late Bronze Age and would be able to probe for the earliest occupation levels right from the start. These, then, would be our first excavation areas. Areas C and D were chosen for

Ashdod excavation team, 1965. Moshe Dothan is in center row, third from left.

another reason: to determine just how far the ancient city had spread. I had instructed Menashe Brosh, the local inspector of the Department of Antiquities, to collect any surface finds that might indicate likely places to dig; these he found in the plain to the south of the tell.

During the seven digging seasons that followed, we would slowly uncover a total of twenty-three superimposed city levels, whose architecture, artifacts, and historical connections allowed us to piece together the story of the rise and fall of ancient Ashdod. In retrospect, we can now see Ashdod's history as a continuous story.

Although we found some Early Bronze Age fragments, we assume that the city of Ashdod did not exist before the Middle Bronze Age, when its area was limited to the acropolis and it was fortified, as were all cities along the Via Maris in Canaan, for protection from the Egyptian enemy. During this period and in the Late Bronze Age, when the city came under Egyptian influence, Ashdod was notable throughout the ancient world for its textile and dyeing trades, a fact known from Ugaritic documents and substantiated on the site. The city was completely destroyed in the thirteenth century B.C. and rebuilt apparently by one of the Sea Peoples. At the end of the thirteenth century B.C., Ashdod became distinctly Philistine, and it was only then that the city expanded from the acropolis to the lower city. Ashdod was again destroyed in the tenth century B.C., either by the Israelites or the Egyptians, but was rebuilt and refortified soon after. The city was again partially destroyed in the eighth century B.C. by the king of Judah, Uzziah, and at the end of the eighth century B.C. it fell to the Assyrians, from whom it periodically revolted. So much for the early history of Ashdod. Our excavations, however, did not proceed so schematically.

FIRST GLIMPSE AT A LATE BRONZE AGE CITY

Area B, the Late Bronze Age level where we started digging, was almost entirely occupied by a single structure, a large public building with a spacious central courtyard surrounded by storerooms. The ground plan showed considerable Egyptian influence, and beneath it we found two previous structures of almost identical form. The discovery of Cypriot and Mycenaean pottery fragments on each of the successive floor levels provided us with a key to dating the structure: roughly from 1450 to 1250 B.C.

Unlike the massive citadel and storerooms at Tel Mor, the structure in Area B seemed to be a large private residence and administrative center, similar in part to the "governor's residency" at Tell el-Farah and even more so to the spacious patrician dwellings found at Megiddo in the north. The location of the structure was also suggestive as it was built close to the center of the Late Bronze Age city's prominently located acropolis. There was no clue to the identity of the occupants, but the significant quantity of Mycenaean and Cypriot pottery, figurines, stone vessels, weights, and spindle whorls, indicative of the trade in textiles for which the merchants of Ashdod were well known throughout the eastern Mediterranean during this period, gave us our first impressions of the character of the wealthy residential quarter of the city in the Late Bronze Age.

Beneath the remains of the successive residencies, the finds were meager, but the presence of Cypriot vessels indicated that this earlier stratum was probably founded around 1500 B.C. and marked the beginning of almost three centuries of international trade, until the coming of the Philistines and the other Sea Peoples at the end of the thirteenth century. As at Tel Mor we had ample evidence for the sudden and dramatic end to this period of prosperity. But what exactly the role of the Philistines was in the destruction of the Late Bronze Age city was not yet apparent.

HELLENISTIC RENAISSANCE AND BYZANTINE DECLINE

In Area A we had hoped to reach the Philistine levels by the end of our first season, and though we managed to dig through ten feet of accumulation, we ended the season still a thousand years away. What we did gain was a picture of both change and continuity in the last centuries of Ashdod's urban life. The earlier commercial importance of the city in the Bronze and Iron ages had been renewed with an overlay of Greek culture, after the conquest of the entire Middle East by Alexander the Great in 332 B.C. And religious practices, particularly the worship of the Philistine god Dagon, seemed to have persisted under a variety of guises through the Hellenistic period. Evidence of the prominent place of the Philistines in Ashdod's early history during our first season of digging came from another quarter, from Area C.

The archaeological experience of earlier generations had taught us that the highest part of a tell generally represented only a small part of an ancient city. While the most important structures—palaces, citadels, administrative centers, workshops, and industrial areas—were often found there, the poorer residential and working areas were located on the surrounding plain. The lower city often provided less spectacular finds than the acropolis, but they did provide information about population growth, the living standard of the inhabitants, and their level of technology. As we soon discovered, Area C was *outside* even the lower city, but—to our great good fortune—it was solidly connected to Ashdod in a way that only archaeologists could appreciate. Area C contained the ancient city's municipal garbage dump!

CLUES FROM THE GARBAGE DUMP

What our diggers uncovered was an oval-shaped pit, about twenty feet wide, in which we found the accumulation of at least two centuries of bones, ash, broken cooking utensils, and discarded Philistine pottery. For anyone interested in the development of the Philistines' artistic tradition, the dump was a gold mine. It contained hundreds of examples of elaborately painted Philistine ware: small bowls, kraters, stirrup jars, and "beer jugs." And what is more, we discovered our first indication of the early Philistine cult: dozens of fragments of libation vessels and various clay figurines.

Among them were modeled bird heads that seemed to be three-dimensional reproductions of the swans that appeared so often in the decoration of Philistine pottery. There were also fragments of strange cylindrical statuettes with beaklike noses, bulging eyes, and distinctive flat-topped headdresses. We immediately recognized their similarity to Mycenaean figurines, but only later did we discover how crucial their importance would be for understanding the cult of the early Philistines at Ashdod.

The lowest levels of the pit contained only the earliest types of Philistine pottery, which would be dated to the period of their initial settlement and expansion in the twelfth and early eleventh centuries B.C. But in the upper levels, from a slightly later period, around 1000 B.C., there was a surprising transformation of their traditions. From her work at Tell Qasile, Trude had assumed that except for the heavy kraters with the crude black spirals, the distinctiveness of the Philistine ceramic tradition had been completely lost by this time. Our garbage pit revealed an unexpected artistic innovation, a previously unknown class of pottery whose "ridged rims" were covered with red slip, burnished and often decorated with thin black and white bands, still bearing some of the traditional Philistine shapes.

The "Ashdod Ware," as we called it, was our first indication that there was a "coherent" Philistine culture along the coast of Canaan. But how far into the succeeding centuries would this influence continue to bear on Ashdod's material culture? A partial answer to this question came unexpectedly in the last of our excavation areas during our first season of digging, in a section of Area D, which we were able to identify as the lower city.

CHAPTER 12

Tragedy:
Threefold Confirmation

Just a few yards away from our headquarters in Area D we began to discover a very different aspect of the history of Ashdod. Area D was a section of the plain about two hundred yards to the south of the acropolis, beyond our Area C garbage dump. In the furrows of a recently planted cotton field, the plowing had turned up hundreds of pottery sherds, dozens of figurine fragments, and unusual concentrations of ash and crumbled bricks, far too extensive to be the result of occasional dumping or erosion. The bricks, in particular, seemed to belong to the substantial structures of an intensively built-up city quarter. And since we were eager to determine the southern limit of the city in its various stages of development, we began digging here while work on the acropolis continued.

The pottery finds included hollow, animal-shaped heads and curved clay cylinders that had come from cultic libation vessels called *kernoi*. There were also typical bowls and juglets from about 800 to 600 B.C. This was the time of the Hebrew prophets who warned of doom at the hands of Assyria and Babylonia. In 721 B.C. the kingdom of Israel was destroyed by the Assyrian armies of Shalmaneser V, and less than a century and a half later, around 587 B.C., the kingdom of Judah was destroyed by the Babylonians under Nebuchadnezzar, who left Solomon's Temple in ruins and carried off most of the Judean population into exile.

For the Philistines, the rise of Assyria and Babylonia was equally catastrophic. During the four centuries that followed their political and military eclipse by King David (c.980 B.C.), the cities of the Philistine coast suffered a series of military disasters, recorded in ancient Assyrian and Babylonian documents and graphically described in the writings of the Hebrew prophets. Around 750 B.C., during the reign of the Judean king Uzziah, Amos warned of Ashdod's impending destruction; Isaiah, writing about forty years later, reported Ashdod's actual destruction by the armies of the Assyrian king Sargon; Zephaniah predicted, around 625 B.C., that "Ashdod's people shall be driven out at noon," and his contemporary Jeremiah warned that "the remnant of Ashdod" would soon drink from the "cup of the wine of wrath." From a Babylonian document called the Istanbul Prism, we know that the king of Ashdod had been taken into captivity at the time of Nebuchadnezzar's conquest of Philistia around 600 B.C., and in the following century, after the Babylonians had left their mark on the country as a whole, Zechariah reported—with a certain satisfaction—that the pride of Israel's traditional enemies, namely the Philistines, had been humbled and that "a mongrel people shall dwell in Ashdod."

DOWN THROUGH THE RUBBLE

As the digging continued on our grid of approximately five hundred square yards in Area D, it became clear from the pottery types and scattered building remains that the last period of major occupation in this area had ended during that same period of Babylonian rule in the sixth century B.C. The few pottery finds reflected the culture of the entire country during this period; there was nothing that we could call distinctively Philistine, and the finds from the first level seemed to substantiate Zechariah's words on the pitiful decline of Ashdod.

In the level below, we still had not reached any substantial structures, but the finds at least indicated some signs of urban life. This portion of the city had apparently been an industrial quarter, as indicated by the many ash-filled pits and remains of pottery kilns. The pottery forms here were similar to those we had found in the uppermost stratum and seemed to point to the fact that these last two periods of occupation were rather short-lived, what might be called the twilight of Ashdod's independence.

According to the *Histories* of Herodotus, the city of Ashdod (Azotos in Greek) had a dubious distinction at this time which may have explained its precipitous decline. Recounting the achievements of the Egyptian king Psammetichus, who ruled from 663 to 609 B.C., Herodotus noted that twenty-nine years of that king's reign were devoted to the siege and final conquest of Ashdod, and that "Azotos held out against a siege longer than any city of which I have heard."

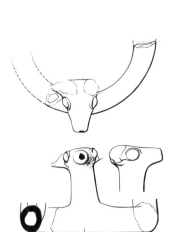

Hollow rings of pottery—kernos rings—used as drinking vessels, with attached heads fashioned in such shapes as pomegranates and bull heads.

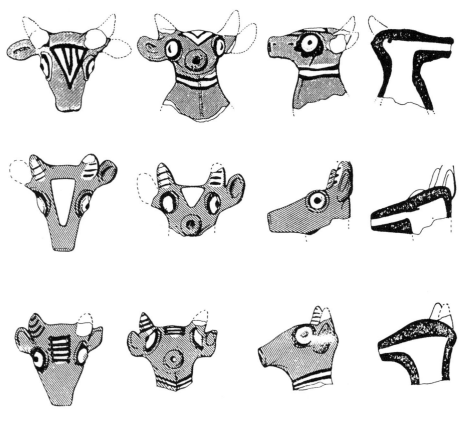

Kernos heads from Ashdod. No one knows for certain how kernos rings were used, but they apparently were filled with liquid during the course of a ritual, shaken up, and then poured out. These range from twelfth century to ninth century B.C.

If our meager finds were any indication, the ultimate conquest put an effective end to Ashdod's economic importance. Up to then, the city had apparently been a faithful vassal, the capital of a province of the Assyrian Empire, since its conquest by the armies of Sargon II in 712 B.C. In that year the Assyrians had launched a campaign to suppress a revolt in the city. After its successful suppression and the punishment of the rebels, the city was accorded a certain measure of independence as long as the expected revenues continued to flow into the coffers of the Assyrian kings.

With little help from historical sources, we began to uncover dramatic new evidence about the city's culture during the time of Assyrian domination. About three feet below the surface we found extensive building remains throughout the entire excavation area. The most important of these was a structure containing at least twelve rooms. We could not be sure of the full extent of the complex since many of the walls extended beyond the area of the dig. There we found an unusual assortment of incense stands, figurines, and the same type of *kernoi* we had found on the surface. Our impression was that this place was connected in some way with cultic ceremonies.

Although archaeologists are often criticized for identifying puzzling structures as cult-connected, we became increasingly convinced that this was the site of a Philistine sanctuary in the eighth century B.C. and before. In its southern wing we found a small room built according to a strange convoluted plan. In its center was a low, blocklike platform, plastered on all of its exposed sides. From the presence of cult vessels and "offering tables" scattered around, it seemed likely that it was an altar.

This place of worship, if it truly was such, was established four hundred years after the Philistines' initial settlement in Ashdod, but the signs from the sanctuary and the surrounding storerooms provided an intriguing indication of the persistence of an earlier Philistine cult. Among the figurines found here were types similar to those we had found in the huge pit filled with earlier Philistine pottery in Area C, more fragments of the rounded, hollow *kernoi* with modeled clay heads of animals serving as spouts, more of the miniature "offering tables," more of the stylized figurines with the flat headdresses, as well as male images with bulging eyes and prominent noses in a style that was unique to Ashdod. One in particular caught our attention: the figure of a man playing a lyre.

The identities of these deities remained a mystery, but the function of the main room in this building as a sanctuary seemed quite clear. The whole building apparently served a fortified industrial quarter of the city, for on its southern side we found a section of a substantial city wall, and on the north, large concentrations of ash and apparent refuse from pottery kilns. The level could be dated to the eighth and seventh centuries B.C. from the pottery, and since we found only fragmentary walls and floors beneath this level, and only meager occupation above, it seemed that during the Assyrian period, despite its repeated destruction, Ashdod succeeded in maintaining an extensive built-up area—and, presumably, a relatively high standard of living.

Figurine of lyre player from Ashdod, dated to the eighth century B.C. Drawings, reliefs, and sculptures of musicians were quite common in the ancient Near East.

SECRETS OF THE ANCIENT CRAFTSMEN

Our first digging season ended early in July 1962. Over the winter I planned for the coming season, when we would be able to follow up our leads from Area D and even open up several more excavation areas. And when excavations began again in June 1963, we returned to the area of the lower city with the intention of uncovering the structures to the north of the shrine. We were particularly interested in determining the nature of the industrial activity that had been carried on there.

As we began to dig down, we immediately encountered a complex of brick structures which, like the shrine and adjoining storerooms, seemed originally to have extended both to the east and west. As the digging proceeded farther to the north, we discovered the well-preserved remains of ancient potters' kilns, some still containing burnt and deformed pottery.

Never before had such an extensive potters' workshop from the biblical period been excavated in Israel. In uncovering the various structures of this complex, we were able to reconstruct the separate stages of the production of the finished vessels. The craftsmen of Ashdod who worked in this area produced an impressive variety of storejars, bowls, jugs, juglets, and cult objects in what seemed to be a mass-production process. Every stage in the process was carried out in a different place, and several could be readily identified.

The large courtyard structures in the southern part of the area appeared to contain the storerooms and workshops in which the raw clay was prepared and the vessels were shaped on potters' wheels. Just a few yards to the north was a line of low unroofed structures that enclosed the pottery kilns. Surprisingly, these kilns were not permanent structures, but consisted of a rectangular fire chamber dug into the ground with an upper part that was meant, intentionally, to be destroyed after every use. From the debris in several of the kilns and from the remains of the lower parts of the kilns themselves, we were able to reconstruct the firing process.

First the ancient potters stacked the fuel and unbaked vessels on the floor of the open kiln and then, apparently, enclosed the kiln with a dome of mud and clay. After lighting the fuel through a small opening, the potter allowed the fire to burn until all the fuel was consumed. And when the kiln had cooled down and the process of manufacture was complete, the potter broke open the upper portion of the kiln to remove the finished vessels.

This method of production must have been used by several generations of Ashdodite craftsmen, for we found thick accumulations of debris from successive kilns that had been built directly one on top of the other. But there was evidence that a sudden change had taken place in the plan of the compound. Not only were there two distinct floor levels in all of the buildings and courtyard, but there was also a change in the orientation of the kilns themselves: in the earlier stage, their opening faced south; in the later, east.

It was, of course, possible that this shift was due to practical considerations. In a heavily built-up area, the thick, acrid smoke of the pottery workshops must have been a public nuisance. A shift in the orientation of the kilns might have been an effort to take advantage of the easterly sea breeze. But there seemed to be another difference. Most of the forms in both levels were common to the entire country during the eighth century B.C., but in the later level there was also a particular bowl shape that was strikingly similar to the shallow, carinated bowls characteristic of Assyrian cities. Did the expansion of the lower city, we wondered, occur before or after the violent conquest of Ashdod by the armies of Sargon II in 712 B.C.?

This was a crucial question for the history of the city since we had both biblical and Assyrian references to the importance of this event. But the appearance of a specific ceramic form could not provide a definite answer. We needed a more general indication. As we dug into the workshop area, we found it, to our grim surprise.

A VIOLENT END TO THE CITY

Just beneath the plastered floor of one of the courtyards we began to uncover a mass of human bones that seemed to be part of a large communal grave. During the previous season we had found the fractured skull fragments of three adult males in the rooms to the north of the shrine, which pointed to some violent event. Now we uncovered the remains of at least forty-five individuals. Signs of violence were unmistakable: many of the bones were sharply cut or splintered, and on the back of a detached skull found among them were the marks of an axe or sword wound.

The unpleasantness of excavating the human remains in Area D grew as we expanded the area of digging and began to grasp the extent of the sudden violence that had swept the city. As we dug into the surface of an adjoining courtyard, we came upon another mass grave, this one filled with *hundreds* of dismembered skeletons. Later anthropological analysis provided us with a possible reconstruction of the manner of the burial: Soon after a violent catastrophe, a large pit was dug in the open courtyards of the potters' quarter and the bodies were thrown in with some personal artifacts—beads, earrings, bracelets, and small pottery vessels. As soon as one level of the pit was filled, a thin layer of earth was spread and more dismembered bodies were thrown in. Some of the long bones bore signs of violent amputation, and there was even grimmer evidence in a refuse pit near one of the kilns. Ten skulls were piled on top of one another, eight of them still connected to the upper two or three vertebrae. Dr. Niko Haas of the Hebrew University Medical School later concluded that in addition to the bones of hundreds of children, adolescents, and adults that could be identified, there were thousands more bone fragments too deteriorated or broken to be confidently identified.

The city of Ashdod had clearly suffered a terrible massacre, dated by the pottery to the end of the eighth century B.C. It seemed likely that the widespread killing had taken place at the time of the conquest of the city by Sargon II. But the subsequent use of that same area over the mass graves seemed to violate the accepted burial practices of ancient times, for after the catastrophe life and work resumed there with little apparent change. The floors over the graves were again laid and plastered, and the workshops and kilns quickly put to use again.

I wondered how the Ashdod potters could be so indifferent to the fact that thousands of people were buried there. Either they didn't care—which seemed extremely unlikely—or they didn't know. There was clearly an element missing in the historical reconstruction. In our next digging season we would find some additional clues in a completely different part of the tell.

During the 1963 season most of our efforts were directed to the excavation of Area D in the lower city, but work also continued in Areas A and B on the southern edge of the acropolis, and in a new area, G, on the northern side of the tell, where we hoped to find information on the city's northern boundary.

Jim Swauger, who had worked with me in Area A during the first season, now directed operations in Area G. Because of the encroaching sand dunes, he decided to begin by digging a long north-south trench down the entire slope to determine the sequence of layers it contained. Swauger soon discovered that the entire northern slope was blanketed by an extensive Byzantine dump that, in some places, reached a depth of more than three feet. This accumulation appeared to be the refuse of the city thrown out by the people living on its summit when it was abandoned in the seventh century A.D. The Byzantine inhabitants of Ashdod had apparently also dug into the earlier layers of their city, for among the artifacts we recovered broken bowls and fragments of the cultic "offering tables" and *kernoi* of the Iron Age. But most of the dump consisted of ash, soil, broken pottery, and discarded stones that Swauger and his team had to clear by hand to get to the undamaged layers of occupation below.

One day, just as I was passing by, one of the volunteers loading a wheelbarrow with debris casually showed me a stone that he thought was unusual. He wanted to make sure that he wasn't about to destroy a piece of valuble evidence inadvertently. I remember looking at the fragment and then looking again, dumbfounded. The volunteer had made one of the most important discoveries of the dig.

Ashdod building stones were all cut from the local light-colored sandstone. This stone was of dark volcanic basalt and the nearest area where basalt was naturally abundant was southern Syria, about 150 miles away. Furthermore, the jagged shape of the stone indicated quite clearly that it was not a simple building stone but a fragment broken from a large stone monument. Carved onto its face were four lines of cuneiform characters, within carefully drafted horizontal lines. If it were

143

part of a royal Assyrian stele, as I thought it might be, its importance would be enormous. We knew that such stelae were commonly erected by the Assyrians in the territories they conquered—and that only one tiny fragment of an Assyrian stele had ever been found in Israel before. I hoped that we would find more.

I made a special point of showing the distinctive basalt fragment to all of the volunteers before we cleaned it and sent it off to Jerusalem, in the hands of David Freedman, to Israel's leading Assyriologist, Professor Haim Tadmor.

ASHDOD IN
REBELLION

Tadmor was particularly interested in the history of Ashdod in the Assyrian period, since he had worked extensively on inscriptions found in Sargon's palace at Khorsabad, near Mosul, Iraq, where several references to the conquest of Ashdod had been found. The cities of Philistia, according to Tadmor, had been reduced to tributary status during the reign of one of Sargon's famous predecessors, Tiglath-Pileser III (744–727 B.C.). The king of Ashdod during this period, Azuri, was specifically mentioned as having sent a tribute of silver, textiles, and papyrus to his Assyrian overlord. This compulsory generosity must have imposed an economic burden on the city, but considering the overwhelming power of the Assyrian Empire there was apparently no alternative. The destruction of the capital of the kingdom of Israel and the deportation of its population to the north, as reported in the Bible, was ample evidence of the consequences of defying the Assyrian king.

Still, as it turned out, Ashdod was to take its chances. Tadmor's reading of the events of the period from the long Display Inscription in the palace at Khorsabad showed that in 713 B.C.,

> Azuri, king of Ashdod, had schemed not to deliver tribute anymore and sent messages [full] of hostilities against Assyria to the kings [living] in his neighborhood. On account of the(se) act(s) which he committed, I abolished his rule of the people of his country and made Ahimetu, his younger brother, king over them.

This enforced change in leadership was not uncommon in the Assyrian Empire, but the response of the people of Ashdod was. Having gotten a taste of independence—and freedom from tribute—the Ashdodites were unwilling to submit to the rule of an Assyrian puppet. Tadmor was able to piece together the next stage in the story from another inscription, found earlier at Nimrud, another Assyrian capital, to the effect that the people of Ashdod

> conceived [the idea] of not delivering tribute and [started] a rebellion against their ruler; they expelled him. . . . Yamani, comm[oner without

any claim to the throne] to be king over them, they made sit down [on the very throne] of his [former] master and [they . . .] their city [for] the at[tack . . .] its neighborhood, a moat [they prepared] of a depth of 20 [?] cubits . . . it [even] reached the underground water in order to. . . .

The description of the city's defensive preparations was fragmentary, yet we would later find a thick city wall at Ashdod that was reinforced at about this time. But the sudden fortification and attempts at fomenting a rebellion among the neighboring vassal states were of little use, for the Assyrian king could not tolerate outright acts of treason against his rule:

> I, Sargon, the rightful ruler, devoted to the pronouncements [uttered by] Nebo and Marduk, [carefully] observing the order of Ashur, led my army over the Tigris and Euphrates at the peak of the(ir) flood, the spring flood, as [if it be] dry ground. Yamani, however, their king who had put his trust in his own power and [therefore] did not bow to my [divinely ordained] rulership, heard about the approach of my expedition [while I was still] far away, and the splendor of my lord Ashur overwhelmed him and he fled. . . .

The people of Ashdod then had to face the might of the Assyrian armies alone. Sargon's troops marched through the countryside and subdued various cities in the vicinity, like Azekah and Ekron, whose sieges were depicted on the reliefs from Khorsabad. The outcome of Ashdod's conquest became a matter of public record on the walls of the palace of Sargon:

> I besieged [and] conquered the citites Ashdod, Gath, and Ashdudimmu; I declared [Yamani's] images, his wife, his children, all the possessions and treasures of his palace as well as the inhabitants of his country as booty. I reorganized [the administration] of these cities [and settled] therein people of the regions of the East, which I had conquered personally. I installed an officer of mine over them and declared them Assyrian citizens and they pulled [as such] the straps [of my yoke].

Thus ended the short-lived rebellion, after which Ashdod became the capital of an Assyrian province and was never fully independent again.

In the context of the Assyrian records, our fragment of the royal Assyrian stele took on special significance. Tadmor recognized that it came from a monument identical in size and shape to the stelae Sargon erected in such far-flung conquered territories as Kition on the southeastern coast of Cyprus and at the city of Asharne in northern Syria. Each was a seven-foot-high monument that bore a depiction in low relief of Sargon himself standing before the symbols of the royal Assyrian gods. Beneath a formalized invocation to those deities, and a long-winded recitation of the king's honors and titles, were detailed descriptions of Sargon's many conquests, which concluded with an account of the specific victory that had led to the erection of the stele. There was little left of the inscription on our first fragment, but by comparing it with the complete stele from Cyprus, Tadmor was able eventually to reconstruct at least a part of its original text. It told of Sargon's decisive victories to the east of the Tigris, in the distant lands of Karallu, Shurda, Media, and Elam. There was no mention of Ashdod's rebellion. For that, we would have to find more fragments of the stele.

ASSYRIAN TRIUMPH AND PHILISTINE EXILE

After our initial discovery, it became my habit to scan the surface of the tell for any sign of basalt. Between Areas A and G the summit of the acropolis was barren, covered by weeds, fragments of pottery and marble, and low stone walls that had once marked the boundaries of the villagers' vegetable plots. The walls were constructed of stones from the various levels of the ancient city. One day, one of the volunteers excitedly reported that he had noticed a dark stone embedded in one of the walls, and he took us to the spot.

The stone was definitely basalt, but since it was too deeply wedged into the rough wall to pry out easily I dug away some of the dirt around it so that I could run my hand over the concealed side. I felt what seemed to be incised characters, and when we finally pried the stone from the wall my senses proved to have been accurate: it was a corner fragment from the Assyrian stele with four lines of cuneiform signs on both of its outer sides.

Before the end of the 1963 season we discovered yet another corner fragment, this one used as a building stone in one of the Hellenistic structures from Area A. Although the three pieces came from levels much later than the time of Sargon's conquest, the text of the second and third fragments contained a few significant phrases relating to the history of Ashdod in the Assyrian period: "ceased his tribute," "speak treachery," "he was sending messages," "he incited them . . . made them my enemies," and finally, "the immense forces of Assyria." They all seemed to confirm the initial supposition that the stele bore an official account of the rebellion of Ashdod and was set up in a public place after the conquest of the city.

The historical records provided the framework into which we could now assess the significance of the puzzling reoccupation of the potters' quarter *above* the mass burials. As was customary, the surviving inhabitants of rebellious cities were exiled to a remote part of the empire and replaced by deportees from other conquered lands. It had worked with the ten northern tribes of Israel, and it apparently worked with the Philistines of Ashdod. Now we could understand why the later potters of the lower city had no compunctions about plying their craft in a graveyard. They simply moved into the depopulated houses and workshops, unaware of the masses of human bodies that lay beneath their feet.

The significance of our finds from the Assyrian period, beyond their obvious drama and tragedy, was unique for Israeli archaeology. In addition to the account preserved in the Assyrian records, the conquest of Ashdod in 712 B.C. had been mentioned by the prophet Isaiah, as noted earlier. Now, with the discovery of a third version from our fragmentary stele, we had a unique *triple* confirmation, the last one from the site itself. The several separate sources could now be joined together to reconstruct the violent end to a long period of Philistine control over the city-state of Ashdod.

Plate 1. *Basalt statue of Ramesses III, from Beth Shean.*

Plate 2. *Captured Sea Peoples: the Philistines, from Medinet Habu.*

Plate 3. *Warrior of the Sea Peoples, with "feathered" headdress, from Medinet Habu.*

Plate 4. *Lid of anthropoid coffin, possibly Philistine, with stylized headdress, from Beth Shean.*

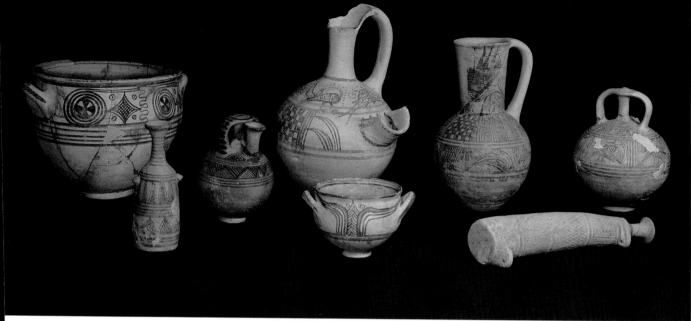

Plate 5. *Assemblage of Philistine bichrome pottery.*

Plate 6. *Assemblage of Philistine bichrome ware with typical bird motif, from Ashdod.*

Plate 7. *Musician stand from Ashdod.*

Plate 8. *Seated Philistine goddess: "Ashdoda."*

Plate 9. *Philistine-made gold disc, Aegean in style, possibly a pommel cover, from Ashdod.*

Plate 10. *Stamp seal with possible inscription, from Ashdod.*

Plate 11. *Cylinder seal with possible inscription, from Ashdod.*

Plate 12. *Female anthropomorphic figurine, from Tell Qasile.*

Plate 13. *Composite drinking vessel, from Tell Qasile.*

Plate 14. *Bird-shaped Philistine bowl, from Tell Qasile.*

Plate 15. *Isometric view of Deir el-Balah showing occupation of the site (and corresponding clay-vessel types) from successive periods: Egyptian Amarna (bottom), Egyptianized Canaanite, Mycenaean, Philistine, Israelite, and Byzantine (top).*

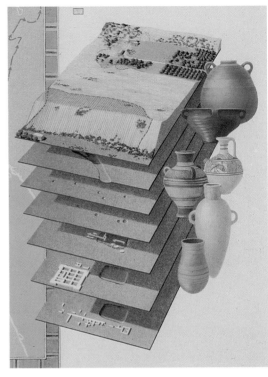

Plate 16. *Trude Dothan and Baruch Brandl on site at Deir el-Balah.*

Plate 17. *Anthropoid coffins in Egyptian tradition, "naturalistic style," from Deir el-Balah.*

Plate 18. *Northeast acropolis of Ekron.*

Plate 19. *Northeast acropolis of Ekron: isometric view of levels of occupation from 13th to 6th centuries* B.C.

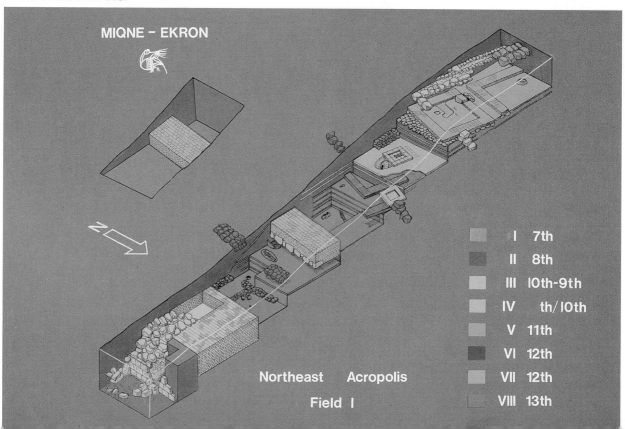

MIQNE – EKRON

N

	I	7th
	II	8th
	III	10th-9th
	IV	th/10th
	V	11th
	VI	12th
	VII	12th
	VIII	13th

Northeast   Acropolis

Field I

Plate 20. *Lion-faced vessel, from Ekron.*

Plate 21. *Elaborate Philistine bichrome bird motif, from Ekron.*

Plate 22. *Mycenaean IIIC:1b pottery assemblage—kraters and bowls, from Ekron.*

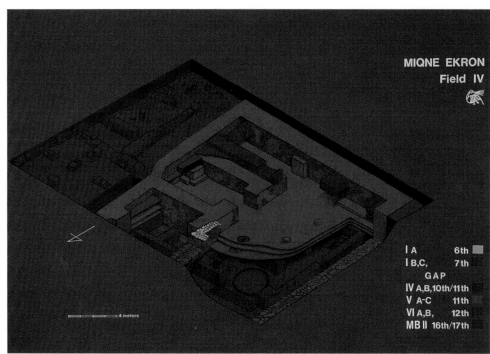

Plate 23. *Isometric reconstruction of Stratum V, Ekron.*

MIQNE EKRON
Field IV

I A	6th	
I B,C,	7th	
	GAP	
IV A,B,10th/11th		
V A-C	11th	
VI A,B,	12th	
MB II 16th/17th		

4 meters

Plate 24. *Hearth sanctuary, Ekron.*

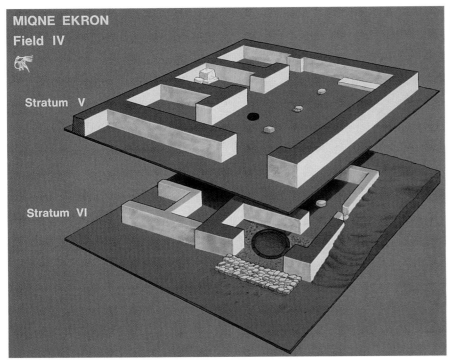

MIQNE EKRON
Field IV

Stratum V

Stratum VI

Plate 25. *Two superimposed buildings at Ekron: 12th and 11th century* B.C. *palace and shrine.*

Plate 26. *Artist's rendition of a hearth room at Pylos, in Greece, showing the central importance of the hearth.*

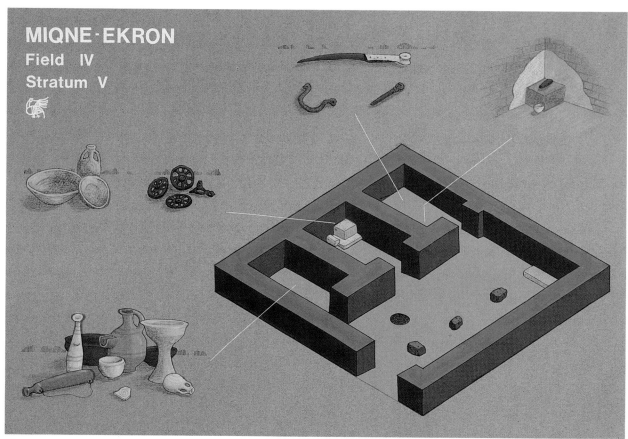

MIQNE·EKRON
Field IV
Stratum V

Plate 27. *Isometric plan of shrine with ritual platform and associated finds, Ekron.*

Plate 28. *Double-headed bronze linchpin of Philistine chariot wheel found in the vicinity of three miniature eight-spoked bronze wheels, Ekron.*

Plate 29. *Student delicately uncovering iron knife with ivory handle, Ekron.*

Plate 30. *Iron knife with ivory handle.*

Plate 31. *Student holding a pomegranate-shaped vessel from the destruction level of the early Philistine city at Ekron.*

Plate 32. *A cache of ivory, faience, and stone objects from the destruction level, Ekron.*

CHAPTER 13

Philistine Foundations

By the end of the 1963 season, we had finally reached levels in which we found substantial amounts of Philistine pottery and some characteristic Philistine artifacts of the twelfth and eleventh centuries B.C. While we still could not explain the meagerness of the Philistine remains at Tel Mor, their abundance at Tel Ashdod was unmistakable; we were eventually able to uncover three quite different parts of the well-fortified city of the earliest Philistines. This provided us with the opportunity of advancing our knowledge of Philistine architecture, crafts, and cultic objects and gaining a new perspective on life in the heart of Philistia during the early Philistine period.

In Area A, on the southern edge of the acropolis, the tell contained the ruins of a massive earlier structure. Only about a foot beneath the uppermost levels we uncovered a series of thick walls, each built of two rows of carefully laid mudbricks, reaching a width of almost four feet. The ground floor was divided into long, narrow chambers, which apparently served as storerooms. The few pottery sherds we found here, among them "Assyrian bowls," corresponded to our finds in the potters' quarter of Area D and suggested a chronological connection to the period following Sargon's conquest. Since two of the stele fragments were found in this general vicinity, it seemed possible that this large structure might have served as the city's administrative center during the Assyrian period. But we soon discovered that this fortified storehouse or citadel was not the work of the Assyrian conquerors. It gradually became evident that by the time of Sargon's conquest, this

THE HISTORY
OF A CITADEL

citadel had already been guarding the southern approach to the city for hundreds of years.

As we dug down alongside the thick outer walls through more than six feet of accumulation, we eventually realized that the major construction in this area began soon after the Philistines' arrival in Canaan, in the twelfth century B.C. (This was later numbered Stratum XII, c.1109–1125 B.C.) There were the remains of what must have been a substantial structure that, in its initial phase, may have served as a large private residence. But since beneath it was a thick blanket of destruction debris from the end of the Late Bronze Age, it also signaled a clear cultural break in the history of the city.

The early Philistine settlers had certainly laid the foundations, yet it was left to succeeding generations to enlarge on the original plan. Above the remains of this stratum we distinguished evidence of rebuilding and expansion, and the construction of the first of the several successive citadels that would dominate the acropolis until the time of Sargon. In Stratum XI (c.1125–c.1050 B.C.) a new outer wall was erected, almost twice the thickness of its predecessor, and although we uncovered only a small portion of this building, its character seemed to be that of a freestanding tower, not necessarily linked with the city's outer fortification wall. This structural isolation was suggested not only by its location in the middle of the upper city, but also by its apparent self-sufficiency. On the floor of the main hall we found silos probably constructed by the citadel's residents to store their own supply of grain.

In historical terms, the first century of Philistine building corresponded roughly to the time of the reign of Ramesses III up to the beginnings of their conflict with the Israelites in the middle of the eleventh century B.C. As we would subsequently discover in other excavation areas, these first hundred years were a time of consolidation and prosperity at Ashdod. The Philistines were and remained a distinct political and cultural entity.

THE CITY IS FORTIFIED

The citadel in Area A was not our only indication of the establishment, expansion, and fortification of the early Philistine city. At the opposite end of the tell in Area G we had finally completed the removal of debris from the Byzantine dump, when we began to uncover a series of superimposed floors and layers of mudbrick. Area G was located exactly on the northern edge of the early Philistine city, and it enabled us to uncover the main line of Ashdod's fortifications and to determine the nature of the structures that had been built immediately inside.

Philistine fortifications were of more than just architectural or military interest. They had a direct bearing on their political and economic

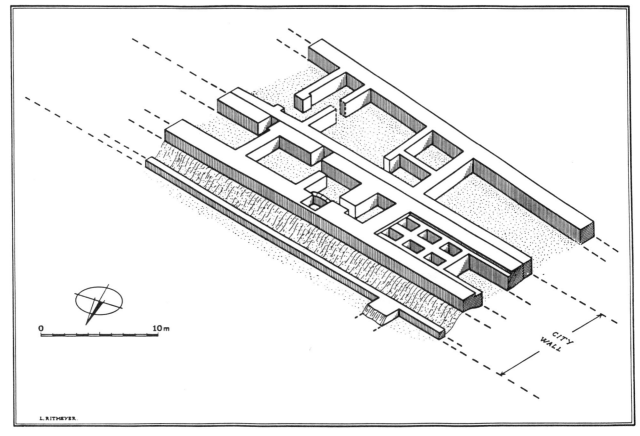

L. RITHMEYER.

history. The construction of city walls seemed to imply that when the Philistines settled along the Canaanite coast with the permission of the pharaoh, they were granted a measure of political autonomy. This quasi-independent status could, in turn, explain the circumstances of their later expansion throughout the inland regions as Egypt ceased to be a serious factor in Canaanite affairs toward the end of the twelfth century B.C.

With the slow expansion of our work in Area G, during the next few years we uncovered persuasive proof that the Philistines had, indeed, a generation or so after their arrival, established a well-planned and fortified city. Carrying on in their Aegean traditions, they soon reached a relatively high level of prosperity.

At the lowest level—that is, Stratum XII—we could trace their first efforts to establish a defensive line around their city. Using the thick walls of a ruined, earlier structure whose historical significance we would later discover, the early Philistines of Ashdod constructed a

Scarab from the time of Ramesses III, twelfth century B.C., found with bichrome Philistine pottery.

substantial double fortification wall, strengthened by an additional thin retaining wall slightly to the north which supported a series of carefully laid earth layers against the main wall's northern face.

Up to the time of our excavations, most scholars dated the beginning of the Philistine invasion to the early twelfth century B.C., using the Medinet Habu reliefs as their main source. In the carefully laid construction levels of Ashdod's northern fortifications we found a rare and direct confirmation of the date of their establishment. Here, in addition to the pottery and artifacts of a slightly earlier period, was a small amount of the earliest Philistine bichrome pottery and a scarab of Ramesses III. These finds not only substantiated the simple fact of the Philistines' settlement here during the early twelfth century B.C., but they also enabled us to reconstruct the period's historical context.

By the end of the twelfth century B.C., defense was apparently no longer the most important priority for the city. Houses were constructed outside the line of the original fortifications and a small alley provided convenient access to the center of town. One of the houses to the north of the city walls contained a series of large rooms surrounding a spacious paved courtyard, a sign that the prosperous residents of this extramural quarter lived in a time of relative tranquility. There was little evidence of any Israelite attacks, although this time roughly matched that of the biblical exploits of Samson. Typical Aegean-inspired Philistine pottery continued to be produced, the workshops were in constant use, and the city continued to expand.

LIFE IN THE RESIDENTIAL QUARTER

Now that we had determined the nature of the early Philistine occupation, at least in its broad outlines, on the northern and southern slopes, we began to dig on the western side, Area H. This was the high part of the ancient city, where the most important buildings would presumably be found. As in Area G, it took several seasons of digging before the layout of this part of the city became clear, but from the start we could see that the area was occupied by two main blocks of buildings, oriented on a uniform north-south axis and separated by a wide street running from east to west. The main street sloped steeply to the west, providing an outlet for drainage toward the edge of the city, perhaps even to a city gate that had by now been completely eroded.

The size and extent of the building complexes in Area H were impressive, with dwelling rooms opening onto a paved interior courtyard. Along its eastern end was a narrow chamber that probably served as a storeroom. Beyond were the remains of what seemed to be a similar residential complex. The finds inside confirmed our initial supposition that these were prosperous Philistine households. In addition to the wide range of elaborately decorated bowls and kraters, there were utilitarian pottery types like cooking pots and "spinning bowls," the latter used in the manufacture of textiles. On the floor of the central courtyard we even found a delicate finger ring, carefully crafted from an extremely thin sheet of beaten gold.

To the north of the street, the special character of the buildings and the finds suggested that they were used in the rituals of an early Philistine cult. The center was occupied by a rectangular courtyard, on the surface of which were the stone bases of two columns and a plastered brick structure that seemed to be an altar for offerings. And in the two rooms adjoining the courtyard we found a very rich assortment of artistic and cultural artifacts: several complete Philistine vessels, scarabs, beads, an ivory cosmetics box, gold and faience jewelry, and two gold-leaf dagger pommels ornamented with delicate punctured decoration, in a style reminiscent of the technique of Mycenaean metalsmiths (plate 9). One of the most intriguing finds was a stamp seal with several cryptic signs, similar to the still-undeciphered Cypro-Mycenaean script of Cyprus in the Late Bronze Age (plate 10). Although a few Philistine words had been identified in biblical texts, they had been transliterated into Hebrew. The nature and alphabet of the Philistine language is a subject of scholarly controversy.

Just beyond the wall that bordered the street we found a highly unusual platform of mudbricks with an outer apsidal outline and a rectangular depression within. Up to then no temples with apses were known in this period, yet its nearness to the small courtyard with the altar suggested that there might have been a cultic connection. And in a nearby destruction level we came upon an artifact whose cultic associations were never in doubt.

Among the ashes and collapsed rubble of one of the Stratum XII buildings we found a clay figurine torso, roughly rectangular in shape, that immediately riveted our attention; its surface was covered with the characteristic black and red painted decoration. Rachel Hachlili, the supervisor of the excavations in this area, instructed the volunteers to sift through the debris for additional fragments, and they soon came up with one of the long-necked figurines with a flat headdress, similar to other head and neck fragments previously found. Furthermore, they found another element: a base similar in form to the small, four-legged "offering tables" we had found in the shrine of Area D. Up to then we had not been able to provide a really tenable reconstruction of the figure. But now all the pieces fit together and offered us a striking, if highly stylized, image of a seated female Philistine deity merged into the form of a high-backed throne or chair (plate 8).

A PHILISTINE
GODDESS

Mudbrick platform with apsidal outline at Ashdod.

After the ash covering was delicately brushed away in our excavation laboratory, we were able to examine the details of the painted decoration, which reflected the same eclectic combination of influences evident on the Philistine pottery of the twelfth century B.C. Over the heavy white slip that covered the clay were alternating zones of horizontal bands and elongated triangles. Trude had already demonstrated how the Philistines' use of the triangle decoration was a stylization of the Egyptian lotus flower motif. And here on the figurine was both stylization and a realistic interpretation: between the small clay breasts on the front of the figurine was a tiny painted lotus flower, in the form of a pendant, suspended from a painted necklace.

This, then, was an example of the image of a deity worshiped at Ashdod at the time of the Philistines' initial settlement, and it was a figurine whose unique form and decoration reflected the adaptation of Aegean traditions in a Near Eastern milieu. When we had first found fragments of our long-necked figurines, we recognized their resemblance to Mycenaean figurines of the preceding Late Bronze Age, commonly found on the Greek mainland, in Cyprus, and in Canaan as well. Some had been of seated deities, sometimes separate from their chairs, sometimes attached. Our figurine seemed to represent a sub-

0 — 2 CM

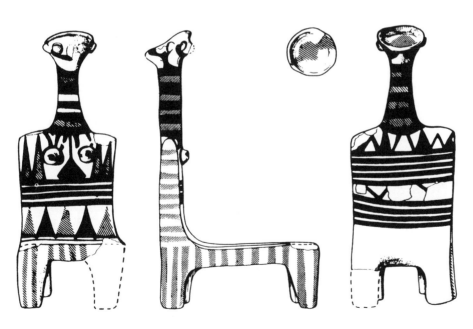

"Ashdoda," a female terra-
cotta figurine, reflecting the origin of Philistine cult beliefs.
The body merges into a four-
legged throne. Her flat, armless
torso and modeled breasts are
outlined on the back of the
throne. "Ashdoda" figurines
embody Mycenaean concepts
borrowed and adapted by the
Philistines. This "Ashdoda" is
the only complete example of
the type.

The "Ashdoda" figure is
probably a schematic representation of a female deity and
throne. It is clearly related to a
grouping known throughout
the Greek mainland, Rhodes,
and Cyprus—a Mycenaean female figurine seated on a
throne, sometimes holding a
child. These figurines are
thought to represent a mother
goddess.

155

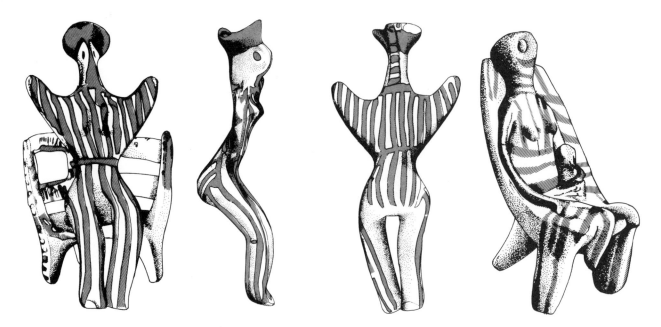

Left, first three views: *Seated Mycenaean figurine;* Right: *Seated Mycenaean figurine with child; from Athens National Museum.*

sequent development and stylization of the Mycenaean prototype, in which the chair and the goddess's body were completely merged.

But our Philistine figurine was distinct from its Mycenaean predecesssors in the same way that the Philistine pottery was itself different from earlier Aegean wares. And because it so clearly represented the essence of Ashdod's early Philistine culture, I decided to give our nameless deity a name or, at least, a nickname. "Ashdoda" seemed appropriate.

In fact, "Ashdoda" provided us with our first indication of the trends in Philistine religion. The veneration of a seated deity continued, apparently, at least until the time of Sargon's conquest—as we had seen in the finds of the Late Iron Age shrine in the potters' quarter in Area D. A significant transformation had taken place, however, sometime during the four hundred years of Philistine settlement in Ashdod. There were many fragments of clay "offering tables" which might have been transformations of the seated deities. And a few examples maintained the original form of the deity-table merger but were *male* cultic images rather than female.

According to the Bible, the Philistines worshiped only male deities, the most prominent among them Dagon (or Dagan). Yet, as some scholars had pointed out, Dagon was from the Canaanite pantheon. Originating, apparently, in Mesopotamia, he was one of the main male gods of Canaan in the second millennium B.C.—that is to say, he was famous long before the Philistines' arrival. It was only after the Philistines began to assimilate local customs, toward the end of the eleventh century B.C., that Dagon became associated with them. Before that, it was "Ashdoda" who held sway: for the first century after their arrival they had remained faithful to the Great Mother goddess of the Aegean world.

In the limited time left of the digging season I suggested that we make a small experimental probe beneath the level of the courtyard where we had found "Ashdoda." This might give us an idea of the nature of the city's transition from the levels of the Late Bronze Age to the Early Iron Age.

As it turned out, we did not find the clear-cut chronological sequences that had been observed at other Philistine sites. We found that the foundations of the first Philistine structures—characterized by finds of the typical bichrome pottery—were superimposed on similar buildings of a slightly earlier period, not on the ruins of the Late Bronze Age. About three feet below the level of the early Philistine courtyard, we uncovered another floor level on which there was no Philistine pottery, only fragments of bowls, kraters, and juglets, similar but not identical to Philistine ware. The color and quality of the clay were different and the decorations were painted in a dark monochrome. This level directly overlaid the destruction debris of the Late Bronze Age city and provided us with our first indication of the previously unknown chapter in the history of Ashdod. Strangely enough, as we were ending the season, there were some similar indications revealed in the lowest excavation levels of Area A as well.

There, just below the earliest of our Philistine structures, on the southern edge of the acropolis, we distinguished a thin layer of beaten earth and accumulation that again marked an intermediate stage of occupation, between the destruction of the Late Bronze Age city and the first appearance of Philistine bichrome ware. Although there were no signs of any structures on this level, we found more examples of what seemed to be the earlier version of Aegean-inspired pottery. We had finally gotten to the crucial period of transition between the Bronze and Iron ages, and we could now see that the circumstances of the transition at Ashdod were unexpectedly complex. There seemed to be another stage that we had not previously recognized. It would be another three years before we resumed the excavations. By then the evidence would become a good deal clearer and the abundant Aegean-inspired monochrome pottery would be our most important clue.

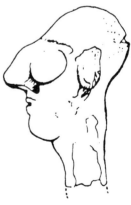

Male cultic images.

CHAPTER 14

An Aegean Connection

We spent the next year at the Institute for Advanced Study at Princeton, during which the Archaeological Institute of America gave me the opportunity of lecturing to its chapters all over the United States. Initial reports in the popular press of the Ashdod excavations had created a good deal of interest among archaeology enthusiasts. I found large and attentive audiences wherever I went, eager to hear about our discoveries at one of the most important cities of the Philistines.

True, the audiences were not always interested in the latest advances in archaeological research. Many of their questions often had to do with Samson and Delilah, David and Goliath, or the Temple of Dagon at Ashdod—subjects about which I could not offer any startling news— and I had to emphasize constantly that our excavations were not intended to "prove" biblical contentions. Our intentions were, I explained, to study Philistine culture from another perspective entirely. And it seems to me that when I showed the audiences slides of the Philistine fortification system, the elaborately painted Philistine pottery, and the stylized figurine of "Ashdoda," so strikingly contemporary in form, they began to understand that the traditional view of the Philistines as predatory barbarians was not, to say the least, historically accurate.

Returning to Israel in the fall of 1966, I was very eager to plan the next digging season at Ashdod. Although we had already uncovered the remains of the early Philistine city in several areas, the evidence of settlement in the period immediately *preceding* the Philistine arrival remained enigmatic. If the Philistines themselves were not the conquerors of the Late Bronze Age city, some of our most basic historical assumptions might have to be revised. In addition, there was the problem of coordinating the city levels at Ashdod with those at the neighboring harbor town of Tel Mor. I hoped to concentrate on these archaeological objectives during the coming summer. But in the late spring of 1967, modern, rather than ancient, history determined our excavation plans.

A military conflict loomed between Israel and Egypt, and, by May, many of our Israeli staff had already been mobilized. War seemed inevitable as news reports brought the unsettling accounts of the blockade of the Straits of Tiran to Israeli shipping and of Egyptian troop concentrations in Sinai. Since our excavations were scheduled to begin in June, I was forced to make a difficult decision. I knew that even if there weren't open hostilities, many of our staff would still be in the army, and in light of the tense Middle Eastern situation we couldn't count on our American student volunteers to come. When I spoke to Jim Swauger in Pittsburgh, he had come to the same conclusion: there was no alternative to canceling the 1967 excavations at Ashdod.

Several weeks later the war did break out. But within six days it was over, and as soon as life in the country began to return to normal I was eager to get into the field for whatever work could be done. Without the American contingent we would have to leave the main excavation areas—and the early Philistine levels—until the next full-scale season. But there was still one archaeological detail that could be dealt with.

The potters' quarters of the lower city in Area D was where we had found the dramatic evidence of Sargon's conquest, and it was important to determine when this part of the city was first occupied. So I brought a small team to Ashdod during the summer to complete the excavation of Area D. Our limited excavations revealed some floor levels of the ninth century B.C., but nowhere in the area was there any evidence of earlier occupation. It seemed clear to us, therefore, that the original Philistine city, like its Bronze Age predecessors, had been restricted to the acropolis.

INVASION FROM CYPRUS

By the summer of 1968, when we finally returned to Ashdod with a full-scale excavation team, we were now primarily interested in concentrating on the puzzling developments that had taken place in the city after the end of the Late Bronze Age. Naturally, our previous excavations in the courtyard building of the early Philistine period (near which "Ashdoda" had been found) indicated that the best place to look for more evidence of that transition was in Area H, on the western slope of the tell. The distinctive early variants of Philistine pottery found beneath the floors of the building suggested that a building phase in this area had *preceded* the Philistines, but because we had uncovered such a small area beneath Stratum XII, we could not be sure that this transitional period was not just a mirage.

As soon as we began to dig beneath the courtyard of the early Philistine building in Area H, it was clear that the transitional period was real. Above the thick blanket of ashes and collapsed debris that covered the ruins of the Late Bronze Age city we found a well-built mudbrick building containing a storeroom with several complete storejars. The original plan of this structure was uncertain, but farther to the north another building of this level, stratigraphically Stratum XIII, was easier to identify. Beneath the walls of the Philistine building with the unique, apsidal structure in Stratum XII, we were able to trace a strikingly similar layout in the building that had existed here in Stratum XIII.

In many places the walls of the Philistine building were founded directly on the walls of the earlier structure, and even more significant they seemed to have been erected according to the same building techniques. They consisted of large, flat mudbricks, laid lengthwise, a single row of them creating a wall. The dimensions of the bricks were identical in both strata, and in some places there was no clear architectural division between the two periods, just a gradual rebuilding of the same walls and relaying of floors. Although here and there were changes and additions in the Philistine period, it seemed evident that the basic layout of this section of the city was already established before the erection of the Philistine fortifications on the northern edge of the tell.

In addition to the similarity between individual structures, there was obviously a common city plan. In Area H, the street that divided the two blocks of buildings in the early Philistine period divided the blocks of the preceding level as well. Since the street and adjoining buildings of Stratum XIII were built directly above the thick level of Late Bronze Age destruction, we were forced to conclude it was then that the basic character of the Early Iron Age city of Ashdod was determined. And from the similarity of the monochrome pottery we found on this earlier level to the later Philistine bichrome, it seemed that the cultural relationship between the Philistines, as we had always identified them, and the earlier settlers was close.

Ever since the thirties, when Walter Heurtley had first attempted to trace the origins of the Philistines' artistic traditions, most scholars had agreed that the closest prototypes for the Philistine pottery shapes and decorations were to be found in the latest class of Late Bronze Age Aegean pottery, whose technical designation was Mycenaean IIIC:1b. Since the farthest east that such vessels had ever been found was on

Cyprus, Heurtley had assumed that the Philistine potters had relied strictly on memory in reproducing their own variants of these wares.

We could now see that this theory needed revision. The floor levels of the Stratum XIII buildings in Area H contained dozens of examples of Mycenaean IIIC:1b ware. Most of the fragments came from open vessels, bell-shaped bowls, and kraters, precisely the types that later became hallmarks in the Philistine repertoire. And the monochrome decorations shared some of the Philistines' bichrome motifs and patterns. The significance of our discovery was enormous, for it seemed that we were now able to distinguish a pre-Philistine Aegean settlement in Canaan. Initially I myself believed that we could now pinpoint the last stopping place of the Philistines, if not their original homeland.

During the years that Trude was working on her dissertation, we had visited the excavations on Cyprus several times. The sudden appearance of Mycenaean IIIC:1b pottery there, apparently in association with the destruction and rebuilding of the major Cypriot cities, had led the archaeologists working there to associate it with the arrival of Aegean immigrants from the Greek mainland after the destruction of the Mycenaean palaces. This population movement had preceded the first recorded appearance of the Philistines by a generation. Yet we now seemed to have evidence that the Aegeans had, at that time, reached Canaan as well. The Mycenaean types in Stratum XIII at Ashdod had exact parallels in Cyprus, particularly at the site of Sinda, near the eastern coast of the island. At first we were so convinced that our Mycenaean IIIC:1b vessels were imported from Cyprus that we even began to call them "Sinda ware." They seemed to provide a direct link between our Stratum XIII settlement and the events in the rest of the eastern Mediterranean—that is, a gradual process of migration rather than a single lightning invasion down the Canaanite coast.

We still could not be sure if the first Aegean settlers at Ashdod were themselves Philistines or one of the other Sea Peoples mentioned in the Egyptian records. The Medinet Habu reliefs did not, apparently, tell the whole story. And as work in Area H continued during the 1968 season, we also resumed the excavations in Area G on the northern slope of the tell. And it was there that we gained new insight into Ashdod's history and found further evidence regarding the first appearance of the Sea Peoples there.

THE RISE AND FALL OF AN INLAND CITY

In Area G, and only in Area G, were we able to dig through *another ten strata*—that is, to the seventeenth century B.C. There, at Stratum XXIII, we finally began to get an idea of Ashdod's establishment, and on our way, so to speak, a glimpse of the city's first centuries of existence, provided particularly by strata XVI and XIV. In the lowest

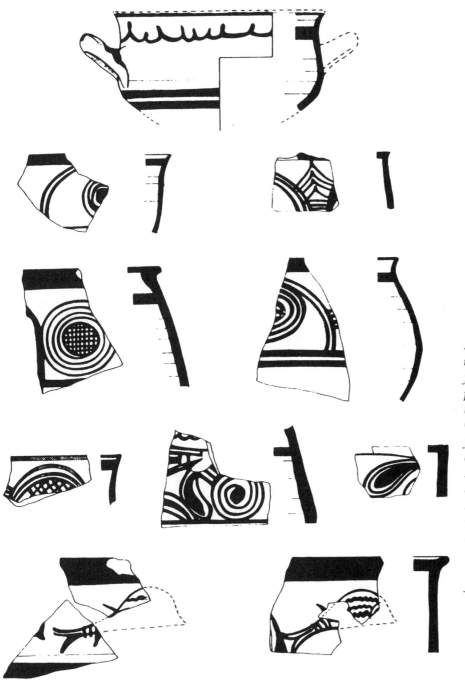

Mycenaean IIIC:1b pottery made locally in Ashdod. In forms, motifs, and color, the pottery is a faithful reproduction of Mycenaean traditions. Of greenish buff ware with a fine hard texture and one-color decoration, it appears on bell-shaped bowls and small kraters, as well as on stirrup jars and strainer-spout jugs. The decoration consists of vertical zig-zag patterns; spirals, some with net-decorated centers; wavy lines below the rims; and fish decorations. This assemblage offered the first glimpse of the prototypes of some Philistine vessels and was clearly made by potters well versed in Mycenaean pottery techniques.

*One of the elaborately deco-
rated Mycenaean IIIC kraters,
closely related in ware, shape,
paint, and decorative concept to
the locally made Mycenaean
IIIC:1b pottery found at Ashdod.*

stratum we uncovered a massive city gate. The natural topography of
Area G, on the steep northern slope of the upper city, determined its
continuing function as the northern boundary of Ashdod throughout
the second millennium B.C. But at the time of its establishment, about
1600 B.C. or a little earlier, that boundary was already guarded by the
solid mudbrick gate and sloping rampart.

The historical events that led the Hyksos rulers of Egypt to establish
the harbor town of Tel Mor and the inland metropolis of Ashdod at
roughly the same time were not particularly relevant to the Philistine
settlement four centuries later. But what did link the two periods was
the expansion of commercial contact with the Aegean world. By around
1450 B.C., Mycenaean as well as Cypriot pottery appeared in the excavated levels, a phenomenon common to all the cities of the Canaanite
coast. As at Tel Mor, we found evidence at Ashdod of Egyptian involvement and, probably, control: above and slightly to the south of
the earliest fortifications in Stratum XVI a large public building was
erected whose storerooms and monumental entrance, with two large
stone column bases, recalled Egyptian architectural models. Apparently
it had served as the city's administrative center or official residence.

The significant number of Egyptian New Kingdom scarabs and a
fragment of a stone doorjamb with a hieroglyphic inscription from the
same period made it seem likely that Egyptian administrators or garrison troops had been stationed there. The inscription read: "Fanbearer
on the right hand of the King." The prosperity of Ashdod and its
harbor town in the fourteenth and thirteenth centuries B.C. was well
known from the evidence of Ugaritic documents, and was illustrated

by our own archaeological finds. Additional texts subsequently discovered at Ugarit indicated that Ashdod even had its own legal weight
standard, the Ashdodite shekel, which further emphasized the city's
commercial importance. But as we uncovered the last of the Late Bronze
Age levels, Stratum XIV, we saw that the city's prosperity suddenly
came to an end in the late thirteenth century B.C.

We knew from Egyptian records from the reign of Merneptah of
attacks by the earliest Sea Peoples in the western Nile delta, and of
famine and population movements in the Aegean and Asia Minor. But
because none of the surviving inscriptions or documents mentioned
Ashdod specifically, we had no written evidence of the fate of the city
during this period. Our evidence was now strictly archaeological. It
suggested that while some international trade continued, there was an
apparent lowering of the city's previous high standard of living. The
once-monumental entrance to the residence was dismantled. One of
the large column bases seemed to have been used to repair an inner
wall. And other slight modifications of the building's interior arrange-
ments represented haphazard, makeshift repairs.

These changes were, apparently, omens of the final destruction of
the prosperous, Egyptian-dominated trading city. A thick layer of ash
and collapsed bricks and building stones marked the end of the commercial center that had flourished for several hundred years. And here,
in the ruins of the massive residence, evidence of the catastrophe seemed
especially violent: most of the thick outer walls were destroyed down
to their foundations, and the upper story had collapsed and blanketed
the surviving ruins.

So far these finds matched those in the destruction level and the heavily
fortified harbor citadel at Tel Mor. But at Ashdod, as we expanded the
excavation in Area G in 1969, we suddenly recognized how the history
of the two places subsequently diverged. At Tel Mor, an Egyptian
presence was resumed after only a brief interruption: a newly built
watchtower and workshops testified to a continuity in the settlement's
character. But in the ruins of the Late Bronze Age residency in Stratum
XIII we found clear signs of reoccupation by new settlers. They had
adapted the remaining inner walls for use as sheds or huts. In the process,
the function of many of the building's rooms was altered. A finely
plastered pool that had once stored rainwater was now turned into a
room. And in the rear, in one of the large storerooms, the new occupants erected several thin walls, partitioning the large space into an
open courtyard and adjoining workshops for various crafts.

Most of the area seemed to have become an artisans' quarter, and in
one of the rooms of this complex of workshops we discovered a potters'

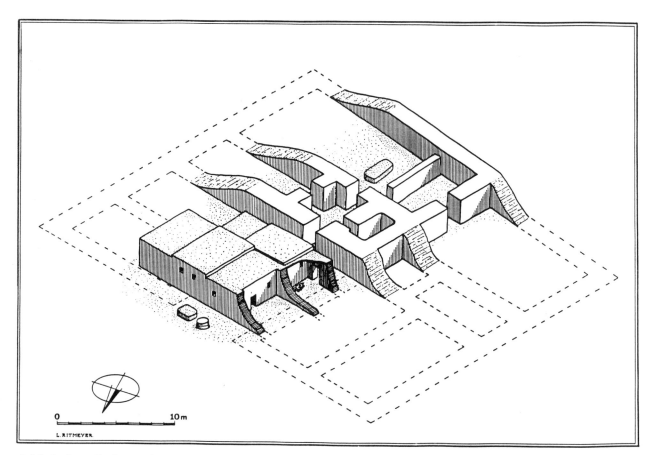

Ashdod, Area G. Isometric re-construction of Stratum XIIIb.

storeroom, with several storejars leaning against the walls and two dozen complete bowls stacked facedown in carefully arranged rows on the floor. These, apparently, were merchandise for sale. The bowls and almost all of the decorated pottery found in Stratum XIII were typical examples of the Mycenaean IIIC:1b style.

So the pottery of the first inhabitants of Ashdod after its Late Bronze Age destruction was extremely close in style to that of the invaders who had occupied and rebuilt cities in Cyprus at approximately the same time. Therefore, Stratum XIII represented a stage of settlement *preceding* the emergence of Philistine culture as we knew it. But we were not sure if these settlers at Ashdod were Philistines or another group of Sea Peoples who roamed the eastern Mediterranean at the end of the thirteenth century B.C.

Our evidence of this earlier settlement was not restricted to pottery. There were also some indications of cult. At the northern edge of the area we uncovered an open-air shrine consisting of a square structure

166

of plastered bricks and a round pillar base revised from the ruined Late Bronze Age residency. There were sherds and small animal bones scattered on the brick structure, and the surface of the column base was blackened by fire. It seemed likely that these installations were used as an altar and the base for an image. The distinctive character of this Stratum III cult was illustrated by a small stone cylinder seal bearing an inscription and a row of highly stylized figures, which was quite different from the Philistine stamp seal found in Stratum XII in Area H (plate 11).

From the accumulation of debris here we estimated that the artisans'

Assemblage of Philistine Mycenaean IIIC:1b ware from what appears to have been a potter's workshop in Ashdod. A large amount of charred wood, probably from a kiln, was found on the floor of one of the rooms. Twenty-seven pottery vessels were stacked upside down on the floor nearby.

Early Sea People or Philistine altar in the open-air shrine at Ashdod.

167

quarter existed for about a generation. But toward the end of that period, which we identified as Stratum XIIIa, a few characteristic Philistine bichrome sherds were found mixed with the more numerous examples of the Mycenaean monochrome pottery. It was difficult to distinguish evidence of a *gradual* artistic development from one to the other. The elaborate style of the earliest Philistine sherds was already developed (plate 6), as if a new artistic tradition had suddenly influenced the city's potters sometime after the establishment of Stratum XIII, and this new cultural impetus soon dominated: over the unfortified artisans' quarter of the Stratum XIII settlement, a new city arose.

Now we could finally begin to understand the historical context of the Philistines' fortification and city planning of the early twelfth century B.C. The earlier complex of workshops and remaining massive walls of the Late Bronze Age residence became the structural base of the new city wall. The painted pottery of this level was almost entirely Philistine bichrome, with only a few Mycenaean IIIC:1b sherds. Moreover, the Philistine builders apparently disregarded the sanctity of the earlier open-air shrine and buried its altar and column base under the tons of their carefully laid revetment levels that supported the city wall's outer face. What was clear, however, was that the Philistine city was built above an earlier settlement that also possessed an Aegean-inspired culture, but of a slightly different character. Our challenge now was to attempt to identify those earlier settlers and, if possible, trace their origins.

TRACE ELEMENTS AND TRANSITION

By the time we completed our excavations in Area G, we had dozens of complete and fragmentary examples of the Mycenaean IIIC:1b pottery. Their shapes and decorations led us to believe that at least a significant number of them had been imported directly from Cyprus. But we still needed some physical evidence of the precise origin of the Ashdod Stratum XIII vessels. Fortunately, a new scientific technique enabled us to do just that.

The technique, called neutron activation analysis, had been adapted for use in testing pottery by Professor Isador Perlman of the Lawrence Berkeley Laboratory of the University of California. Perlman was a nuclear physicist whose personal interest in archaeology had led him to develop the means by which the geographical origin of ancient pottery could be determined with considerable accuracy. The principle of Perlman's technique was that the clay of a particular region had a distinctive chemical "fingerprint." Once he had collected a "library" of clays from around the eastern Mediterranean, he would irradiate a small sample of the pottery in question and determine the proportion of its various trace elements—the heavy metals measured in parts per million.

During previous digging seasons Perlman had tested and proved his technique on Ashdod sherds whose origin was clear to us. Now we assumed that Perlman's tests would confirm our hypothesis that they were imports, and he might even be able to pinpoint their exact origin. The results, however, contradicted our hypothesis: not a single one of the pottery samples was imported. Their composition showed that they were all manufactured at Ashdod!

In other words, the Stratum XIII settlers had brought their ceramic know-how with them rather than actual wares. They were then migrants and not traders. I referred to these "proto-Philistines" as the "Anakim," taking my cue from the Bible. The Anakim are mentioned a number of times in Deuteronomy and in Joshua, both dated to before the Philistine conquest. One of the passages in Joshua [11:22] reads: "There was none of the Anakim left in the land of the people of Israel; only in Gaza, in Gath, and in Ashdod did some remain." It is possible that they later assimilated into Philistine culture.

Cyprus may well have been their last stopping place, but since Mycenaean IIIC:1b style was widespread at the time they might have brought their traditions with them from the Greek mainland, Rhodes, Asia Minor, or the north Syrian coast. The sheer range of these possibilities forced us to view the settlement of Ashdod in the context of the early movements of the Sea Peoples, who ranged throughout the entire eastern Mediterranean.

While Tel Mor was still apparently a strategic point for the Egyptian administration in its attempts to guard the commercial maritime traffic along the coast, the immediate inland regions were left by default to the new settlers, who, because of the increasing weakness of the Egyptians, were able to establish firm footholds there.

It was clear that the ancient Egyptian records—which claimed that the Philistines and the other Sea Peoples arrived in Canaan in one massive invasion during the reign of Ramesses III—could not be taken at face value. The Medinet Habu reliefs and inscriptions had apparently telescoped the events of a protracted process of Aegean immigration, the destruction of cities along the coasts of Asia Minor and Syria, and the migrants' eventual settlement on the southern Canaanite coast.

Our archaeological evidence now seemed to suggest that this process extended over a long period—from at least the end of the reign of Merneptah, at the end of the thirteenth century B.C., to the time of the rise of the XXth Dynasty, toward the end of the eleventh century B.C.

The finds of the Stratum XIII settlement represented the earliest stage in the Aegean immigration. It may have begun while the Egyptian administration still maintained a nominal presence along the coast. It was only later, however, with the last and most threatening wave of invasion—in which the Philistines and their allies reached the Nile delta—that the Egyptians were finally forced to act. That, apparently, was the historical context of Ramesses III's great land and sea battles against the Philistines and their allies. It was the culmination of a long and complex process.

CHAPTER 15

The Age
of Philistine Power

Five seasons of digging might have seemed like a long time for a single project, but during our fifth season at Ashdod in 1969 we felt as if we had only begun. By the terms of our agreement with the Smithsonian Institution and the Carnegie Museum, this was to be our last large-scale dig. As things turned out, we continued for another three years.

We had by now gained an understanding of the circumstances of the Philistines' arrival in Canaan, but we had yet to explore more fully the subsequent period of their inland expansion and conflict with the Israelites. This chapter was, of course, the most well known from a biblical standpoint, beginning with the stories of Samson and ending with the victories of David, who put an end to the Philistines' hegemony.

Long before archaeological excavations, historians of the biblical period had established an approximate chronological framework for the conflict, and elaborated on the sometimes sketchy and often obscure details of the biblical narrative. Despite the Bible's theological intentions and its legendary components, it preserves a basically reliable record of the great conflict between the two peoples. By synchronisms between the reigns of later Israelite and Judean kings and the king lists of Assyria, the conflict could be roughly dated to cover the last half of the eleventh and the beginning of the tenth centuries B.C.

The earliest encounters between the Israelites and the Philistines consisted, apparently, of mere border skirmishes, typified by the stories of Samson. Single-handed, he raided the Philistine cities of Timnah, Ashkelon, and Gaza, until he was finally captured and put to death [Judges 14–16]. That the border at this period was reportedly at the edge of the Judean hill country meant that a significant Philistine inland expansion from their original coastal enclave had taken place. This was soon to lead to Philistine domination and a head-on territorial clash.

According to 1 Samuel [4:1–10], the first clash took place at Ebenezer, near the sources of the Yarkon River on the Sharon Plain, around 1050 B.C. If the biblical descriptions are accurate, it was an uneven match from the start. The well-organized Philistine armies, with special detachments of archers, charioteers, infantry, and cavalry, faced a lightly armed Israelite volunteer force. The Israelite villagers were quickly defeated; their desperate summoning of supernatural intervention by bringing the Ark of the Covenant to the battlefield made matters only worse: the Ark was taken as booty by the Philistines. According to the narrative, the Ark caused a plague in the Philistine cities of Ashdod, Gath, and Ekron, and was eventually restored to the Israelites at Beth Shemesh. But the Philistines established garrisons throughout the hill country and maintained close control over the region's population and trade routes.

It would appear that Philistine domination lasted for about a generation, from c. 1050 to c. 1020 B.C. During that time the Israelites' unity had been kept alive by the prophet Samuel, who traveled throughout the hill country encouraging resistance to the Philistines and adherence to the rituals of the Israelite cult. It was then that the Israelites recognized their need for a leader to overcome the Philistines, and Saul, from the northern tribe of Benjamin, was anointed first king of Israel.

The events of Saul's reign in the last decades of the eleventh century B.C. are shrouded in legend, but the stories of the Israelites' victory at Michmash, north of Jerusalem, and David's miraculous defeat of Goliath [1 Samuel 14, 17] suggest that the Philistines suffered a series of serious setbacks. And even after one last counterattack by the combined armies of the Philistine cities, in which Saul was defeated and killed near Beth Shean [1 Samuel 31], the Israelite monarchy endured. The Philistines had regained control of the Valley of Esdraelon and still exercised control over the coast and a large part of the hill country, but David was now destined to break their hold.

The turning point was apparently David's capture of the Jebusite city of Jerusalem in the central hill country and its transformation into the Israelite capital, around 1000 B.C. When the Philistines met his forces in the Valley of Rephaim on the southern outskirts of Jerusalem, they were routed and driven from the hill country once and for all.

Ashdod's role in this protracted conflict was central, at least at the beginning. It was to the Temple of Dagon at Ashdod that the Philistines brought the Ark of the Covenant. There is no specific mention of Ashdod later, except insofar as it provided troops for the battle against Saul in the Valley of Esdraelon.

Our challenge as archaeologists in the excavation of Ashdod was not to contest or substantiate the biblical version of events but rather to study the city's development and its material culture during this period. Evidence of biblical personalities could not be expected to appear in the archaeological record, but fortifications, cult practices, and urban growth could, in this most significant era of Philistine history.

The most important events of the Philistines' wars with the Israelites would perhaps be reflected in the evidence in Stratum X. We already had an idea of general trends from our finds at this level. In Area A, on the southern edge of the acropolis, we had noted the substantial strengthening of the citadel during this period, and, even more suggestive, in Area G we could distinguish the signs of a complete transformation in the city's plan around 1050 B.C.

Before this time we had observed how houses were built outside the line of the original fortifications, an indication of peace and prosperity. And, indeed, this concurs with the Israelite view in the Samson stories of a prosperous alien population of Philistines settled in the cities of the coast. But now, at the peak of their power, the houses that had dotted the northern slopes of the acropolis were systematically leveled to make way for a new, even more massive line of fortifications, a solid wall of mudbricks, almost fifteen feet thick. We traced the course of the Stratum X wall for more than forty feet in an easterly direction as it ran along the northern edge of the tell. A sharp corner at the eastern edge of the excavation area suggested the presence of external bastions or an alteration in the line of the wall as it seemingly enclosed an area far wider than just the acropolis. And when we later opened another area in the lower city it was clear that sometime after 1050 B.C., Ashdod became one of the largest cities in the entire country.

The need for the defense of this Philistine capital at the time of the first large-scale military confrontation with the Israelites might have been expected and was, in a sense, a confirmation of the biblical information. And in another area, we uncovered a suggestive human illustration of at least one facet of the Philistine military tradition at Ashdod.

Close to the highest point of the acropolis, in Area K, we uncovered a large, open courtyard that was bounded on all sides by substantial brick walls. As we cleared the level of the courtyard, we uncovered a

A WARRIOR'S BURIAL

grave containing a single adult male skeleton and, nearby, the complete skeleton of a horse. The burial of a single man and his horse inside the city was an unusual phenomenon, and at such a location underlined the importance that the inhabitants had apparently ascribed to this individual. We would later uncover evidence that linked this area to the cult rituals of the Stratum X city.

But of additional interest was the presence in the grave of a heavy dagger with a thick iron blade. Since Goliath's spearhead was said to have been made of iron [1 Samuel 17:7], many scholars had suggested that the Philistines had brought the secret of iron smelting to Canaan from their Aegean homeland. Earlier excavations of Philistine sites had, it will be remembered, contradicted this theory: few iron objects were found in Philistine settlements and they were mostly luxury items— rings and bracelets—rather than weapons or tools. The spread of iron-working seemed rather to be the result of changing technology, due to the collapse in the trade of tin, an essential raw material for the production of bronze. At the time of the Philistines' arrival in Canaan, bronze was still the most common metal. Iron became common throughout the entire region only toward the end of the eleventh century B.C.

But the dagger in this eleventh-century B.C. grave was of interest not so much because it was made of iron but because of its distinctive shape. The blade was slightly curved toward its point, unlike the straight Canaanite daggers. It was a kind never found in Israel before. As we later learned, this form was characteristic of Greek daggers of the early "Dark Ages," around 1000 B.C., another piece of evidence of possible contact between the Philistines and the peoples of the Aegean, even as late as the time of their wars with the Israelites.

THE MUSICIANS OF ASHDOD

Although we didn't discover the famous Temple of Dagon at Ashdod, we found evidence of a significant cult transformation that occurred in the city at this time. Throughout the area of the northern fortifications we found a number of fragments of the small clay "offering tables," similar to those of the later shrine of Area D. There we found our earliest examples of the circular, animal-headed *kernoi*, close in style to the libation vessels of the Canaanites. A few fragments of "Ashdoda"-like figurines indicated that the Aegean cult traditions were still present, as did the motif carved on the face of a stone seal. Although only half of this artifact was preserved, its top was carved in the form of a recumbent lion, and on its engraved lower surface was the image of an "Ashdoda" type playing a lyre.

These Aegean cult traditions, however, seemed to be fading by the end of the eleventh century B.C. We had already noted that the characteristic decorated Philistine pottery was quite rare in Stratum X. The dominant pottery types were of the red-burnished "Ashdod Ware" that had a close stylistic relationship to the pottery of the cities of Phoenicia and the inland centers of Israel. A similar phenomenon of cultural assimilation could be observed in the cult objects of this period: in addition to the Canaanite-style libation vessels, a number of male images began to appear. As we already knew, Dagon himself was a Canaanite deity whose worship was not originally a part of the Philistine cult. And as we expanded the excavations in Area K, we found a clear indication of the extent to which the Philistine cult had been altered by the time of their wars with the Israelites.

There were clear signs of destruction and burning all over the Area K courtyard, an indication that this part of the city, near the summit of the acropolis, had suffered a sudden, violent end. The enclosed walls had collapsed and were covered with a thick layer of ashes. A few yards from the warrior's grave we found evidence of cultic practices: deeply embedded storejars and fragments of an elaborate cult stand (plate 7).

This latter artifact was completely reconstructed. Beneath the deep, carinated bowl, which may have been used for incense or offerings, were five stylized figures, each playing a musical instrument: two played double flutes, another cymbals, another a tambourine, and the last a lyre. It seemed clear that they represented a group of temple musicians, of a type apparently familiar to the inhabitants of Ashdod. It was the earliest depiction of musicians on a cultic vessel ever found in Israel. It also provided us with an unexpected similarity between the religious practices of the Philistines and the contemporary Israelites in the late eleventh century B.C. In 1 Samuel [10:5–6], Samuel instructs Saul to look for a particular sign of his divine election as the first king of Israel:

> You shall come to the Hill of the Lord where there is a garrison of
> Philistines; and there, as you come into the city, you will meet a band
> of prophets coming down from the highplace with harp, tambourine,
> flute, and lyre before them, prophesying. Then the spirit of the Lord
> will come mightily upon you, and you shall prophesy with them and
> be turned into another man. . . .

The passage underlines the importance of music as a means of achieving divine revelation for the Israelites at the time, a tradition familiar to us from the legends of David and Solomon as well. So, despite biblical emphasis to the contrary, there were similarities in cult practices between Israelites and Philistines.

The initial finds in Stratum X had given us a hint of the nature of

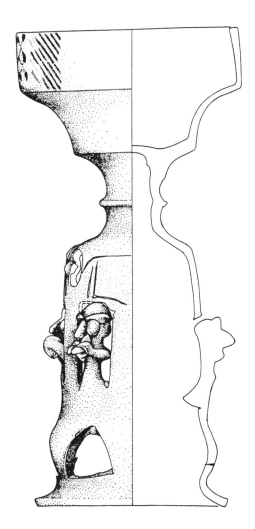

A cult stand, with five musicians around its base, from Ashdod. Four are modeled in the round and stand in window-like openings, fixed by the peg-like lower parts of their bodies. The upper parts of the figures, though schematic, are more realistic. The heads are disproportionately large with bulging eyes and exaggeratedly large noses. The fifth and central figure is distinctive, with larger dimensions and a different style and construction. The figure's outline was cut out, after which the individual features were modeled and added. Its face is grotesque, and its head is a flattened version of the modeled heads of the other musicians. The eyes and protruding ears are asymmetrical. A procession of three animals is rendered above the musicians.

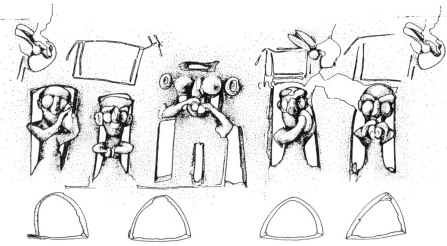

the transformation that Philistine culture was undergoing at the time of the wars with the Israelites. Their Aegean heritage was almost forgotten, and local influences had become predominant after a century and a half of assimilation. We had also gotten a sense of the power of the Philistine city of Ashdod in this period, with evidence of its expansion and sudden fortification at the end of the eleventh century B.C. Yet as we would soon see, the most impressive monument of this powerful Philistine capital was not to be found on the acropolis, but in an area of the lower city, several hundred yards away.

DISCOVERY IN THE ORCHARD

During our first season of digging, six years earlier, we had excavated a trial trench, E, on the summit of the eastern hill, near the ruins of the medieval mosque. But because the earliest remains there were from the Byzantine period, we could not determine if the Philistine city had ever spread that far to the east. Beyond that eastern hill lay the apricot orchard of Kibbutz Hazor, which bordered on the main north–south highway.

All through the years of digging at Ashdod, Menashe Brosh of the Department of Antiquities had conducted extensive surface surveys in a continuing search for any signs of ancient occupation in the outlying areas. Although he often brought back pottery sherds and artifacts, he never found signs of any substantial settlement beyond the immediate vicinity of the acropolis. But this year, as the kibbutz plowed the western edge of their orchard in preparation for spring planting, he found an extraordinarily high concentration of Iron Age sherds and figurine fragments in the freshly turned furrows.

When we examined this pottery we found many types similar to those found in the potters' quarter in Area D. And because there were many crumbled brick fragments in the sample, it seemed that Brosh had located a previously unknown part of the ancient city. Our subsequent visits to the area confirmed this supposition, and even though this was to be our last season at Ashdod, I felt the opportunity too intriguing to ignore. If the area of the orchard turned out to be part of ancient Ashdod, it would completely change our understanding of the city's size in the various stages of its development. Accordingly, we sought and received permission from the kibbutz to dig there. We called the site Area M.

By the end of the 1969 season, our finds in Area M surpassed even our most optimistic expectations. The abundant pottery finds came from the massive fortifications of the city's eastern defensive line! Beneath the uppermost layers we began to trace a series of superimposed city gates and adjoining structures which, by their changing forms, gave us the tools to reconstruct the character of the city's eastward expansion from late in the Byzantine period back through the centuries to the time of the Philistines' wars with the Israelites.

ENTRANCE TO A PHILISTINE CITY

Since Area M covered some two and a half acres, its excavation could not possibly be completed in one season; we worked on for another three.

The finds in the lowest levels of Area M enabled us to distinguish the stages of Ashdod's initial expansion. Before the construction of the city wall and gate, there were signs that this site, several hundred yards from the acropolis, had been used, in its earliest period, as an industrial area. Just above the virgin soil, eight feet beneath the surface of the orchard, we found pottery kilns and clay basins filled with refuse of manufacture—ash and broken, deformed vessels, both fired and unfired.

We found silt-filled depressions throughout the entire level, an indication that one of the main reasons for the choice of this area was the availability of natural clay. The successive floor levels of ash and pebbles around the kilns suggested that this was not a brief occupation but the beginning of permanent settlement here. The vessel types found in this first, unfortified pottery compound matched those of Stratum XI elsewhere. There were sherds of the Philistine bichrome type, but the dominant types were of the later "Ashdod Ware," and included basins, cult stands, storejars, and even toys. The location of this area of workshops so far from the fortified acropolis underlined the extent of Ashdod's prosperity and expansion toward the end of the eleventh century B.C.

It was then that the workshops were leveled and the kilns, walls, and refuse pits buried under the foundations of the city's new defensive line. We now finally had the continuation to the east of the huge mudbrick city walls of Stratum X that had been constructed along the northern edge of the city. We had never supposed that the urban core of the city extended so far east. Although this section was a quarter of a mile from the highest part of the acropolis, it was here that one of the main entrances to the city was built. In the center of Area M we uncovered a massive city gate consisting of two towers, each containing two guardrooms, adjoining the central passageway. Few city gates of this period had been found anywhere in the country, and ours provided a particularly vivid indication of the Philistines' power at the time of their wars with the Israelites.

This massive mudbrick structure, measuring approximately forty-five by fifty feet, was reinforced by stone facing and stone foundations at its most vulnerable points. Its orientation was east-southeast, toward the foothills of Judah, the possible threat.

Insofar as we could connect these archaeological finds with the parts of the biblical narrative, the character of this powerful Stratum X city offered a tangible complement. They matched the stories of the Philistines' first conflicts with the Israelite forces and their conquest and control of the hill country. Yet the last stage of the conflict, the victories of David and the collapse of Philistine power, was more difficult to distinguish in the archaeological record. Though the Stratum X gate and the city's fortifications were subsequently destroyed and left in ruins, we were to find unexpected evidence that the Israelites may not have been directly responsible for the conquest of Ashdod in the early tenth century B.C.

CHAPTER 16

Fortifications, Survival, and Decline

The Stratum X gate complex was not the only—nor even the largest—fortification system we uncovered in the apricot orchard, known as Area M. It actually took us two seasons of digging through the levels of a later and even more massive structure before we even detected the presence of the fortifications from the time of the Philistine-Israelite conflict. The crumbled brick and pottery fragments that Brosh had found on the surface belonged to the *later* gate structure, and most of our work in Area M concentrated on tracing the history of the city in the centuries during which, despite the massiveness of the fortifications, there was only meager written evidence.

In the four centuries that followed the rise of the kingdom of Israel, Ashdod maintained a distinctive culture and identity, despite being repeatedly attacked and conquered. As late as the sixth century B.C. the Ashdodites were reported to have been ruled by their own king, and a century later were still speaking their own peculiar dialect. We knew, of course, that Ashdod's political independence had been effectively ended by the eighth-century B.C. Assyrian conquest, but it seemed that even later, after that disaster and the exile of much of its population, memories of Ashdod's Philistine heritage remained.

Professor Mazar was one of the foremost proponents of the theory that by the end of David's reign (c.1000–960 B.C.), the cities of Philistia had become virtual vassals of the Israelite kingdom. At Tell Qasile, he

WHO FIRST BROKE THE POWER OF THE PHILISTINES?

181

believed he found evidence for this in the sudden and violent destruction of the city's first great period of commercial prosperity. The latest pottery types preserved in the destruction of Stratum X there (which was close in date to Ashdod's Stratum X) suggested that the destruction had occurred in the early tenth century B.C.

We, too, had evidence of the violent destruction of Ashdod in the same period. The citadel on the southern edge of the acropolis contained a thick layer of ash and crushed vessels, and in the north, in the area of the fortifications, the structures inside the city were destroyed and abandoned at the same time. The situation of the Area M city gate completed the picture: sometime in the first half of the tenth century B.C. this vital part of the city's defense system was destroyed completely. On its surface, three superimposed clay ovens had been subsequently built, a sign that the eastern gate was left in ruins for an extended period of time.

Archaeologically, it appeared that the power of Ashdod had been broken, but, as was noted in the last chapter, it was not clear to us by whom. Although David defeated the Philistines in the neighborhood of Jerusalem and ended their control over the hill country, the Bible makes no reference to a later campaign in the heart of Philistia or to the conquest of Ashdod. In fact, the latest pottery types in the Stratum X complex were known to continue well into the tenth century B.C. This suggested that at least the final blow to the Philistines might have been struck by an Egyptian pharaoh, whose campaign to Philistia in the mid-tenth century B.C. is vaguely alluded to in the Bible.

During the eleventh century B.C. the political unity of Egypt had been shattered. The south was controlled by the high priests of Amun at Thebes, while the north was ruled by a succession of kings, known as the XXIst Dynasty, at the city of Tanis in the Nile delta. There were indications in Egyptian records from around 1100 B.C.—the "Onomasticon of Amenope" and the "Report of Wen Amun"—that the Philistines maintained peaceful contacts with the rulers at Tanis. But in the following century, after the Philistines had lost their inland trade routes to the kingdom of Israel, their relationship with Egypt apparently changed.

The Bible is primarily concerned with crediting the God-fearing Israelites with the destruction of the Philistines. But according to 1 Kings 9:16, an unnamed "Pharaoh, king of Egypt, had gone up and captured Gezer and burnt it with fire, and had slain the Canaanites who dwelt in the city, and had given it as a dowry to his daughter, Solomon's wife." The marriage of Solomon to an Egyptian wife obviously signified the establishment of an alliance between Egypt and Israel. But the reference to Gezer as a Canaanite city was puzzling: it had long been referred to in the Bible as a Philistine city.

Almost a century before the Ashdod excavations, an artifact was found at Tanis that might have shed light on the biblical passage and provided a historical context for the destruction of the Stratum X gate at Ashdod. It was a badly damaged fragment of a royal relief of Pharaoh Siamun, whose reign, c.978–959 B.C., overlapped that of both David and Solomon. On the relief, Siamun is shown smiting a captive in a manner reminiscent of the stylized stance of Ramesses III at Medinet Habu. One of the captives is stretching forth his hand in the same gesture of submission used by the Philistines.

An attack by the Egyptians on Ashdod around 970 B.C. would accord with the archaeological evidence. At Tell Qasile, and now at Ashdod, we had come to appreciate the intimate link between the Philistines' power in Canaan and their singular role in the country's trade. But their position declined, first with the rise of Israel, then with the appearance on the scene of an energetic Egyptian ruler, eager to reassert control over his country's former possessions. The already weakened cities of Philistia must have been an easy target.

From the very beginning of our Area M excavations, we knew that we had discovered a truly monumental structure. Just beneath the surface of the orchard, the team uncovered a large pottery kiln of the Hellenistic period, the base of which was dug into solid, reddish brick material. But the bricks didn't seem to have just been dumped there. They were carefully laid in rows and were part of the most massive structure that we had discovered at Ashdod. The thick brick walls extended to the edges of our initial excavation area, and in at least one place there was a small chamber enclosed by unusually massive walls.

Instead of trying to dig downward in a limited area, we had to concentrate on uncovering as wide an area as possible in order to reveal the extent of the huge structure. Eventually we delineated two towers of a city gate of Stratum IX, each tower containing three eleven- by eight-foot interior chambers or guardrooms. Its overall dimensions, approximately seventy by sixty feet, were almost twice those of its predecessor and in themselves significant: they closely resembled the massive city gates discovered at the royal cities of King Solomon in Hazor, Megiddo, and Gezer. What, then, was a "Solomonic" gate doing at Ashdod?

The Ashdod Stratum IX gate complex was just as impressive an example of Iron Age engineering as were the gates of the royal cities of Israel, whose architectural unity had been recognized by Yigael

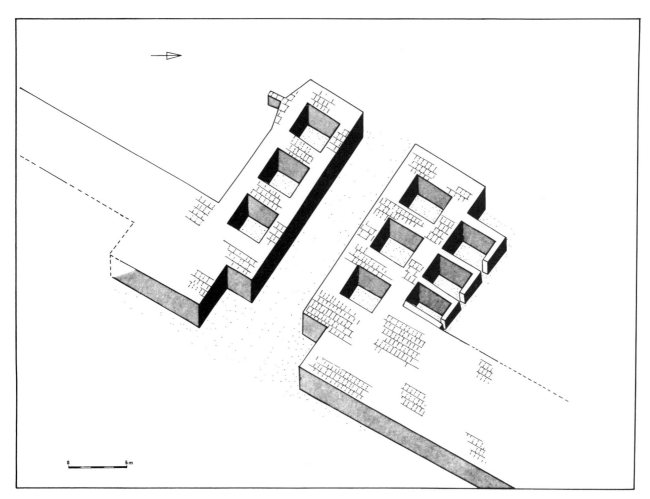

0 ___ 5 m

The Ashdod gate complex closely resembled the massive city gate of Solomon's royal cities in Hazor, Megiddo, and Gezer.

Yadin. Huge ashlar stones strengthened the junctions of the external walls and were used as facing on both the front and the rear. The passage itself was well paved with a mixture of crushed stone, pebbles, and potsherds, with a slight rise in the center to prevent damage to the foundations of the gate from the runoff of rainwater from inside the city.

It was evident, however, that even if the Ashdod gate had been constructed during the reign of Solomon and reflected Israelite control of the coast, it remained one of the key points in Ashdod's defensive system long after Solomon's kingdom collapsed. From the successive levels of paving and from the spacious plaza inside the city, it was clear that Ashdod enjoyed an unprecedented prosperity for nearly two centuries *after* Solomon. The Philistine "renaissance" at Ashdod during this time was entirely absent from biblical accounts of this period, but it was commensurate with contemporaneous international developments.

Toward the end of the tenth century B.C., after the death of Solomon, the armies of the XXIInd Dynasty of Pharaoh Shishak had invaded and destroyed many of the cities of the kingdom of Israel. In one of the lower levels of the gate we discovered an Egyptian scarab of the XXIInd Dynasty which, while not conclusive in itself for dating purposes, suggested the possibility that Ashdod and the other Philistine cities regained their full independence in the wake of Shishak's invasion, resuming control of the main coastal trade route and their role in the maritime commerce along the eastern Mediterranean coasts.

In addition to a hoard of iron carpenters' tools, one of the storerooms constructed inside the gate contained the bronze pans of a scale and a collection of thirty-one stone and metal weights. These were evidence of extensive commercial links with other regions: they included the Egyptian *kite/deben* standard, the gold and silver shekels of Mesopotamia, and the shekel of the cities of the Phoenician coast.

These finds indicated that the defeat of the Philistines at the hands of the Israelites had been only a temporary setback. With the weakening of the Israelites after the division of the United Monarchy into the two kingdoms of Judah and Israel, the Philistines had apparently been able to reassert themselves as a commercial power. The city gate of Stratum IX represented a new era of Ashdod's prominence, only a century after their great defeats.

The subtle archaeological evidence we distinguished around and inside the gate towers of the fortifications indicated that the gate had apparently remained in its original form for almost two hundred years. The repeated raising of the floor levels in the storerooms and guard chambers and the repaving of the entrance roadway represented continuous occupation with the normal accumulation of debris. Here and there we could distinguish minor repairs to the structure, as might be expected for such an extended period. But near the end of the period of the gate's existence, there was a change in its plan that dramatically altered its function. A substantial brick wall on a stone foundation was built across the entrance to the city, providing a narrow and indirect entrance to the gate itself, barely large enough to accommodate a single person. We could date the pottery of this last phase to the mid–eighth century B.C., a time when the people of Ashdod were threatened and had to make hurried preparations: King Uzziah of Judah was on the warpath.

The traditional hostility between the Judeans and the Philistines was well known in the later prophetic writings, but throughout the later

Iron Age there were few specific references to concrete historical conflicts. One of the few was Uzziah's campaign to Philistia around 750 B.C.: "He went out and made war against the Philistines, and broke down the wall of Gath and the wall of Jabneh and the wall of Ashdod" [2 Chronicles 26:6]. Our archaeological finds corroborated this reference.

Uzziah's reign was devoted to restoring Judean control over the long-distance Arabian trade routes. To that end he rebuilt and fortified the city of Ezion-Geber, near the site of modern Eilat on the Gulf of Aqaba. But for this strategy to be successful, he also needed an outlet to the Mediterranean. Since the northern kingdom of Israel, with which he was in conflict, blocked his outlets to the ports of Phoenicia, he had to gain control of the northern Philistine coast. The biblical account of the campaign in Chronicles reports that "God helped him against the Philistines," but we could see from the excavations that in addition to divine intervention, Uzziah's Judean army was aided by the well-placed blows of a battering ram. The thin blocking structure fell quickly and the outermost wall of the northern gate tower was then pounded until it collapsed. The thick layer of ash, charred beams, and collapsed brick was evidence of the devastation that ensued.

As we had already discovered from our excavations in the potters' quarter in Area D with its mass graves and late eighth-century B.C. destruction level, there soon arose another threat to the city of Ashdod far more dangerous than that of the Judean king: the mighty Assyrian Empire. And, indeed, toward the end of the eighth century B.C., the people of Ashdod fortified their city again. The city had apparently recovered from Uzziah's attack. It was then that Ashdod reached its greatest stage of expansion. The city itself was enormous. To the south was the potters' quarter with its own fortifications, and to the east, the gate complex of Stratum VIII. Nearby on the coast, excavations made by Dr. Jacob Kaplan had revealed impressive fortifications indicating that this area might have been Ashdudimmu in Assyrian—"Ashdod of the Sea"—the stronghold of the rebel Yamani of the Assyrian annals.

From the Stratum VIII level came our first indication of Philistine script at this time, from two inscribed pottery vessels. We had an example of twelfth-century B.C. Philistine writing from Stratum XII which showed it to be similar in character to the Cypro-Minoan scripts of the Late Bronze Age. Four hundred years later it was obvious that the Hebrew alphabet had come into use, although we could not be sure of the nature of the Philistine language. One of the inscribed fragments bore the word p-h-r in Hebrew, probably meaning poher, "the potter," appropriate in light of the extensive potters' quarter in the lower city at this time. The other, also in Hebrew letters, was more enigmatic.

It bore a name, *d-g-r-t* or *Dagarat*, which was not Semitic and may have been the remnant of an earlier Philistine heritage.

In Area M, the only significant change in the rebuilt gate complex of Stratum VIII was a thick external reinforcement of the northern gate tower. Here the builders had constructed a massive brick wall at precisely the point at which the tower had been breached previously. This conscious attempt to strengthen the fortifications could be seen as evidence of the city's preparations for yet another attack, this time—if we were correct in ascribing the gate complex to the Area D potters' quarter—against the Assyrian assault of Sargon II. As we already knew, Ashdod did not stand up to the might of the Assyrians, and the Stratum VIII gate was destroyed in some places down to its foundations.

The conquest of Ashdod by Sargon in 712 B.C. changed the city from an independent kingdom to an Assyrian vassal with a substantial foreign population. Nonetheless, as we had already seen in the potters' quarter in Area D, after the massacres, destruction, and deportations, its prosperity quickly returned. The fortifications were restored and there were signs of reconstruction in the gate area. If the information preserved in the Assyrian annals was reliable, the revival of activity in the city took place during the reign of a king called Mitini, who faithfully sent his tributes to the Assyrian treasury. From small finds in this level, we could see that Ashdod continued to trade with Judah and Cyprus, and its prosperity apparently continued to the end of Assyrian power and the beginning of a new wave of conquests in Philistia in the mid-seventh century B.C.

In all of our excavation areas, the remains from the post-Assyrian period were poorly preserved. They had either been affected by erosion or later building, so our picture of Ashdod's subsequent history was hazy. The contemporary levels in the Area M gate complex were also badly damaged, but because they were linked to the long sequence of the development of the city's fortifications, we could at least suggest a possible connection between the archaeological evidence and the major events of the time.

The most famous event was, of course, the twenty-nine-year siege of Ashdod by Pharaoh Psammetichus, described by Herodotus as the longest siege he had ever heard of. Unfortunately, this record-breaking conflict left little trace in the archaeological record outside the fact that the destruction of the gate roughly coincided with Psammetichus's campaign, around 640 B.C.

By the end of the seventh century B.C., the gate stratum was destroyed and never rebuilt. The debris filling the guardrooms and storerooms included pottery types similar to those found at Judean sites destroyed at the time of the Babylonian conquest. It would appear, therefore, that the campaigns of Nebuchadnezzar, which ended the existence of the kingdom of Judah, also marked the end of Ashdod's prominence.

Above the late seventh-century B.C. destruction level, we found only pits, pottery kilns, and fragmentary walls. While we could not be sure of the later extent of the lower city—since the apricot orchard covered most of the area—the city of Ashdod apparently shrank back to the acropolis and remained, for the rest of its ancient existence, just a small town.

Although the area of the former city gate continued in use as a work area for potters, and a small agora was erected on the acropolis, the trade and urban life of the surrounding region apparently moved to a new Persian-Hellenistic city on the seashore, Azotos Paralios, "Ashdod of the Coast." The ancient city, now known as Azotos Mesogeios, "Inland Ashdod," continued to decline. By the Byzantine period, as we could see by the few scattered traces of occupation, the once powerful Philistine capital had become just a tiny village, with a population that included Samaritans. Its rural character hardly changed in the thousand years that followed, as its locus shifted to the eastern hill, and its name was changed to the Arabic variant, Isdud.

In the summer of 1972, by the time we completed the Ashdod excavation project, the new city of Ashdod had come to life. The initial plans for the construction of a major international port for southern Israel were nearing completion. To the south of the new harbor, near the banks of the tidal river that had once provided a connection between Tel Mor and Ashdod in the Bronze Age, there was now a modern commercial center and industrial area, and expanding residential districts.

Ashdod's excavations had not, of course, solved all the problems connected with the history of the coast and the culture of the Philistines, but they had at least established a sound stratigraphic and chronological basis with which to continue the work. We had traced Ashdod's development from the time of its establishment as a Canaanite city at the end of the Middle Bronze Age, through its growing commercial importance during the Late Bronze Age under Egyptian domination, through its transformation into one of the cities of the Philistine pentapolis. And having uncovered the rise and fall of one of the great Philistine capitals, our search would grow wider: we would now try to see the Philistines in the context of other places and other Sea Peoples.

PART V

BROADENING THE CONTEXT

TRUDE DOTHAN

CHAPTER 17

To the Island
of Cyprus

In 1970, as Moshe was nearing the end of the Ashdod excavations, I had the opportunity to get back into the field with a new excavation project. That year the Institute of Archaeology at the Hebrew University was reorganized and its first director, Professor Yigael Yadin, wanted to encourage an expansion of Israeli archaeological research within a broader geographical framework. The numerous excavations already carried out by the university and other Israeli institutions underlined the close connections of the country to the cultures of the surrounding regions throughout ancient times. So far, because of the political situation and the sheer extent of Israel's archaeological remains, we had concentrated our efforts within Israel itself. Yadin succeeded in raising funds and getting official sanction for an Israeli expedition to Cyprus, a country that had become one of the most important centers in the eastern Mediterranean for international archaeological work.

From the time of the plundering expeditions of the American consul in Larnaca, General Luigi di Palma Cesnola, in the latter half of the nineteenth century, the tombs and ancient cities of Cyprus provided museums and collectors all over the world with a treasure trove of artifacts, whose mixed styles demonstrated the island's position as a bridge between the ancient Near Eastern and Aegean worlds. In time, with more systematic excavations, it became clear that it was a maritime center for Egyptians, Aegeans, Hittites, Syrians, and Canaanites. There

had been references in ancient cuneiform texts to the copper-rich land of Alashiya, which many scholars had assumed to be Cyprus, and the rich finds unearthed at the ancient coastal cities of Enkomi, Kition, and Hala Sultan Tekke, among others, confirmed the island's prosperity during the Late Bronze Age.

Our own work in Israel had highlighted an important facet of ancient Cypriot commerce: in the Late Bronze Age levels of almost every excavated Canaanite city, the most distinctive types of decorated pottery were Cypriot ware. The unmistakable sherds of white "milk bowls" and the dull, dark juglets called "bilbils," along with the Mycenaean vessels shipped through or even manufactured on Cyprus, were only the most durable remains of what had obviously been a flourishing trade. The exchange of Cypriot copper and manufactured goods for the agricultural products of Canaan brought about a far-reaching cultural and economic interaction, and was, indeed, an important factor in the rise of urban civilization along the Canaanite coast.

My interest in the culture of the Philistines had naturally drawn my attention to the finds on Cyprus: with the sudden end of Bronze Age trade in the region, new settlers arrived on the island, rebuilding and reoccupying some of its great coastal cities. This was distinguished most clearly in the archaeological record by the appearance in Cyprus of Mycenaean IIIC 1:b pottery. Most scholars linked this to the movements of the Sea Peoples, suggesting that the new settlers on the island were Achaean refugees from the destroyed Mycenaean civilization on the Greek mainland. And since this type of pottery was so close to the types that Moshe had recently discovered in the earliest Sea Peoples' level at Ashdod, it was clear that the cultural connection between Cyprus and Canaan continued during the disturbances and migrations at the end of the Late Bronze Age.

Cyprus was, therefore, an ideal locale for the first Israeli expedition abroad, and once Yadin received the blessing of Archbishop Makarios, then the president of the Republic of Cyprus, it was agreed that I should co-direct the excavations with my colleague Dr. Amnon Ben-Tor. That summer Yadin, Joseph Aviram, then the administrative director of the institute, Ben-Tor, and I made an exploratory visit to Cyprus to look over possible locations and consult with the Cyprus Department of Antiquities.

IN SEARCH OF A NEW PERSPECTIVE

This was not my first trip to Cyprus. Almost two decades before, as graduate students, Moshe and I had visited the island with Professor Mazar. This was soon after the end of the first phase of digging at Tell Qasile. At that time the most important excavations on Cyprus were at the huge site of Enkomi, near the eastern coast of the island. They were being carried out by a French expedition headed by Claude Shaeffer, the excavator of Ugarit, and a Cypriot expedition headed by Porphyrios Dikaios of the Department of Antiquities. In contrast to archaeological sites in Israel, the rich and enormous ruins of Enkomi were not situated on a mound but were located in a huge depression, near the marshy outlet of the Pedeios River. Earlier excavators had assumed that Enkomi was an ancient cemetery and not a city, but Shaeffer and Dikaios had proved them wrong: they had unearthed fine ashlar buildings, enormous quantities of Mycenaean pottery, and elaborate carved ivory and bronze artifacts—testimony to the trade and craftsmanship that had been carried on there.

In the following years we followed developments at new sites along the coast, and returned several times to visit the collections of the Cyprus Museum and the excavations at Kition, Paleapaphos, and Enkomi. Now I was back on the island with my colleagues, faced with the task of finding a site that would offer a reasonable chance of success in the framework that we had begun to formulate, for beyond our strictly archaeological objectives, our Cypriot excavations were planned as a study dig for the students of our institute, to enable them to gain experience in a different cultural and archaeological milieu. And because of our limited resources, we did not want to attempt too ambitious a project as our first undertaking outside Israel.

Soon after our arrival in Nicosia we met with Dr. Vassos Karageorghis, director of the Department of Antiquities, a man deeply involved, from his work at Kition, in the problem of Cyprus's Bronze Age culture and the coming of the Sea Peoples. We were particularly interested in the ancient sites on the southern and eastern coasts, from which direct trade with Canaan was presumably carried on. But Karageorghis urged us to dig somewhere in the central plain of the island, across which the ancient overland trade routes from the copper mines had run. He had a specific site in mind: Bomboulari tis Kououninas, a tiny yet intriguing site just outside the village of Athienou.

The site, some twelve miles south of Nicosia, had been briefly excavated before. In 1958, Porphyrios Dikaios and Chrystomos Paraskeva of the Cyprus Department of Antiquities had carried out a two-day trial dig there, uncovering a number of tiny pottery vessels that probably served cultic purposes, some huge smashed pithoi, signs of intense burning, and lumps of copper ore. These finds, together with a bronze model of a cultic chariot found some years earlier on the surface, were suggestive of the site's connection to Cyprus's Late Bronze Age cult and copper industry. Its geographical position on the main road leading from the mountains made it the perfect way station between the mines and the trading cities of Kition and Enkomi. As late as the early twentieth century, Athienou was an important stop for the island's mule teams, Cyprus's main means of transport before the coming of the automobile.

The ancient site itself, located a few hundred yards from the village, was surrounded by olive groves and fields. The site was disappointingly small, rising only about seven feet above ground level and covering less than five acres. But it had certain advantages: we could establish our headquarters in the village and count on it for our food and supplies. At the time we could certainly not imagine how rich and unique a site it would turn out to be.

LATE BRONZE AGE CULT AND INDUSTRY

In the summer of 1971, after all the preliminaries were behind us, we arrived in Athienou and established ourselves in the village school. Our team included about thirty students and specialists from the Institute of Archaeology in Jerusalem. We were soon honorary members of the friendly village. We enjoyed the Greek-Cypriot cuisine of our cooks, Maria and Elemi, the daily rides and weekend trips provided by Andreas in the village bus, and the supplies of water brought in huge jars on mule to the excavation site. We sat at the open-air taverna of the village in the evening and were welcome guests at weddings and other local celebrations. Furthermore, that summer and the next we established contact with the many foreign scholars—American, Swedish, Swiss, Italian, and Greek—digging all over the island.

At the beginning we had to acclimatize ourselves to the summer heat, more intense even than what we were used to in Israel. We would begin the day at four in the morning and return to headquarters for pottery sorting, registration, and photography by noon. We opened our first major excavation area just to the south of the highest point on the site. Since the total depth of accumulation at Athienou proved to be only about three feet, we were immediately confronted with evidence of intense cultic activity from the fourteenth and thirteenth centuries B.C. The sheer amount of evidence was almost impossible to handle at first.

Just a few inches beneath the surface, we began to uncover large heaps of tiny vessels, some less than half an inch in height. Dikaios and Paraskeva had found only a few of them. We discovered hundreds. By the end of the excavation, we had retrieved more than two thousand complete examples and large fragments of others that brought the total to approximately ten thousand.

For the most part, they were crudely made and were probably votive offerings deposited at the cult site by ancient visitors seeking divine approval for their pursuits. There were also hundreds of tiny skillful reproductions of Late Bronze Age pottery types: the common Cypriot "milk bowls," white-shaved juglets, base ring vessels, and Mycenaean ware. The nodules of copper ore we found among the pottery offerings indicated that copper smelting was also carried on here. Although similar collections of votive vessels had been found before on Cyprus, ours was by far the largest. Yet the total absence of cultic figurines and the paucity of standing architecture—much of which had been removed over the centuries for building materials—confronted us with an enigmatic starting point from which to reconstruct the history of the site.

In time, however, we were able to reconstruct at least part of the original plan of the site. About sixty feet square, it included large square rooms at its northwestern and northeastern corners, and what seemed to be a main entrance on the north. It was apparently a center for cultic rituals and, perhaps, smelting. To the east of the main building we uncovered finds in several deep pits which indicated the extent of the site's overseas commercial connections as well.

There we found full-sized vessels, local Cypriot "milk bowls" and "bilbils," and Mycenaean bowls and jugs of the highest quality. In addition to the everyday pottery, there were distinctive containers for the valuable trade commodities of imported oil or perfume. Among the most indicative objects of this type were two large stirrup jars decorated in the Late Minoan style of Crete. Minoan objects of the Late Bronze Age were relatively scarce on Cyprus, yet this connection was given additional substance by our discovery of a portable stone brazier and a basin with a bull's-head spout that also reflected a Minoan background.

Athienou's cultural contacts with the Greek mainland were no less conspicuous. Beyond the full-sized and miniature Mycenaean vessels, we found a body fragment of a large storejar impressed with a typically Aegean cylinder seal scene of galloping animals. We found further evidence of links to Egypt: a bronze ring with a hieroglyphic inscription and a blue frit scarab bearing a lotus pattern of New Kingdom date.

This mix of influences had been distinguished before at the great trading cities of Enkomi and Kition, but we were surprised that this cosmopolitanism had reached as far inland as the cult and industrial center of Athienou. One particularly vivid illustration of this was a small ivory rhyton: while its shape and function were inspired by similar vessels in the Aegean and the large cities of Cyprus, its incised rows of human heads, gazelles, birds, plants, and fish were executed in a primitive, folk-art style, perhaps by a local craftsman.

From all the evidence it was obvious that the Athienou shrine had reached its greatest prosperity by the end of the thirteenth century B.C. It provided us with another vantage point from which to view the complex and close-knit trading network of the eastern Mediterranean

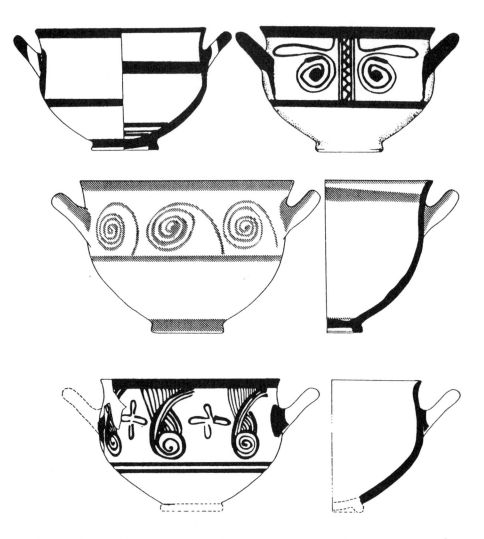

Mycenaean vessels from Athienou.

in that period. Although we could not come to any immediate conclusions about the specific cult practices or industrial activity, it was clear that Athienou was an important station along the internal copper routes of Cyprus. For me, it was even more exciting, as we soon discovered that the site had been reoccupied and rebuilt at the time of the arrival of the Sea Peoples on Cyprus at the end of the thirteenth or beginning of the twelfth century B.C.

A SEA PEOPLES'
OUTPOST

Neither the 1958 trial excavations nor our own preliminary surveys at Athienou had revealed any trace of the Sea Peoples' occupation of the site after they settled on Cyprus. We had assumed that the site had been destroyed and abandoned at the time of the collapse of the Bronze Age trading network. But as we continued the excavations, it became

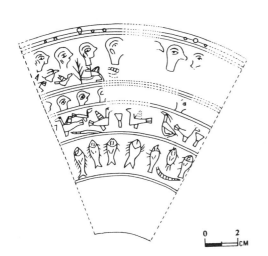

Ivory cup from Athienou.

clear that the site had been occupied by the Sea Peoples, and its industrial activity had intensified. The main building continued to be used well into the twelfth century B.C., and new rooms and floor levels were added. Although the piles of votive vessels in the central courtyard were apparently covered and forgotten, there was evidence of a continuing cultic connection. A pit in the central courtyard contained a characteristic Mycenaean IIIC:1b bowl of the Sea Peoples together with a pair of bull's horns, whose cultic associations on Cyprus were well known.

But the most dramatic changes in this period took place to the east of the main building. There we discovered a complex of plastered platforms against the eastern wall of the main building. These platforms were constructed of a thin layer of stones and broken pottery on which the thick lime plaster had been laid. Their original layout was difficult to reconstruct, not only because of the effects of erosion, but also because of the complex nature of the industrial operations for which they were apparently designed. Low partition walls marked off at least ten distinct working areas, some of which were further divided by raised curbs in the platform surfaces themselves. Further, throughout this area were signs of burning, suggesting that the industrial operations had required sustained and intense fire. The fact that the enigmatic networks of built-in channels were filled with large chunks of copper ore reinforced our supposition that the entire complex was connected with copper smelting—a process carried out by Sea People craftsmen with considerable sophistication, and a facet of their culture only hinted at in Israel. Nonetheless, the cultural traditions of the settlers in both regions were extremely close.

Of particular interest was our discovery of nearly half a ton of copper ore in various stages of processing, from large chunks of almost sixty pounds to small nodules of a few ounces. These by-products of the site's once-active metal industry offered us the chance to gain a better understanding of the techniques by which Cypriot copper was smelted and the possible changes in technology brought about by the arrival of the Sea Peoples. And after submitting examples to specialists in ancient metallurgy at the University of Pennsylvania, we were able to establish that the site's Late Bronze Age metalworkers had anticipated Rome in this field by more than a thousand years.

After two consecutive seasons of digging at Athienou, we had uncovered more than 90 percent of the surface area of the site and were further able to identify a Late Bronze and Iron Age cemetery. Occupation of the site apparently continued well into the twelfth century B.C., but within about fifty years of the arrival of the Sea Peoples the main building on the site was burned and abandoned, and the site itself reoccupied only briefly again in the eighth century B.C.

As was the case in Canaan, the arrival of the Sea Peoples to Cyprus marked a transitional stage of existence, bridging the period of the collapse of traditional Late Bronze Age civilization and the period of the crystallization of the economy and culture of the Iron Age. Although Athienou was a small site, our excavations there had shown the extent of the transformation brought about by the Sea Peoples and provided us with much food for thought on the developments that took place in Canaan at the same time.

CHAPTER 18

Tombs and Traditions, Egyptian Style

One of the most sensitive indicators of the religion and culture of a people is its burial customs. Yet in the decade of excavation and exploration at Ashdod, Moshe and his team had been unable to locate the Philistine city's main cemetery. As a result, scholarly interest in the subject had remained centered on the earlier discoveries at Beth Shean, Tell el-Farah, and Azor. At Azor, it will be remembered, the diversity of burial customs had produced puzzlement, and the custom of anthropoid coffins, common to Beth Shean and Tell el-Farah, was still a matter of controversy. While some scholars were ready to attribute all anthropoid coffins in Canaan to Philistine mercenaries, others were skeptical of any connection at all. The simple fact was that this controversy and the broader question of Philistine funerary customs could never be resolved until additional Philistine burials, with or without anthropoid customs, were discovered.

In 1967, soon after the Six-Day War, the Israel Department of Antiquities was faced with a massive influx of illegally dug artifacts from ancient tombs and settlements on the West Bank, which had now come under Israeli control. The staff of the department attempted to stop the plunder and, at the same time, conduct salvage excavations. At one such excavation, at Tell Aitun, about ten miles southwest of Hebron, a series of tombs cut into the soft native limestone was unearthed. Although partially plundered, one of them had apparently escaped

notice and was found to contain artifacts that shed light on the spread of Philistine burial customs during the twelfth century B.C.: rare iron bracelets, stone beads, conical seals, and early Philistine pottery. One jug, in particular, was reminiscent of the Mycenaean IIIC:1b decorative patterns found only on Cyprus and Crete. It was decorated with a unique stylized bird and fish, each surrounded by an outline of dots, unknown so far in the Philistine repertoire.

Although Tell Aitun was relatively far from the main Philistine cities, the extent of Aegean influence on the burial customs was evident. Later, when I was able to locate a number of artifacts from the site in private collections, I recognized an unusual class of female figurines, isolated examples of which had previously been found at Ashdod, Azor, and other sites along the coast. These figurines, executed in a simple, naturalistic style, were originally attached to the rims of large Philistine kraters. Although in technique they were reminiscent of the common Canaanite images of fertility goddesses, their pose was entirely different: instead of their hands supporting their breasts, they were raised over their heads, over their long flowing tresses.

In seeking a parallel for these artifacts in archaeological literature, I eventually located a class of similar figurines in the Mycenaean IIIC-

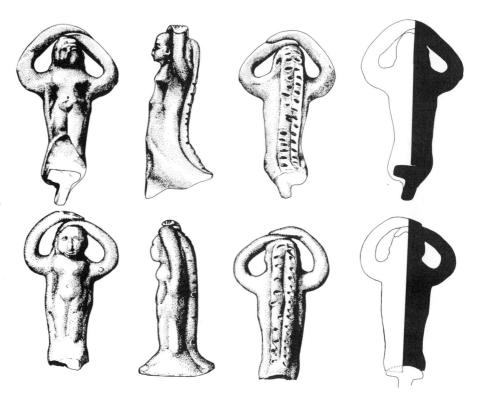

Aegean in inspiration, these terra-cotta mourning figurines from Tell Aitun were mounted on the rim of a krater with the face sideways along the rim. They were hand-molded in the round with a combination of appliqué and incision. The face is broad, with a small pointed chin. The eyes and nose are accentuated, the mouth faintly indicated. The hair is arranged in a straight fringe and falls behind in two long plaits that reach the rim of the krater. The figures wear long garments, open down the front to reveal the naked body.

200

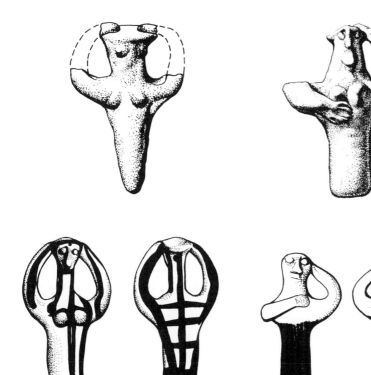

Mourning figurines from Tell Jemmeh (top left), Azor (top right), Naxos (bottom left) and east Crete (bottom right). There are two different gestures of grief in this group: both hands over the head, or one hand on the breast and the other on the head. The two gestures represent different stages in the same act.

period cemeteries of Perati on the Greek mainland and Ialysos on Rhodes, and at other Aegean sites. The tomb offerings at Perati and Ialysos included a number of large, open bowls called *kalathoi*, with clay figurines attached to their rims. The excavator at Perati, Professor Spyridon Iakovidis, believed they were placed in tombs as physical representations of the mourners' grief. He further noted their similarity with a depiction of female mourners found on the sides of decorated clay coffins, or *larnakes*, discovered near Tanagra in Boeotia, whose hands were placed in grief on top of their heads.

The discovery of Aegean-inspired "mourning vases" in Canaan, some of them decorated in the characteristic Philistine bichrome style, indicated a previously unrecognized Mycenaean element in the Philistines' funerary rites. The other mourning figurines found throughout Philistia suggested the widespread observance of this custom, though with local variations. Of course the Aegean background was only part of the picture: the connection of the Philistines to the Egyptian-style coffins of Beth Shean and Tell el-Farah still had to be explained. Here, too, a case of tomb robbing provided us with clues that would eventually lead to a unique and incredibly rich ancient site.

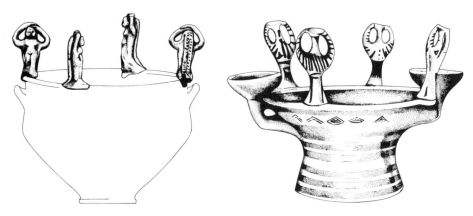

Left: *Reconstruction of Philistine krater with mourning
figurines. Right: Aegean bowl
with mourning figurines from
the Mycenaean cemetery in
Perati, Greece. The figurines
are attached to the rim by pegs.*

THE TRAIL TO DEIR EL-BALAH

In the spring of 1968, not long after the Tell Aitun excavation, a colleague alerted me to a new flood of antiquities filling the shops of the Old City of Jerusalem. Despite his enthusiastic descriptions I was not prepared for the archaeological treasures that I saw. In addition to many complete Mycenaean and Cypriot vessels, there were dozens of Egyptian scarabs, gold and carnelian necklaces, alabaster and bronze vessels, and funerary stelae with hieroglyphic inscriptions of types rarely found outside Egypt.

Most of these artifacts seemed to date from the thirteenth century B.C., the final period of New Kingdom domination of Canaan, immediately preceding the arrival of the Philistines. And in one of the shops I spotted the lid of an anthropoid coffin which the dealer assured me—perhaps to pique my interest in buying it—had been found with the other, more precious artifacts. Unfortunately, when he learned I was an archaeologist and not a potential customer, his tactics changed and he tried to mislead me as to its origin. But I could see from the yellowish sand still clinging to the pitted surface of the coffin lid that the finds obviously came from somewhere along the coast of the country. In time I learned that they came from the Gaza Strip, also now under Israeli control. The task of locating the cemetery would be extremely difficult since the military authorities in the area were far more concerned with security matters than with archaeological exploration. And it was certainly not a task I could undertake alone. But as the influx continued and the artifacts quickly disappeared into private collections, I was unwilling to abandon hope of finding the cemetery. The Department of Antiquities did not have official jurisdiction over the area, so I decided to seek help from someone who did: Moshe Dayan, the minister of defense.

Dayan's reputation as an antiquities collector was already legendary. He had extensive contacts among all of the antiquities dealers and was usually aware of the source of their finds. Many objects from Azor and Tell Aitun had already found their way into his private collection, so when I called him to ask for his help I assumed he already knew about the rich, ancient cemetery in the Gaza Strip. Much to my surprise, he had not yet heard about it and he promised to check. Quite some time passed and the plundering of the cemetery continued unabated. Just as I was about to lose all hope, I got a call from Dayan early in 1968. The cemetery, he informed me, was a few miles south of Gaza, near the village of Deir el-Balah, and if I wished I could visit the site the next morning.

I canceled everything and arrived at the military checkpoint on the border of the Gaza Strip early in the morning. I was met by an officer and a contingent of soldiers in two armored cars. This was my first trip to Gaza, and as we drove through the empty streets of the city, past row upon row of shuttered shops, I could feel the tension and the hostility. But as we continued southward into an area of lush orange and palm groves, clusters of mudbrick houses, and a patchwork of fields, close in appearance to what I expected of Egypt, the atmosphere changed. After crossing the quiet town square of Deir el-Balah, we took a bumpy road and finally arrived at an isolated field in the middle of sand dunes.

We were greeted there by the owner of the property, a Gaza lawyer, and several of his bedouin tenants. The initial appearance of the site was not impressive, but as we began to walk over the pitted surface of the fields my excitement grew: there were dozens of Cypriot, Mycenaean, Egyptian, and Canaanite pottery fragments and thick, heavy pieces of anthropoid coffins. My goal now was to organize an excavation team to uncover what burials still remained in the plundered field, and to place them and the earlier, illegal finds in their proper archaeological perspective. Unfortunately, it took another four years before the security situation improved sufficiently to permit the organization of a dig.

In 1972, just as I was preparing for my second season at Athienou, Dayan informed me that it would be possible to organize a dig at Deir el-Balah. During the intervening years, as illicit digging had continued at the site, some of my efforts had been directed into cataloging the finds and the coffins that had made their way into private collections. In any case, a few months before leaving for Cyprus, I organized an exploratory expedition, jointly sponsored by the Hebrew University and Tel Aviv University.

My staff consisted of several graduate students who were working with me at Athienou, among them Baruch Brandl, who would be actively involved in all the seasons of the dig (plate 16). The team also

Alabaster "lotus" goblet from Deir el-Balah. The lotus flower is a Philistine adaptation of a motif prevalent throughout Egyptian art.

included a surveyor, a photographer, a physical anthropologist, and a number of preservation specialists. Because of the security situation in the Gaza Strip, we were housed in the military garrison at Deir el-Balah and allowed to work only during daylight hours. I still hoped that we would be able to find some undisturbed coffins rather quickly, but the local bedouins we hired to help us were taking us only to places that had already been picked clean. After this went on for two weeks, we began to suspect that our guides themselves were involved in the tomb robbing. Nonetheless, we had no alternative and kept our suspicions to ourselves. This turned out to be wise because one day our bedouin operations chief, Hamad Abu Shmas, whose technique was to probe the soil with a long iron rod, suddenly informed us that our luck had changed.

CLUES IN THE SAND

Indeed, the next morning, digging where Hamad had probed, we found a large four-handled storage jar buried upright in the sand. This, he apparently knew, was the sign of an anthropoid coffin. As we cleared the sand beneath the storejar, we distinguished a dark patch of soil about five feet wide by seven feet long. As we slowly excavated this layer, two clay hands, serenely crossed as if in death, came into view. This was the lower portion of an anthropoid coffin lid, and it also bore a beautifully modeled frowning face with a heavy Egyptian-style wig.

It had been our intention to take any undisturbed coffins back to Jerusalem where they could be opened under laboratory conditions. But we soon realized that this would be impossible: the coffin was shattered into dozens of fragments and had been held together only by the sand that had seeped into it during more than three thousand years. We had no choice but to open the coffin immediately while photographing and recording the precise positions of the artifacts and skeletal remains inside.

No intact anthropoid coffin burial had ever been systematically excavated before, and we assumed that, like the Egyptian mummy cases they resembled, each coffin was designed for a single body. But to our surprise, ours contained two complete skeletons and the remains of two more. The body of an adult male had been placed on top of the remains of a younger individual, who was, in turn, laid on the remains of another adult and child. Burial gifts and personal possessions had been deposited with them.

The artifacts were characteristic of New Kingdom Egyptian culture. Near the feet of the skeleton we found a bronze razor handle, a papyrus cutter, a delicate bronze knife with its handle cast in the shape of a cloven hoof, and a bronze juglet, strainer, and shallow bowl, known as an Egyptian "wine set."

Near the hand of the uppermost body we found five enigmatic pellets, perhaps pieces of the ancient Egyptian game of *senet* or *aseb*. Near the head we found items of personal adornment: a gold earring, gold and carnelian beads, and a gold amulet in the form of the mummified, composite god Ptah-Sokar. Most important for the dating of the burial were three scarabs in delicate settings of silver and gold, one of which bore the first name of Ramesses II, who ruled during much of the thirteenth century B.C. What was most apparent was that this coffin at least had no connection whatsoever with the culture of the Philistines.

In June we made another small excavation at Deir el-Balah and succeeded in locating another three coffins. It seems that approximately another forty-five had been found during the course of the grave robbing in preceding years. Dayan himself had acquired most of them and they comprised by far the richest group outside Egypt. Dayan had his own contacts with Hamad, and although a great deal of information was unnecessarily lost as a result of this unauthorized digging, our subsequent study of the coffins in the Dayan collection enabled us, at least, to construct a provisional typology.

MORE COFFINS AND BURIAL OFFERINGS

Most of the coffin lids were naturalistic in style; others bore stylized exaggerated features, far removed from the original Egyptian prototypes (plate 17). This variation was evident even in the four coffins we had unearthed. In all of the coffins Egyptian influence was overwhelming. It was evident that the tradition of anthropoid coffins came to Canaan in a purely Egyptian milieu and the stylistic differences had only limited chronological significance. From a rectangular carnelian seal found in one of the coffins—inscribed with the name of Ramesses II and bearing the images of the divine triad Min, Horus, and Amun on one side, and an image of the pharaoh driving his royal chariot on the other—it appeared that some of the people buried here were Egyptian or thoroughly Egyptianized Canaanite functionaries of a nearby administrative center of the Egyptian Empire. Neutron activation analysis of the coffin lids confirmed that they were manufactured locally, and this created a problem: no Late Bronze Age city was known to exist in the immediate vicinity.

Many scholars had already identified Ramesses II as the notorious pharaoh who made life so hard for the Israelites prior to their exodus from Egypt. There is an anachronistic reference to the "land of the Philistines" in Exodus [13:17–18], the short route to Canaan which the fleeing Children of Israel had to avoid "lest the people repent when they see war, and return to Egypt." Instead the Israelites took a circuitous route by way of the Red Sea. But the reference is an indication of the extent of Egyptian occupation of the coastal strip between Egypt and Canaan

ALONG THE ROUTE OF THE EXODUS

at the time, an area that would later become Philistine territory.

We hoped that extensive exploration of the vicinity of the Deir el-Balah cemetery would reveal the whereabouts of the settlement, but the outbreak of the Yom Kippur War with Egypt in the autumn of 1973 delayed us considerably. It was impossible to return to Deir el-Balah until 1977.

When we finally did return, the objectives of our first season were twofold: first, to determine the borders of the cemetery and the full range of its burial customs, and second, to explore the surrounding area of sand dunes and gullies for evidence of architectural remains. About 350 yards to the east, at the base of one of the sand dunes, our survey team found a promising area. Late Bronze Age pottery sherds were scattered on the surface, and we discovered, after a trial excavation, a complex of mudbrick structures containing fragments of cooking pots, ovens, and grinding stones. Although it seemed unlikely that such unassuming buildings could be the homes of the wealthy people buried in the cemeteries, they could be nothing else. Our problem was that it was impossible to excavate any farther in the dunes.

The sand here rose more than forty feet above us, and our budget could not possibly be stretched to hire the bulldozers and dump trucks required to remove the hundreds of tons of accumulation over the archaeological remains. But when I discussed the situation with the owner of the property, we devised another solution. He would open his property temporarily as a sand quarry. Later, once we and the sands were gone, he would be able to extend his agricultural domain.

A year later we were able to excavate an extensive area of the Late Bronze Age settlement, and in the years that followed we eventually uncovered the superimposed strata of a settlement that provided a dramatic picture of Egyptian occupation of the coast region of Canaan and, surprisingly, the subsequent settlement during the early Philistine period (plate 15).

The layout and finds of the earliest settlement at Deir el-Balah substantiated the supposition that during the mid-fourteenth century B.C., the el-Amarna period, it was an important Egyptian administrative center. The complex of spacious structures adjacent to what we identified as an artificial pool or reservoir recalled the plans of residencies constructed at Pharaoh Akenaton's royal city, modern Tell el-Amarna. And though we were unable to uncover the entire area, the significant quantities of imported Cypriot and Mycenaean pottery, as well as the distinctive "Amarna blue" vessels—extremely rare in Canaan—testified to the close connections of the residents to the centers of culture in the eastern Mediterranean in this period and, of course, to Egypt itself.

The residence was, however, more than just a wealthy private dwell-

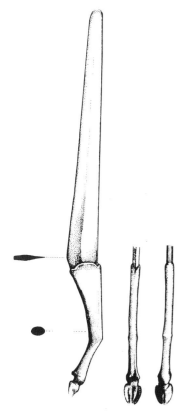

Bronze knife with cloven-hoof handle found at Deir el-Balah.

ing, as we knew from the elaborate bedstead, characteristic of the furnishings of the Egyptian aristocracy in the el-Amarna period, and from the carnelian and gilded blue frit fragments of a ceremonial flail or staff. In a pit outside we found a clay *bulla*, or seal impression, an indication of the presence here of official papyrus archives. The seal bore hieroglyphic symbols similar to those used in the royal archives of Tell el-Amarna.

Above the remains of the first residence and pool we uncovered a truly monumental structure, a sixty-foot-square, heavily fortified citadel with protruding bastions at each of its corners, of the late fourteenth century B.C. It was similar to both the one at Tel Mor from the same period and another recently excavated by Professor Eliezar Oren of Ben Gurion University, at Haruvit in northern Sinai.

All of them were of Egyptian design and highly reminiscent of the high-bastioned citadels and adjoining reservoirs drawn in considerable detail at the Temple of Amun at Thebes. There, on one side of the outer walls of the temple's hypostyle hall, the ancient Egyptian artists had commemorated Pharaoh Seti I's victorious campaign to Canaan by illustrating his progress and stopping points along the "Ways of Horus." One of those stopping points on the way to Gaza was surely Deir el-Balah.

The character of the structures changed completely during the thirteenth century B.C., when Egyptian influence, if anything, became stronger. Sometime during the reign of Ramesses II the fortress was abandoned and the reservoir filled with ash and rubble. Over them an artisans' compound was built, contemporaneous with many of the anthropoid coffins in the nearby cemetery. There was evidence that the workshops here provided virtually all of the craft services required in the elaborate funerary rites. We found unfired pieces of anthropoid coffins and kilns containing coffin bases; *ushabti*, a figurine slave for the deceased's soul; "divine concubine" figurines, identical to some we found in the coffins; scrap metal used in the production of bronze vessels; discarded carnelian beads; and "spinning bowls." To top it all, there was a heavy pottery stamp bearing the image of Ptah, the mummified patron deity of Egyptian artisans.

We could hardly have hoped for a more striking illustration of the cultural milieu in which the custom of anthropoid burial came to Canaan. The Egyptian context was overwhelming and reflected the social prestige it still possessed in the period immediately preceding the arrival of the Philistines. The earlier attempts of scholars like Vincent and Petrie to link the custom of anthropoid burial to the Philistines through the gold masks of Mycenae were clearly mistaken. This was a purely Egyptian tradition, with no trace of Aegean influence.

As we saw at Beth Shean and Tell el-Farah, Philistine mercenaries or civilians may have adopted Egyptian funerary rites, but at other Philistine sites less directly exposed to Egyptian influence, like Azor and Tell Aitun, Aegean burial traditions predominated.

In several places in Deir el-Balah we discovered pits filled with characteristic Philistine bichrome pottery dug into the earlier remains. This pointed to the possibility that a Philistine settlement had been founded in the vicinity in the twelfth century B.C. From the direction of the erosion, however, it appeared that the remains of that settlement now lay under the dunes. The presence of many Egyptian-style vessels alongside the Philistine indicated that the Philistine settlers did not enter a cultural vacuum: Egyptian tradition, so prominent for two centuries, continued to exert an effect on the remaining Canaanites as it did on the Philistine newcomers.

CHAPTER 19

In Search of Other Sea Peoples

The discovery of Mycenaean IIIC:1b ware at Ashdod was important, since, as already pointed out, it provided us with a key for distinguishing the presence of other Sea Peoples. Although there was no foolproof way to determine whether this distinctive pottery signified the earliest arrival of the Philistines or the arrival of an earlier, somewhat different ethnic group, the fact that it was found at Beth Shean and other sites to the north indicated that the Sea Peoples' settlement of Canaan may have been far more extensive than previously thought.

We know that the invasion and settlement of the Philistines in Canaan in the early twelfth century B.C. was part of a long historical process. During the two centuries preceding the Philistines' arrival, various other groups of northern Sea Peoples had made their way to the lands of the eastern Mediterranean. References in the Tell el-Amarna Letters indicated that as early as the fourteenth century B.C., Shardana warriors were already serving as Egyptian mercenaries at Byblos in Phoenicia, and the seafaring Lukka were raiding cities on the eastern coast of the Mediterranean. In the early thirteenth century B.C., at the Battle of Qadesh, memorialized on the walls of the Temple of Luxor, Shardana mercenaries fought for Ramesses II against the Hittites, aided by the Lukka, Derden, Masha, Pitasha, Arawanna, and Karkisha.

During the reign of Merneptah, the son of Ramesses II, new names were added to the list of the Sea Peoples: the Ekwesh, Teresh, and Sheklesh. The appearance of the Philistines, Shiqalaya (or Tjekker), Dannuna, and Weshesh during the reign of Ramesses was merely the climax of the Sea Peoples' increasing pressure on Egyptian territory. Because of the Philistines' conflicts with the Israelites and their prominence in the biblical narrative, their later history could be traced. As for the others, some could be tentatively identified with peoples mentioned in Greek myth, but most of them never again appeared in written records. The beginning of archaeological interest in the Philistines in the nineteenth century, however, encouraged scholars to look for evidence of the fate of the other Sea Peoples.

In 1973, while I was involved in the anthropoid coffins, Moshe was appointed professor of archaeology at the Department of Maritime Civilizations at Haifa University, which was just then inaugurating a program in both land and underwater archaeology. And as soon as the Ashdod excavations were completed, he began to contemplate the excavation of Tel Akko, the northernmost port in the country. Happily, the coastal area between Akko in the north and Tell Qasile in the central area was no longer terra incognita, thanks to a nineteenth-century Russian, our early twentieth-century English excavator John Garstang, and a recent joint Israeli-Japanese excavation in the area.

AMENOPE'S
TRAVEL
GUIDE

In 1891 Vladimir Golenischeff, a prominent Russian Egyptologist, obtained a cache of ancient papyri found at el-Khibeh in Middle Egypt. One of the documents in the cache, the "Onomasticon of Amenope," was an encyclopedic enumeration of subjects such as the natural elements, offices, foreign peoples, towns, buildings, land, beverages, and food. The Philistines were recorded as living in Ashkelon, Ashdod, and Gaza, and in a separate list of ethnic communities living in territorial enclaves along the Canaanite coast were, enumerated in north-to-south order, the Shardana, the Shiqalaya, and again, the Philistines.

The Shardana and Shiqalaya had been allies of the Philistines in their attack on Egypt at the time of Ramesses III, and both had reportedly been settled as mercenaries in Egyptian garrisons after their defeat. Now the Onomasticon hinted at the location of their settlements. In another document obtained by Golenischeff, the "Report of Wen Amun," a rather colorful ancient travelogue, the city of Dor was described as "a harbor of the Shiqalaya."

The remains of that ancient city, whose later history was known from Greek and Roman records, were confidently identified with the mound of Khirbet el-Burj, Hellenistic Dora, about twenty miles south of the modern port of Haifa. The first excavations at Dor were made by John Garstang in 1923 and 1924. But the massive accumulation of later periods hindered his progress, as it did at Ashkelon.

From his limited finds—a few fragments of Early Iron Age vessels that seemed to have been executed in the same style as bichrome Philistine pottery—Garstang suggested that the Shiqalaya culture was similar to that of the Philistines in their adaptation of Aegean tradition. But Dor proved to be too much of a challenge, and at the end of his second season Garstang attempted a trial excavation at the small inland site of Tel Zeror. There, too, his results were inconclusive. Only forty years later, when Tel Zeror was excavated by a joint Israeli-Japanese expedition, did the apparent outlines of Shiqalaya culture emerge.

Naturally, this expedition had all the benefits of later archaeological work in Philistia. They were able to determine that the city had been established in the Middle Bronze Age, and had later been a small artisans' village that was destroyed at the end of the thirteenth century B.C. There then came a period of abandonment, followed, in the middle of the eleventh century B.C., by the construction of a fortress. This appeared to reflect the same inland expansion and fortification that was taking place at the time in the Land of the Philistines. With small variations, the repertoire of pottery vessels followed the same range of types as Philistine ware, and Aegean-type weapons were found. Tel Zeror seemed to offer evidence of the settlement in Canaan of another Aegean-influenced group. And, now, Akko held out the hope that traces of that third elusive Sea People, the Shardana, might be uncovered.

Tel Akko—in Arabic, Tell el-Fukhar, or "hill of the potsherds"—was one of the largest mounds in the country, dominating both the city and the bay of the modern port of Akko. Ancient Akko's position on the only natural bay on the northern Canaanite coast and its location at the outlet of several major inland trade routes made possession of the city crucial to the control of eastern Mediterranean trade. Mentioned first in the Egyptian Execration Texts (c.1900 B.C.) as a city hostile to the Middle Kingdom pharaohs, Akko later became part of the New Kingdom empire, when it was conquered in 1479 B.C. by Thutmosis III. It was frequently mentioned in the Tell el-Amarna Letters as an Egyptian naval base and supply center. In the thirteenth century B.C. several people from Akko are mentioned in Ugaritic economic documents, suggesting that, like Ashdod, Akko supported a colony of commercial agents in the harbor of Ugarit. The decline of the city at the end of the Late Bronze Age is harder to pinpoint. Akko was conquered by Seti I (c. 1300 B.C.), and his son, Ramesses II, is shown in a relief

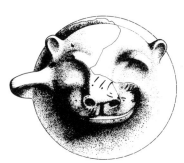

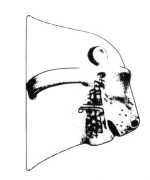

Lion-headed cup from Tel Zeror.

"HILL OF THE POTSHERDS"

211

in the Temple of Karnak breaking down the gates of the city.

After extensive excavations, ten digging seasons to be exact, Moshe and his team were able to construct the basic outline of the city's history. Akko began as a fortified maritime center in the Middle Bronze Age (c. 2000–1550 B.C.) and its massive ramparts continued in use into the Late Bronze Age. The wealth of the city, as suggested by numerous Late Bronze Age texts, could be seen in the elaborate tombs of this period and in the closely packed storehouses and buildings that faced the city's estuary anchorage on the southern side of the tell. Its extensive trading contacts were evident from the imported Cypriot and Mycenaean pottery, scarabs, and metal and ivory objects. But toward the end of the thirteenth century B.C. its prosperity seemed to decline. Signs of destruction were distinguished in various parts of the city, perhaps relating to the conquest by Ramesses II. There was evidence of almost immediate reoccupation of the area of the anchorage, indicating some continued maritime activity. But on the northern side of the city there was a complete change in the character of the occupation.

There they found an unfortified area of workshops, constructed partially on surviving Late Bronze Age structures. This phenomenon was strikingly similar to what had been found at Ashdod with the settlement of the earliest Sea Peoples. Here there was evidence of metalworking—crucibles, bellows pipes, copper and bronze scrap and slag; dyeing—crushed murex shells and the fragment of a large vat still stained with purple; and a complete pottery kiln. In the kiln and in the ash layers that surrounded it was Mycenaean IIIC:1b pottery, by now the hallmark of the Sea Peoples. But in addition to the types of this pottery found in Philistia, there were other distinctive varieties, suggesting that the settlers may have had a different origin.

Some forty yards to the west of the workshop compound, in an excavation area directed by Dr. Michal Artzy, a small mortarlike altar with a concave upper surface containing small quartz pebbles and ash was discovered. Geological analysis showed that the pebbles were not of local origin and the altar itself appeared to be easily transportable. Furthermore, the sides of the altar bore schematic depictions of seagoing vessels, not unlike the ships that had been scratched on the outer walls of the contemporaneous Temple of Kition in Cyprus.

In one of the lowest ash levels in this area, there was a scarab inscribed with the name of the widow of Seti II, Queen Tewosret, who, toward the end of the thirteenth century B.C., at a time of dynastic struggle, did what few women in Egyptian history did: she herself assumed the title of pharaoh. From previous archaeological evidence, the reign of Tewosret was considered to be the last possible period in which the Late Bronze Age Mycenaean IIIC:1b pottery was produced. When pieced together, it appeared that the arrival of the earliest Sea People in Canaan took place at least sometime before the invasion recorded in the Medinet Habu reliefs.

THE PIECES FIT

But exactly who were the Sea People who had founded the workshop compound at Akko? It was evident from the "Onomasticon of Amen-ope" that three Sea Peoples had occupied the coast of Canaan: the Philistines in the south, the Shiqalaya at least as far north as Dor, and the Shardana even farther north, although the boundaries of the latter two were uncertain.

In the Onomasticon, the territorial term *i-s-r* was placed close to the mention of Shardana. Some scholars believed that it referred to Assyria, but most preferred to associate it with the Israelite tribe of Asher, which, according to Joshua [19:24–29], was allotted the coastal territory, from the Carmel range northward to Tyre. And since Judges [1:31] reports that "Asher did not drive out the inhabitants of Akko," it seemed possible, even probable, considering all the archaeological evidence to support it, that indeed the Shardana were settled in the city-state of Akko.

As we have already noted, the Shardana were mentioned in the Tell el-Amarna Letters as mercenaries in the Egyptian garrison at Byblos, in Phoenicia, around 1375 B.C. Almost a century later the distinctive weapons of the Shardana were noted, as was their role as Egyptian mercenaries at the Battle of Qadesh. Other groups of Shardana apparently roamed throughout the eastern Mediterranean in the same period, some serving as mercenaries or, perhaps, royal retainers at the Syrian port of Ugarit. Others were described by the Hittites as dangerous raiders "of the sea." Not long after, still other groups of Shardana were fighting against the Egyptians, joining the hostile confederacy of Sea Peoples and Libyans who invaded the western Nile delta during the reign of Merneptah.

The "flexibility" of Shardana allegiance reached its climax more than a generation later at the time of the Philistine invasion. In the Sea Battle depicted at Medinet Habu, Shardana ships fought alongside those of the Philistines and the Shiqalaya, while in the Land Battle, Shardana mercenaries fought at the side of Ramesses III's troops. The Shardana were easily distinguishable from their fellow Sea Peoples: while the Philistines, Shiqalaya, and Dannuna wore identical feathered head-dresses, the Shardana were characterized by heavy, horned helmets, sometimes surmounted by a disc between the horns.

This distinctive headgear provided a connection between the Shardana and finds at Mycenae itself: there the famous "Warrior Vase" depicted marching soldiers with horned helmets. Furthermore, in one of the ashlar buildings at Enkomi on Cyprus ascribed to the Sea Peoples,

Detail of the Shardana warriors from the Medinet Habu reliefs. They are distinguishable from the other Sea Peoples not only by their horned headdress but by their downward curving ribbed corselets, joined in the middle of the chest over a shirt. Their weapons were the same as those of the other Sea Peoples: long, straight swords and rounded shields.

there was a bronze statuette with a distinctive headdress that was dubbed "the Horned God." The suggested presence of the Shardana on Cyprus at the time of the Sea Peoples' invasion seemed to fit in well with their identity as wide-ranging seamen and raiders.

There was as well linguistic and archaeological evidence connecting them with the island of Sardinia, where Mycenaean IIIC:1b pottery was found. Sardinia may have been either their original homeland or, more probably, one of their final points of settlement. There seemed to be a possible maritime connection between the eastern and western Mediterranean at that time. The people who had manufactured and used the Mycenaean IIIC:1b pottery at Akko and in coastal sites in Sardinia all occupied sites that overlooked natural anchorages. Another possible indication of maritime trade in this period was the discovery of identical copper ingots on Sardinia, on Cyprus, and off the northern coast of Israel. There may have been a route from the rich copper deposits of Sardinia to the Sea Peoples' metal workshops in the eastern Mediterranean.

What is evident, almost beyond the shadow of a doubt, is that the settlement of three of the Sea Peoples—the Philistines, the Shiqalaya, and the Shardana—along the coast of Canaan, and even inland, was part of a complex process of population movement from the Aegean to the eastern Mediterranean sometime around 1200 B.C., a process that had a major influence on the history and culture of the region.

As for the Dannuna, there lies a tale of great fascination. It relates to the story of Samson and Delilah, the inspiration for so much great art (and a number of banal cinema spectacles). In 1956, Professor Yigael Yadin published an article in which he tried to assess Samson, not only in light of the biblical narrative, but in light of Greek legend and archaeological evidence as well. This was just at the time we were working together at the excavations at Hazor and, needless to say, the subject intrigued us all.

In Hebrew tradition Samson was a revered judge, although in fact he was a fun-loving frolicker with the girls next door and loved to plague the boys with riddles. In the first chapter of this book we noted that the legend of Samson and Delilah closely resembled the story of the Megaran king Nisus, whose power-giving lock of red hair was shorn by his deceitful daughter Scylla, when she betrayed him to King Minos of Crete. There is another myth of relevance to Samson, the myth of the riddle-loving Mopsos, and we want to put it into its archaeological context before we discuss Yadin's article.

In 1943 a small expedition from the University of Istanbul was excavating a site called Karatepe, Turkish for "black mound," located on a hill above the Ceyhan River in southern Turkey, in the region of ancient Cilicia. There the excavations uncovered a small Iron Age citadel whose elaborately decorated gate bore two stone slabs with texts in two languages, Phoenician and hieroglyphic Hittite. The Phoenician inscription of sixty-one lines, the longest ancient Semitic inscription found up to then, was written in the ninth century B.C. and revealed that the founder of the ancient city at Karatepe, Azitawatas, claimed the title "King of the Dannuniyim."

Scholars recognized this as a Phoenician form of the name Dannuna, a group of Sea Peoples listed on the Medinet Habu reliefs as one of the Philistines' allies. The Dannuna were identical in appearance to the Philistines and the Shiqalaya: all three wore kilts, body armor, and the feathered headdress. Other scholars had noted the phonetic similarity of Dannuna to one of the common designations for the Greeks in the *Iliad*, the Danaoi.

This cross-cultural identification had long been regarded as mere speculation in the absence of any supporting evidence. The Karatepe inscription provided, at the very least, some circumstantial confirmation: Azitawatas, in addition to his title of King of the Dannuniyim,

215

proudly proclaimed his ancestry from the "House of Mopsos." Mopsos was a colorful figure from Greek myth.

MOPSOS THE RIDDLEMAKER

In one version, Mopsos was noted for having defeated the Greek sage Calchas in a contest of riddles. He was also known as a traveler for whom numerous cities and cult places were named. Among his alleged talents was his ability to speak the language of the birds.

The last version of his biography was preserved by the fifth-century B.C. Lydian historian Xanthus. Xanthus placed Mopsos's greatest feat at the Philistine city of Ashkelon, where Mopsos cast the local goddess and her son into the pond of the city, thereby destroying the power of the local cult. The story may have had its roots in some dim memory of the early incursion of the Sea Peoples into Ashkelon.

In his article Yadin attempted to explain Samson's unique attributes. Samson, he noted, was different from the other Hebrew judges in a number of ways. For one, his raids and rampages against the Philistines were not meant to defend either his own tribe, the Dan, or the Israelite confederacy: they were aimed solely at avenging personal insults and injuries. For another, relations between the Philistines and Samson's tribe were quite friendly. Samson's father willingly arranged his son's marriage to a Philistine woman, and even after the marriage ended Samson's attraction to Philistine women did not wane. He was known to have visited a prostitute in Gaza, and he ultimately paid with his life for his tryst with Delilah, the seductive secret agent of the Philistine lords.

No other Hebrew judge, Yadin went on, was remembered for his physical prowess (or erotic exploits) as were the Greek heroes. Samson's spiritual strength—if it could be called that—was of a completely different nature: he delighted in posing riddles.

In this respect he resembled Mopsos. But there were other parallels. His exploits at various places were memorialized by names, such as the "Hill of the Jawbone," where he slew a thousand Philistines with the jawbone of an ass, or the "Spring of the Caller," where after an appeal to God his thirst was quenched. Finally, like Mopsos, in a daring raid on another Philistine capital, Gaza, Samson laid low the prestige of the local god Dagon.

THE EVIDENCE PILES UP

These narrative parallels might be explained, continued Yadin, through an examination of the biblical evidence relating to the origins of Samson's tribe itself. If Samson, Dan's judge, was unusual, it was perhaps because the tribe of Dan was unusual among the tribes of Israel. In the "Blessing of Jacob" [Genesis 49], where the fates of all the tribes were laid out, Jacob says: "Dan shall judge his people *as* one of the tribes of

Israel" [emphasis ours]. This may be understood to mean that previously Dan had *not* been judged as a tribe of Israel.

In Judges [18:1] it was reported that after the death of Samson, the tribe of Danites, unlike all the other tribes of Israel, "was seeking for itself an inheritance to dwell in; for until then no inheritance among the tribes of Israel had fallen to them." This was an outright contradiction to what appeared in Joshua [19:40–48], where the Danites were explicitly allotted a territory: it included not only the inland towns of the hill country where Samson was to perform his exploits, but also the Philistine city of Ekron and various sites around Jaffa and the Yarkon River, in the immediate vicinity of Tell Qasile, where a number of Philistine settlements had been found.

One of the earliest surviving passages of Hebrew poetry, "The Song of Deborah" [Judges 5], further compounds the mystery. The prophetess alternately praises and chastises the tribes according to the zeal each had displayed in coming to the aid of the threatened Israelite confederacy. At the climactic battle—a bloody engagement with the Canaanite chariotry near Mount Tabor in the north—the men of Dan were conspicuously absent. The prophetess angrily asks, when the battle is over: "And Dan, why did he abide with the ships?"

The picture was becoming clear to Yadin. An Israelite tribe engaged in seafaring? An Israelite tribe that had not been considered Israelite before? Its judge a larger-than-life hero more similar to the heroes of Greek mythology than to the judges of the Israelite God? Yadin concluded that there must have been more than a coincidental connection between the Sea People called the Dannuna and the tribe of Dan. And the evidence seemed to point in that direction: after their appearance in the Great Land and Sea Battles at the time of Ramesses III, the Dannuna who arrived in Canaan mysteriously disappeared.

Since the Philistines, the Shiqalaya, and the Dannuna were identical in their physical appearance on the Medinet Habu reliefs, Yadin presumed that they were closely related and would have settled near one another along the Canaanite coast. Since the Philistines settled areas from Gaza to Ashdod, the Shiqalaya farther to the north around Dor, and the Shardana the coastal area even farther north, around Akko, the only place left for the Dannuna would, therefore, be the area around Jaffa—precisely that area allotted to the tribe of Dan in the Book of Joshua.

The archaeological discovery of the Philistines' inland expansion permitted Yadin to suggest that the Danites may have come under pressure from the neighboring Philistines, and it was in this subordinate position that Samson's encounters with the Philistines apparently took place. At the time, as the Samson stories seem to indicate, the Danites were related in language and culture to the Philistines. In fact, other Israelites may not have even considered them to be kinsmen: when Samson took refuge from the Philistines in the territory of Judah, the Judeans felt no compunction about tying him up and handing him over to the Philistine authorities [Judges 15].

It was only after the death of Samson in Gaza that the Danites completely changed their way of life. Leaving their struggles with their former neighbors, the Philistines, behind them, they began a communal migration, "putting the little ones and the cattle and the goods in front of them" [Judges 18:21] in a manner strikingly reminiscent of the Sea Peoples' overland trek, pictured at Medinet Habu. Far to the north, they established a new enclave at the former Canaanite city of Laish, which they now renamed Dan. During this migration they may have also adopted a new religious identity: the family of Jonathan, reportedly a grandson of Moses, were made official priests of the tribe of Dan.

The Bible fails to report an extensive genealogy for the tribe of Dan, and this may point to their foreign origin. Yadin supposes that Samson's hostility to the Philistines was directed only against the increasingly tyrannical rule of the Philistine lords and that his own people may have been closely related. If so, their only distinction from the Israelites' traditional enemies seems to be their eventual abandonment of their Aegean traditions to become Israelites themselves. This eventual mixing and assimilation of cultures in Canaan is precisely what our archaeological excavations have confirmed.

IMPORTANT INFLUENCE

The apparent connections between the Sea Peoples and the peoples of Canaan are many. These connections invest the Sea Peoples with a far wider role in the history of the area than was imagined when we began our search for the Philistines. The conclusions to be drawn from the unique coincidence of pottery styles, social organization, and cultic practices can no longer be considered a regional phenomenon of interest to Egyptologists, biblical scholars, and Aegean archaeologists alone. The Sea Peoples mentioned in the records were apparently active in the Mediterranean during the political upheavals and population movements that marked the transition from the Bronze Age to the Iron Age.

What precisely engendered the disturbances at the center of Mycenaean civilization at the end of the thirteenth century B.C. may range from a radical change in climate to the pressures of population movements southward from Europe, and from internal uprisings to a complex administrative collapse. Whatever the causes, the gathering momentum of the disruption to the long-standing trade and political balance of the Late Bronze Age Aegean had increasing effects far beyond the Mycenaean homeland.

Although the sequence of events is still disputed, the evidence points to the arrival of groups from the Aegean soon after the destruction of the Mycenaean palaces. The culture of Cyprus was dramatically transformed by the new arrivals, as was that of the eastern Mediterranean coast. In some places, like the city of Ugarit, they may well have been responsible for the city's destruction and may have briefly reoccupied its ruins. In Akko, Tell Keisan, and the cities of Ashdod, Ekron, and, perhaps, Ashkelon, they established permanent communities, some larger than others but each attempting to maintain the traditions of their Aegean homelands.

The archaeological evidence seems to substantiate the fragmentary details of the Egyptian records of the time and corresponds to the situation depicted in the Greek legends of the aftermath of the Trojan War. The stories of the heroes returning from Troy told of attacks and migrations by roving bands of seaborne warriors, and of the conquest of lands and the establishment of cities throughout the Mediterranean world. King Menelaus and his Spartans, returning from Troy, reportedly raided the coasts of Cyprus, Syria, and Egypt. Odysseus and his crew reached Syria and Egypt in the course of their wanderings. Teuros, the Trojan leader, founded the city of Salamis on Cyprus, and Agapenor, king of Tegea in Greek Arcadia, reportedly established the city of Paphos on the island's western coast. Warriors who had served under King Nestor of Pylos founded cities in Italy, and veterans from Rhodes established colonies in Spain. Whatever the historical value of the stories, they all describe the situation that became increasingly familiar to archaeologists all over the region: the sudden establishment of settlements characterized by the distinctive Mycenaean IIIC:1b pottery. In the course of time, we became aware of the twin phenomena that succeeded the settlement of the Sea Peoples: their enormous influence on the other inhabitants of the region and, finally, their eventual assimilation.

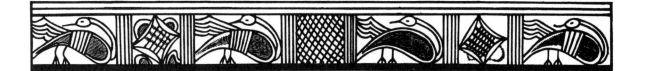

PART VI

BACK TO THE PHILISTINE HEARTLAND

TRUDE DOTHAN

CHAPTER 20

The Tip of the Iceberg

While I was still at work at Deir el–Balah in the seventies, trying to understand the influence of Egyptian funerary practices in Canaan, some intriguing new discoveries were made at Tell Qasile about the Philistines' religious practices which reriveted my attention on this enigmatic people. The director of the new excavations there, Amihai Mazar, was a member of the younger generation of Israeli archaeologists. He happened to be one of my own graduate students at the Hebrew University, as well as the nephew of my former teacher, Professor Mazar—a rather rewarding kind of archaeological daisy chain.

More than two decades had passed since our first excavations at Tell Qasile, and during that time the modern city of Tel Aviv had spread, completely surrounding the site of the tiny Philistine city on the banks of the Yarkon River. When we had excavated the site not long after the establishment of the State of Israel in 1948, we had only a dirt road and concrete pumphouse to remind us of modern civilization. Now high-rise apartment buildings and the country's major north-south highway skirted the site. The sprawling Museum of the Land of Israel, dedicated in 1959, abutted the eastern slopes of the tell.

While the main phase of our excavations had ended in 1950, Professor Mazar had returned for further small-scale excavations, first in 1959 and then again in 1962. Since then, much had been discovered about the Philistines' culture and their relationship to the other Sea Peoples. Amihai Mazar had first come to the tell for a small emergency excavation in 1971, after which he decided to resume digging on the summit. After a few false starts he and his team began to uncover the walls of

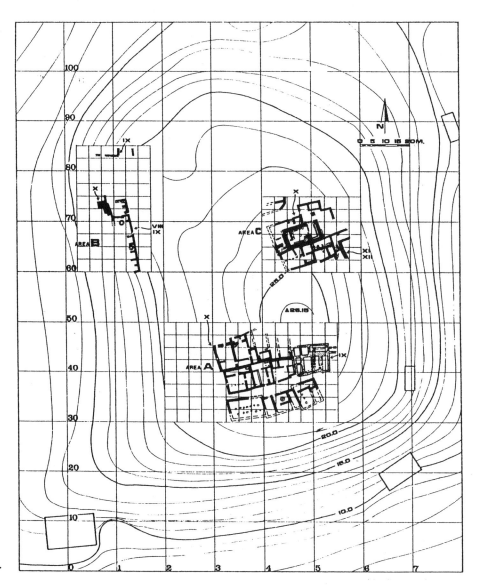

Contour map of Tell Qasile.

a mudbrick structure that were relatively well preserved. In fact, the thick walls, associated by now with late Philistine pottery, were more massive than any that we had previously found at the site.

SANCTIFIED
GROUND

With this promising indication, Amihai Mazar returned the following year. It was then that he recognized the character of the massive structure: it was a Philistine temple, constructed during the height of Philistine culture, around 1050 B.C. (Stratum X). Oriented more or less on an east-west axis, with an altar and storeroom for ritual objects,

224

facing in the direction of the sea, this temple provided the most complete picture of the nature of the Philistine cult.

The Tell Qasile temple proved to be a reconstruction of a series of earlier cult buildings, all built on the same spot since the foundation of the city by the Philistines. It provided us with a unique, continuous picture of Philistine religious development over a period of about two hundred years.

The area was a well-planned complex of a number of units, and was evidently the cultic center of the Philistine city. In each of the three strata, XII, XI, and X, a new temple was erected, and with each new structure the temple was enlarged farther to the east. The western wall, the orientation toward the Mediterranean, and the focal point of the ritual remained unchanged throughout.

The earliest temple building—Stratum XII, c.1150 B.C.—was a one-room brick structure with plastered benches along the walls and a beaten-lime floor. A plastered brick platform approached by two steps was located at the western end of the building. Offering bowls and votive vessels lay on the temple floor. The special finds in the spacious courtyard or *temenos* east of the temple included an ivory knife handle terminating in a suspension ring bearing traces of an iron blade, fastened to the handle by three bronze rivets. This is the earliest iron implement at Tell Qasile, associated with the initial phase of Philistine settlement, and one of the earliest iron knives found anywhere in the country. The wide diffusion of knives of this type points to a connection between the Philistine culture and contemporary Aegean and even European cultures. A similar knife was discovered at Enkomi in Cyprus on the floor of a twelfth-century B.C. workshop. Another parallel comes from a Mycenaean IIIC tomb at Ialysos in which Mycenaean mourning figurines were found. It is striking that the association of mourning figurines and an iron knife occurs in the Mycenaean IIIC and the Philistine cultural complexes.

After the destruction of the Stratum XII temple, a new and larger temple was built directly above it (Stratum XI, around 1100 B.C.). It too consisted of a single room with a plastered floor and brick benches along the walls. The focal point of the cult was in the northwest corner, where the altar stood. On the southwest side of the temple was a corner room over which lay organic material containing an abundance of pottery, cult vessels, and bones. The cult vessels included an anthropomorphic mask, an ivory bird-shaped cosmetic bowl, a conch used as a horn, terra-cotta figurines, beads, and dozens of small votive bowls. Red-slipped bowls now appeared with the pottery.

The inhabitants of Tell Qasile evidently expanded the temple a half-century later, for the temple of Stratum X (c.1050 B.C.) seemed to be

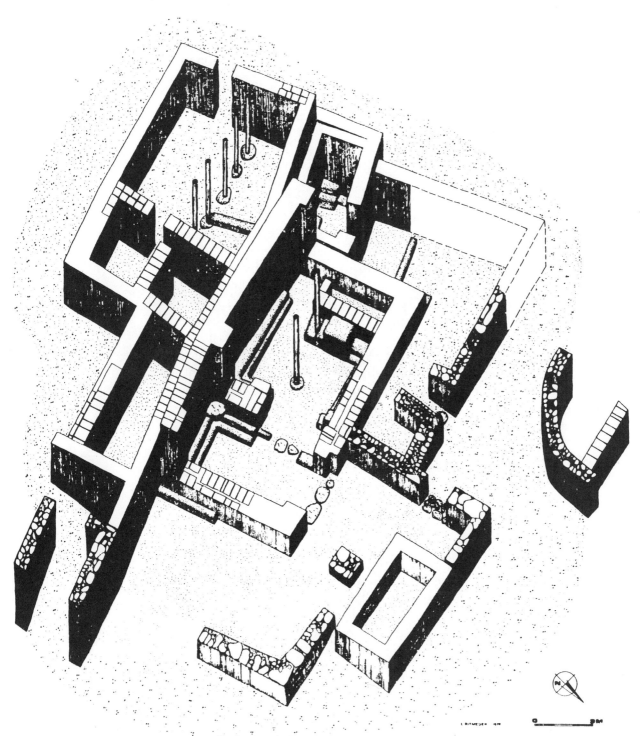

Exonometric view of Area C, Tell Qasile.

Artist's reconstruction of shrine containing cult stand, Tell Qasile.

Pottery assemblages found on the floor of the shrine at Tell Qasile. Characteristic of the second half of the tenth century B.C., the pottery was red-slipped and burnished and included Phoenician imports and pottery decorated in the Philistine tradition.

227

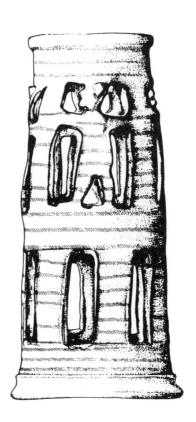

Cylindrical cult stand with human figures found at Tell Qasile.

merely an enlargement and rebuilding of the previous temple on a different plan. No trace of a burnt layer was found, indicating a peaceful transition. The temple now was an elongated building oriented to the west and divided into two main parts: an antechamber and a main hall. The altar was located opposite the central opening of the main hall. It

228

should be noted that the stratum X altar was built directly above the cult installations of both previous temples, despite differences in the plans. The ceiling of the large central sanctuary was supported by cedar columns, reminiscent of Solomon's cedar beams in the Temple of Jerusalem. As in the earlier temples, there were benches along the walls for offerings.

On the temple platform, a cylindrical cult stand with human figures was found. Two rows of rectangular and trapezoidal windows were cut into its walls, and in each window a schematic human figure could be seen striding with outstretched hands, the head in profile. The motif of a such a procession, "Marching Men," is well known in the area from the second millennium B.C., although representations of human figures on cult stands are rare. Other known examples are from Beth Shean and Ashdod (the "Musicians' Stand").

The Stratum X temple was destroyed by a great conflagration, presumably at the time of the conquest of the city by King David around 980 B.C. The building was obviously plundered before it was destroyed by fire, for no valuable objects were found. Two metal objects were uncovered, a socketed bronze double axe, on the steps of the altar, and an iron bracelet. Such axes were rare in the Near East and seem to have had Aegean prototypes. The bracelet is of a type known from Early Iron Age sites when metal was rare and used mainly for jewelry.

In Stratum X the *temenos* reached its peak of development: the open courtyard was now enclosed by a wall, within which there was a square stone base, apparently the foundation for a sacrificial altar. Around the altar, the team discovered the bones of goats, sheep, camels, cattle, and even hippopotami, common in the marshes of the Yarkon Valley in the Early Iron Age.

The open courtyard extended to the west up to a miniature temple, adjacent to the western wall of the main temple. It was a brick-walled room with an altar at the southwest corner. Three projections along the central axis probably held cult vessels. Three cylindrical cult stands with geometric decorations and with rectangular or oval windows were found in the southwest corner. Ritual bowls still stood on two of them, and a third bowl was found on the porch. Two of the bowls were "bird bowls" with molded heads, backs, wings, and tails (plate 18). Birds were apparently sacred to the Philistines, as to the other Sea Peoples, perhaps because of the role they played in navigation.

The miniature temple was destroyed by the collapse of the brick walls and not by fire. It is possible that it remained standing and continued in use even after the general destruction of Stratum X. If so, this would indicate a somewhat unusual phenomenon—a religious con-

229

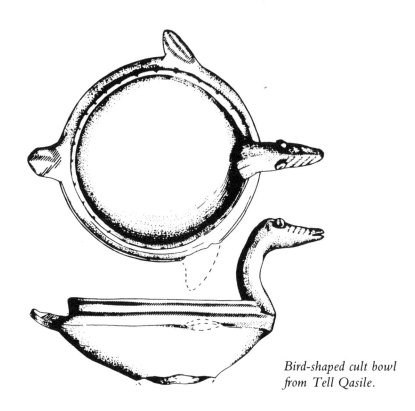

Bird-shaped cult bowl from Tell Qasile.

Cylindrical cult stand with bird-shaped libation bowl from Tell Qasile. The stand tapers upward with a two-ridged everted rim. Two small oval windows were cut in the body. On the stand rested a bird-shaped bowl. The tail is split and the short wings turn backward. The shape of the beak identified the bird as a shoveler duck.

tinuity that was unexpected, since it was assumed that Tell Qasile was occupied by the Israelites at this time.

Another feature of the courtyard is a pit lying below the altar of Stratum X. It is not clear whether it existed simultaneously with the temple of Stratum XI or whether it was dug during the transition phase. The pit is probably a *favissa*, for the burial of cult vessels. One of the buried objects was an anthropomorphic vessel of a female figure whose nipples served as spouts, which bore traces of painted decoration (plate 12). Another important vessel found was a ceramic lion's head with open mouth and modeled fangs, decorated with typical Philistine motifs in red and black. There were also abundant pottery vessels, among them two bottles and an elaborately decorated horn-shaped vessel.

The temples at Tell Qasile show a fusion of architectural styles. No exact parallels for the temple plan have been found in Israel, although many features continue the Canaanite tradition evidenced in the temples of Lachish and Beth Shean. Small sanctuaries excavated at Mycenae and Phylakopi (on the island of Melos) resemble that of Tell Qasile both in general layout and in details. A thirteenth-century B.C. temple from Kition in Cyprus also has similar architectural features.

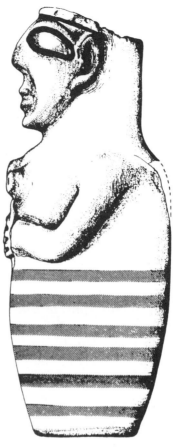

Female anthropomorphic figurine from Tell Qasile. Although the figurine lacks any divine symbol, it probably represents a fertility goddess. The vessel was used by filling it through a special funnel and pouring the liquid through the breasts.

Lion-headed cup from Tell Qasile.

231

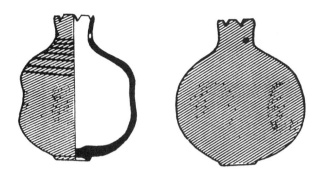

Pomegranate-shaped vessel from Tell Qasile. This is a pressed square with a concave depression on either side and a narrow high neck whose rim is cut in pointed zigzags. Two small holes were pierced in the neck so that the vessel could be hung.

The local Canaanite tradition could be seen in the tall cylindrical cult stands of the temple. Egyptian influence could be seen in a pottery plaque representing the facade of an Egyptian-style temple, framing the fragmentary figures of two deities. The kernos rings with attached pomegranates, birds, and animal heads had parallels in both Canaan and the Aegean, as did a lion-shaped rhyton, or flagon, and the large anthropomorphic female libation vessel. There were, further, a number of composite and multispouted vessels that seemed to be uniquely Philistine (plate 13).

The identity of the deity worshiped in the Tell Qasile temples remained uncertain, though the large libation vessel in the form of a female suggested that the central deity might have been an adaptation of the Great Mother of the Mycenaean world. At Ashdod, "Ashdoda" figurines had filled that function, but "Ashdoda" played no role in the cult of Tell Qasile: this small harbor town on the northern periphery of Philistia had developed its own variant of the shared Aegean heritage.

Clearly, Tell Qasile was a well-planned and fortified city with private dwellings, workshops, and a central temple situated in a sacred area, at least in strata XI and X. More evidence will be required to justify

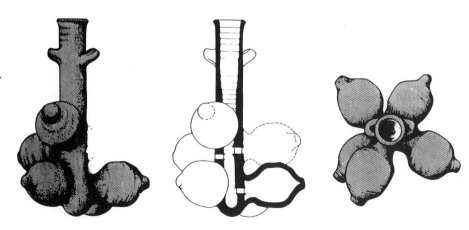

Composite drinking vessel from Tell Qasile. It is composed of a tube, with six elliptical, hollow bodies, ending in "nipples," attached to the lower part. The six were connected to the tube by pierced holes. It is probable that the lower part depicts a kind of fruit, such as a lemon or fig.

the same assumption about Stratum XII. But together they form a cultural unit based on Canaanite traditions merged with features of the Philistine culture that appeared at the very beginning of the settlement.

These were truly spectacular discoveries, for they provided us with a very different picture of Philistine religious traditions from those Moshe had discovered at Ashdod. Here the cult seemed to be a strange combination of Canaanite, Cypriot, and Egyptian rituals. In fact Amihai Mazar's excavations indicated that the Philistine culture, despite its uniformity in pottery, was more complex and regional in its other aspects. The challenge that now lay ahead of us was to understand the differing patterns of this development in each of the Philistine cities and to assess their implications for Philistine history. In order to do this properly, it was imperative for us to seek evidence by excavating one of their *inland* capitals. For if this was the case at the small site of Tell Qasile, it would be interesting to know just what the situation had been at one of the major Philistine capitals, such as Gath or Ekron.

As we were finishing the excavations at Deir el-Balah in 1980, I was given just such an opportunity. Professor Seymour Gitin, director of the W. F. Albright Institute of Archaeological Research in Jerusalem, the center of American archaeologial work in Israel, had often spoken to me about a joint Israeli-American dig and the mutual benefits that both students and scholars could enjoy. Americans and Israelis had often worked together on archaeological digs, but there had never been a project in which both groups equally shared the responsibility for all facets of the expedition. None of us recalls who suggested it, but before we knew it we were talking about a joint Albright/Hebrew University archaeological expedition, and soon we had passed from the conception to the actual planning.

Gitin was interested in the cultural interaction between Israelites and Philistines in the later biblical periods, or Iron Age II (1000–586 B.C.). My own interest was in the transition period between the Late Bronze Age (late Canaanite at the end of the thirteenth century B.C.) and the initial stages of early Philistine settlement and its subsequent consolidation and assimilation during Iron Age I (1200–1000 B.C.). As a result, we decided to look for a site that would produce data for an interregional study of Philistia and Judah in Iron Ages I and II. The obvious choice for a site that would cover both our fields was the Philistine city of Gath.

Gath was the birthplace of Goliath and later the residence of the Philistine king Achish, who gave shelter to David when he fled from the wrath of King Saul [1 Samuel 21:10]. In later times it was annexed to the kingdom of Judah, and still later suffered destruction by the

233

armies of Sargon. Despite its historical prominence, however, its precise location could be determined only by comparing the geographical details of the various biblical mentions with the location and relationship of the various ancient sites that were known. This dangerously subjective enterprise had resulted in the identification of Gath with various tells over an area of twenty-five miles of the coastal plain.

Strangely enough, at the turn of the century, when the archaeological search for the Philistines was just beginning, there was much less controversy about the location of Gath. Most scholars unhesitatingly believed that it had already been excavated at Tell el-Safi by Frederick Bliss and R.A.S. Macalister in 1899. It was there that Philistine pottery had first been identified. But as the distinctive pottery was found at one ancient site after another, the identification became less certain. In any case, both Gitin and I felt that a new excavation at Tell el-Safi might settle the controversy once and for all, and we decided to take a look at the site to consider the practical prospects for undertaking our joint project there.

Certain changes had taken place in the eighty years since Bliss and Macalister had arrived at the tell on horseback. The high mound, with its gleaming white chalk cliffs, was still the most conspicuous feature of the landscape in this part of the southern coastal plain, but the buildings of the Arab village on the summit were eerily unoccupied. Leaving our car at the foot of the tell, we climbed the steep path to the summit, where the view was truly spectacular. To the east were the stony gray hills of Judea and to the west, green fields, orchards, and beyond them, the sea. From the standpoint of size and strategic location, Bliss and Macalister seemed to have been correct in their supposition. The massive mound, with its command of the borderland between Judea and Philistia, had to be the city of Gath.

From a more practical perspective, however, we could see that there would be serious problems in a renewed excavation. Gitin knew this from personal experience at Gezer, where Bliss and Macalister had also dug. They had used the system of trench digging, stripping away the upper levels in one long rectangular section and then filling it in with dump from the next. The first problem would be to determine where exactly these trenches had been.

As we walked through the thistles and ruins on the summit, Bliss and Macalister's maps in hand, we discovered that the maps were disappointingly vague. To make matters worse, one of the most important areas of the mound at Tell el-Safi was partially covered by the ruins of a huge Crusader citadel, far too massive to be dismantled. In fact, there was no unobstructed place on the tell where we could really begin to excavate for Philistine levels. The identification of Gath would have to be left unresolved. We decided to turn our attention to the last of the Philistine capitals, the even more elusive Ekron.

The likeliest candidate for the site was Tel Miqne (Khirbet el-Muqanna in Arabic), although in the last hundred years scholars and archaeologists had located it, among other places, at Aqir, to the east of Yavne, or at Tel Batashi, a few miles from Beth Shemesh. Tel Miqne lies on the western edge of the Inner Coastal Plain that separated Philistia and Judah, overlooking the ancient network of highways leading from Ashdod to Gezer and inland, via Nahal Sorek, to the ancient city of Beth Shemesh. In 1924 William F. Albright noted the existence of the ten-acre upper tell, but because of its size mistook its identity. In 1957 Nathan Aidlin of nearby Kibbutz Revadim discovered that the site included not only the upper tell but also a forty-acre lower tell. He notified Joseph Naveh, of the Israel Department of Antiquities, who surveyed the site. Naveh's analysis of the archaeological evidence, including massive Late Iron Age fortifications, led him to conclude that the entire site could be confidently identified as Ekron.

From the viewpoint of our interregional interest, the site had a number of advantages. It was strategically located on the northeast border of Philistia. It is first mentioned in the Bible in Joshua as part of "the land that yet remains" to be captured by the Israelites [13:2–3], and then again as defining the northern border of the tribe of Judah [15:11]. In Judges, Judah is described as having taken "Ekron and its territory," although this is immediately modified: "Judah took possession of the hill country, but could not drive out the inhabitants of the plain [where Ekron is situated], because they [the inhabitants of the plain] had chariots of iron" [Judges 1:18–19]. The Greek Septuagint translation corrected the Hebrew, stating that Judah did *not* conquer Ekron and its territories. However one reads these conflicting testimonies, the fact is that Ekron was a focal point of important events during the time of the Judges, that is, Iron Age I, when it was in Philistine hands. When, for example, the Philistines captured the Ark of the Covenant [1 Samuel 5:10], they took it to Ekron. Further, in the David and Goliath story, we are told that the Israelites pursued the Philistines to the "gates of Ekron" [2 Kings 1:3]. The Bible also refers to the god of Ekron, the infamous Beel-zebub, Prince of the Demons, or "Lord of the Flies," assumed by many biblical scholars to have been an ancient Canaanite oracle who offered omens on matters of life, health, and death, through the movements of his sacred insects. In later periods both the Israelite king Ahaziah, c.845 B.C., and Jesus of Nazareth were accused by their detractors of consulting the pagan deity.

In any case, biblical references to connections between Ekron and the Philistines provided geographical details that led to its later identification with the site of Tel Miqne: the route by which the Ark traveled on its return to the Israelites at Beth Shemesh led along the Sorek Valley, near whose banks the mound of Tel Miqne lay. Ekron is also referred to in extrabiblical records and in various Assyrian annals. It was assumed up until then that Ekron, unlike the other excavated cities of the Philistine pentapolis, was founded on virgin soil. What was evident was that its geographical position as the northernmost of the Philistine capitals would make Ekron a focus of intercultural contact.

Unfortunately, on our first visit to the site, we found a problem even more serious than at Tell el-Safi: at the place marked on the map of Israel there was no area of ruins at all. For several hours in the heat of the day, we wandered around the fields of Kibbutz Revadim in what seemed to be a hopeless search for the site of ancient Ekron. In desperation we went over to the kibbutz and sought Nathan Aidlin, their resident amateur archaeologist. Aidlin told us that for some reason the official survey maps had incorrectly positioned the tell—a mile away from its actual site! Furthermore, unlike the mounds of Gaza, Ashkelon, Ashdod, and Gath, which rose from the surrounding terrain, Tel Miqne was a "low profile" site: its summit rose almost imperceptibly above the adjoining cotton fields. Low profile it was, but appearances can be misleading, as we soon found out.

Our early visits to Tel Miqne convinced us that a dig there would uncover rich new information on the later Philistine period: the extremely impressive Late Iron Age fortifications and buildings that Naveh had surveyed some twenty-five years before were still visible at the foot of the southern and eastern slopes. Since the fifty-acre area of the city was apparently not occupied after the end of the Iron Age, this would make access to the late Philistine levels immediately possible. There is nothing that an archaeologist likes more than total destruction and abandonment, which provide instant access and a wealth of buried remains.

Because it is located four miles from the highway, the site could be reached only by tractor or a four-wheel-drive vehicle. This difficulty was to our great advantage: Tel Miqne had never been touched. On the other hand, a road had to be built if we were to carry out a full-fledged expedition, and, indeed, by the summer of 1984 a road was finished. Till then we carried out only two seasons of pilot excavations—a deep stratigraphic section on the northeast acropolis, supervised by Ann Killebrew from the Hebrew University (plate 18).

A MIDDLE BRONZE AGE BEGINNING

As the dig proceeded through these two seasons, Ekron provided us with evidence that neither Gitin nor I—nor any other scholar for that matter—had anticipated: the city of Ekron, we discovered, had a history that extended far earlier than the time of the Philistines' initial settlement. Tel Miqne was just the tip of an archaeological iceberg. Geological probes of the area indicated that alluvial deposits had blanketed the lowest levels of the tell. By 1986, although we had begun to dig in various fields, we still had not reached the early periods of occupation suggested by the stratigraphic trench. But characteristic sherds from the lowest levels of our trench revealed architectural evidence of *continuous occupation from the Chalcolithic period* in the fourth millennium B.C. Especially intriguing was the presence of a Late Bronze Age settlement on the upper tell. This was the period immediately preceding the arrival of the Philistines and the emergence of Israel in Canaan. And the abundant examples of imported Cypriot and Mycenaean fragments, as well as New Kingdom objects, testified to the fact that Ekron, like Ashdod and Ashkelon, maintained extensive trading connections and possessed a cosmopolitan flavor.

It took another four years until we reached the earliest periods of occupation, in the heart of the lower city. The work here was supervised by Yosef Garfinkel from the Hebrew University. By then it was abundantly clear that a Middle Bronze Age Canaanite city had existed at Tel Miqne although only scant architectural features were distinguishable at that level, among them living surfaces and below them three child burials in storejars, a hallmark of the period. We assumed that the tell had received its square shape from the original outline of Canaanite fortifications. Counting downward, we numbered this lowest level, which included the entire fifty-acre area, Stratum IX, occupied in the period 1750–1550 B.C.

Stratum VIII, the Late Bronze Canaanite city on the upper tell (plate 19), dates to the fourteenth and thirteenth centuries B.C. and ceased to exist at the end of the Late Bronze Age. Like other Late Bronze Age cities, it was very limited in size yet it conducted a vigorous international trade.

In this level we were able to distinguish sherds of distinctive gray burnished kraters of a type whose ultimate origin had long been associated with Troy. The destruction of the Late Bronze Age city of Troy had been seen as the historical basis for the later Homeric epics and was perhaps, as we previously noted, the beginning of the disturbances that had swept across the eastern Mediterranean world. The exact sequence of events was, of course, still uncertain, but what made our discovery of the gray "Trojan ware" so suggestive was the discovery of other examples of this type of pottery on Cyprus immediately before the settlement of Sea Peoples there.

In Stratum VII, c.1200 B.C., the character of Ekron dramatically changed. The imports from Cyprus and the Mycenaean pottery from

**ENTER: THE SEA
PEOPLES**

the Aegean suddenly ended. The unmistakable pottery style of the Sea Peoples/Philistines appeared: locally made Mycenaean IIIC:1b ware. The quantities were overwhelming. They gave us to understand that here at Ekron, relatively far from the Mediterranean, the early Philistines had established a large and well-fortified city, covering both the upper tell and the larger lower city, which had lain barren for four hundred years. This Iron Age I city, which lasted throughout the twelfth and eleventh centuries B.C. and spanned strata VII to IV, was destroyed around 1000 B.C.—that is, at the beginning of the tenth century B.C. The following occupation of the city, dating from the tenth to eighth century B.C., was again confined to the upper tell. The city returned to its former glory only at the end of the eighth or beginning of the seventh century B.C., during which it reached the zenith of its economic growth and prosperity: it was the largest industrial center for the production of olive oil in the ancient Near East. In 603 B.C. the city was destroyed and abandoned as part of Nebuchadnezzar's campaign to conquer Philistia.

In short, Philistine Ekron was founded, on the site of a previously settled Canaanite city, at the beginning of the Iron Age and evolved through a four-stage process of growth, contraction, regeneration, and partial abandonment, reflecting its changing role as a border city on the frontier separating Philistia and Judah. Throughout its history many of the original concepts of the town plan were repeated. A variety of influences can be ascertained throughout its six-hundred-year history, all of which were common to the distinctive character of the Philistine coastal plain.

CHAPTER 21

Ekron Reclaimed

Our first major season of excavation took place in the summer of 1984, with a staff of thirty and over seventy volunteers from all over the world. For such a large crew, we needed special facilities and, indeed, prior to our arrival, two permanent buildings and all necessary facilities had been built in what would become every summer for the next six years a veritable tent city. If our camp city could be said to have been well planned and executed, the same could be said for the Iron Age I Philistine city of Ekron, which emerged during those years. We were provided with a clear glimpse into the history of a large urban center with a rich material culture. The city expanded far beyond the boundaries of the Late Bronze Age city, and its expansion was according to a well-conceived master plan, based to a certain extent on a keen awareness of ecological factors, a fact that was demonstrated again in the Iron Age II city.

The fortifications of Ekron, the work on which was supervised by Professor Barry Gittlin from the Baltimore Hebrew University, consisted of a mudbrick wall over ten feet thick, with adjoining tower rooms in the south, which may relate to the famous "gates of Ekron" from the biblical text. The fortifications, repaired and strengthened during the course of time, eventually encompassed an area of fifty acres, in both the upper and lower cities.

The inhabitants of this new city, apparently very early on, conceived of the city as divided into different zones: an industrial belt—pottery kilns, metalworking, and smelting; a central area with monumental

A PLANNED CITY

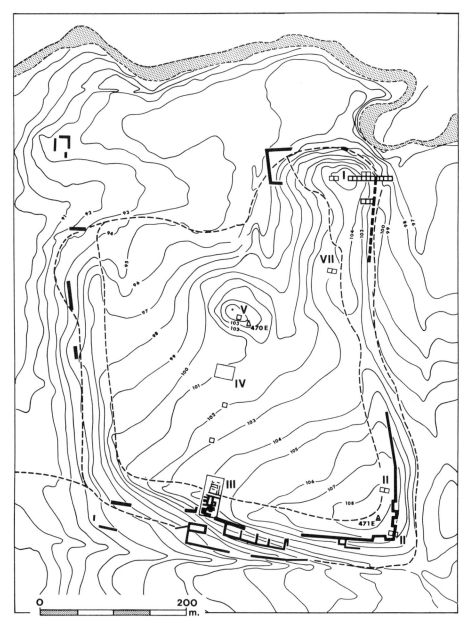

Contour map of Ekron with zones of occupation.

public buildings and shrines; and a domestic area—although we have as yet received only a glimpse of it.

The expanding industrial area, in the upper city next to the wall, contained square and horseshoe-shaped pottery kilns. Large quantities of locally made Mycenaean IIIC 1:b pottery were found here (plate 22), as well as crude figurines in the Mycenaean tradition. Their spreading headdresses and birdlike faces prefigured the style of "Ashdoda." These objects reflected the firsthand know-how the new settlers brought with them from abroad. They used their skills to make fine tableware—bell-shaped bowls and kraters with horizontal handles, jugs with strainer spouts, and stirrup jars, all decorated in monochrome with a repertoire of decorative Aegean motifs, prominent among them variations of the spiral motif. But in addition to these elegant vessels, they made every-day kitchenware, such as cooking pots and large, undecorated *lekane*. It appeared as if the new settlers wanted to feel at home. While Canaanite

Artist's representation of a square kiln from Ekron. This is the best-preserved example of the many kilns found in the upper city. The stoking hole in front of the kiln leads into the lower chamber, where the fuel was loaded and where flues brought air to the fire. A mud-brick platform separates the lower chamber from the upper one, in which pottery was placed to bake and harden. Vast amounts of pottery were found in the vicinity of the kiln.

241

ceramic tradition continued in such forms as storejars, juglets, bowls, lamps, and cooking pots, the new style accounted for more than half of the pottery.

On the periphery of the industrial belt and perhaps in what was part of the residential area, we uncovered a small shrine, built on the remains of a previous cultic installation, which showed the persistence of the tradition of sanctified areas. It had a wide plastered floor, benches, and a platform and, in a disposal area outside, in addition to bichrome pottery, a number of animal and human figurines (plate 21). Among them was the fragment of a lion-headed vessel, similar to the one found at the temple at Tell Qasile (plate 20). On one of the earlier levels we found a miniature votive vessel, identical to some of those among the thousands we had found in the cult center at Athienou on Cyprus. Another connection to Cyprus came with four bovine shoulder blades that bore enigmatic incisions along their edges. These bones were used apparently either for oracular purposes or to make musical sounds, and were common in the temples of Enkomi and Kition.

Adjacent to the fortifications in the lower city was yet another industrial area, this time for metalworking: a crucible with traces of silver was found in a huge installation, lined with *hamra*, a red, sandy plaster. Apparently, these industries catered to local needs.

In "downtown" Ekron, that is, the lower city, what we called the "elite zone"—since this remained its character throughout early and late Philistine occupation—there was an unusually airy, elegant, and monumental palace, the first public building of the new settlers (plate 23). It had heavily white-plastered, rounded corners and plastered floors with a pebbled bedding. The walls of this apparently one-story building were only one brick thick and had an impressive entrance from the northwest corner, leading into a "hearth-room," which contained two superimposed well-built hearths (plate 24). This special unit was massively built, with double brick walls that may have supported a second story in order to protect the hearths, indicating the importance attributed to them. The hearths, built with a round brick frame, one brick

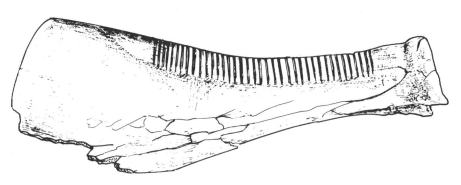

Cow scapula or shoulder blade from Ekron shrine, incised with parallel lines along its upper edge, probably used by the Philistines to divine a message from the deity.

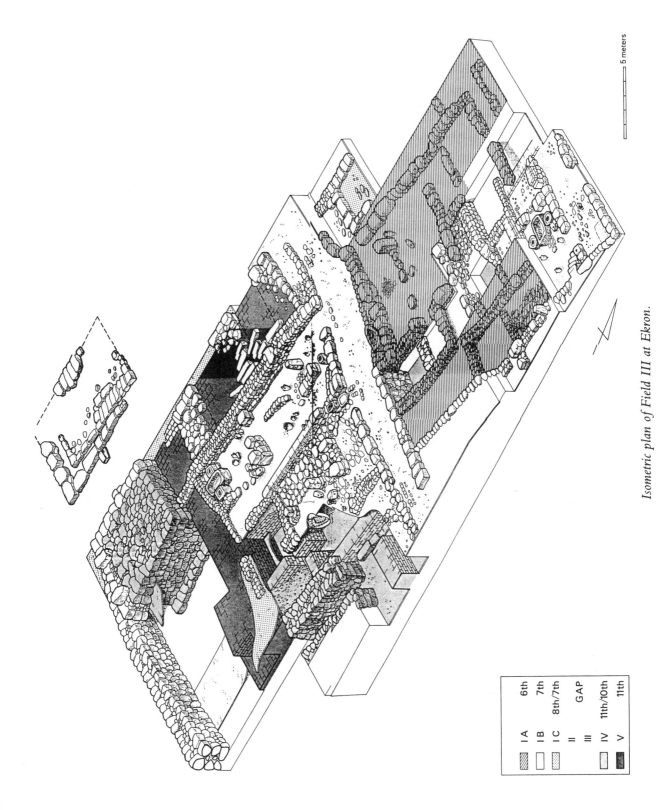

Isometric plan of Field III at Ekron.

I A		6th
I B		7th
I C		8th/7th
II		GAP
III		
IV		11th/10th
V		11th

5 meters

243

Palace and shrine in Field IV at Ekron.

Hearth sanctuary at Ekron. The "hearth-room" contained two superimposed monumental hearths. The hearth appears in the earliest Iron Age–phase settlement in the elite zone of the city and continues through several phases of the palace shrine.

high, and containing heavy layers of ash, were more than eight feet in diameter.

The hearth was not common in Canaan: only one other example was found in the Philistine temple at Tell Qasile. In its initial phase, the concept and central function of the hearth brought by the new inhabitants of Ekron was closely related to the large hearths of the Aegean palaces (plate 26). More than an architectural element, it represented a tradition that reflected the social structure and habits of everyday life in the Aegean (and Cypriot) palaces and shrines. The building could be dated to the twelfth century B.C. by the finds of Mycenaean IIIC:1b pottery and continued to be in use with the appearance of elaborate bichrome Philistine pottery. We also found the elaborately incised ivory lid of a pyxis (cosmetic box) depicting animal combat among a griffin, a lion, and two bulls. It was executed in thirteenth- and twelfth-century Aegean style, and reflected the sophistication of Philistine society.

As the city prospered, a second and larger superimposed building enveloped the first building, although the original architectural conception was maintained, with the same entrance, large hall, and adjoining rooms (plate 25). We could follow a dramatic change in the character of the superimposed building, no doubt the outcome of the peaceful consolidation of the Philistine city, triggered by economic and political stability. Near the southeast corner of the large hall, just below floor level, we discovered a foundation deposit—similar to one in the earlier building—that included a lamp inside two bowls. Similar deposits at other excavated sites have been associated with the ceremonial founding of new buildings—incorporating a local Canaanite-Egyptian practice.

As for the hearth, there is a striking discrepancy between the large hearths of the earlier building and the smaller hearths of this period. They were only three feet in diameter and with their pebbled surfaces seemed to be only a remote reflection of what had come before. Symptomatically, by the second half of the eleventh century B.C., with their Aegean heritage fading into the past, the people of Ekron no longer used the hearth. And in the last phase of the building the hearth was no longer in evidence.

The massive, four-foot-wide foundations of the later building and the boulder-size stones used for them suggest that it was more than one story high, although only the foundations and part of the first floor have survived. The aboveground walls, also four feet thick, were made of white-plastered mudbrick, which had been frequently replastered and perhaps painted.

Right: *Elaborately incised ivory cosmetic box lid from Ekron, about 13 cm. (5 in.) in diameter. The narrow center band is decorated with a rosette, the outer with a scene of animal combat. The designs are finely incised lines that could have been filled with color. Below right: Reconstructed complete cosmetic box based on Aegean example.*

A wall painting from Tiryns in ancient Greece depicting a priestess holding a similar box.

EKRON RECLAIMED

Oil lamp nestling inside two bowls, from Ekron.

Shrine with offering platform from Ekron. On the plastered mudbrick offering platform were two bowls and a flask with red concentric circles. In the next phase of this room, two offering platforms and a bench were found along with a treasure trove of finds.

The architectural features and the artifacts point to the probability that it was predominantly a temple (plate 27). On the north-south axis of the main hall, there were two pillar bases (and possibly a third), one located exactly in the center. This configuration resembled that in the Philistine temple at Tell Qasile, where support pillars stood about six feet apart. It also corresponds with the scene in the Bible [Judges 16:29–30] in which Samson, blind and in chains, brings down the Philistine temple on himself and his enemies by pushing the two pillars apart. Our pillars were seven and a half feet apart.

There were three rooms on the eastern side opening onto the main hall. In the middle room, the focal point of cultic practice, was a plastered, mudbrick *bamah*, or offering platform, that was preserved to a height of three feet. Near the bottom of the *bamah* was a bench that ran around its base. The *bamah* was part of the local Canaanite tradition, but was also well known from Cyprus and the Aegean.

CULT AND ARTIFACTS

Among the small precious items found with the offerings in this sanctuary were a faience ring and a gaming piece in the shape of a chess pawn, and a variety of pottery vessels, including a beautifully decorated Philistine krater. The floors were strewn with animal bones, among them the fang of a wild pig. (Brian Hesse, the archaeozoologist on our team, noted that the Philistines brought culinary changes with them, introducing pork and beef in place of goat meat and mutton.) Among other finds in this building were numerous lumps of unbaked clay, biconical or rounded in shape, used as loomweights in weaving. Loomweights of this type were also found in recent excavations at Ashkelon in twelfth- and eleventh-century B.C. contexts and are known from Kition and Enkomi in Cyprus.

Our knowledge of Philistine cult practices was particularly enhanced by the discovery of three bronze wheels with eight spokes each, a frame fragment of a stand with a loop for the insertion of an axle, and a small pendant in the shape of a bud, all made of cast bronze. These finds were undoubtedly part of a square stand on wheels, a design known from Cyprus in the twelfth century B.C. A basin or laver, in which the offering was placed, would be set on top of the square stand, which provided a supporting frame. This was the first—and, so far, only—example of a wheeled cult stand found in Israel.

The cult stand—in its shape, workmanship, and decoration—was reminiscent of the biblical *mechonot*, or laver stands, made for Solomon's Temple in Jerusalem by Hiram, king of Tyre, with their "bronze wheels and axles of bronze" and "supports for a laver." [See 1 Kings 7:27–33.]

The stands from Solomon's Temple, decorated with cherubim

Wheels, corner, and pendant from bronze cultic stand from Ekron.

A cultic stand from Cyprus used the same kind of wheel as that found at Ekron.

249

(sphinxes?), lions, oxen, and palm trees, must have been similar to the earlier Cypriot stands. On the biblical evidence it can be assumed that in the Syro-Palestine area their manufacture continued at least into the tenth century B.C., the finds from Ekron providing a chronological sequence.

Another unique find was a double-headed bronze linchpin (plate 28). Originally part of a real chariot, the linchpin secured one of the chariot wheels to its axle. The length of the linchpin would fit a normal-sized wheel, not the miniature wheels of the laver stand. The upper part of the linchpin consisted of two faces looking out in opposite directions, closed above by a flat cap covering both heads. Stylistically, the double heads and flat cap strongly resemble the sphinxes that decorate wheeled ceremonial stands from Cyprus, and are clearly Aegean in origin. Elaborately fashioned linchpins are known elsewhere in the ancient Near East, especially from depictions of Egyptian chariots.

Among the other outstanding finds was a complete iron knife affixed by bronze rivets to an ivory handle with a ring-shaped pommel (plates 29, 30). Its cultic or ceremonial significance is indicated by its elegant craftsmanship and the context in which it was found: on the floor of one of the shrine rooms with a *bama* dating to the first half of the eleventh century B.C. Three additional ivory knife handles of the same type were found at Ekron, one of whose insertion slot still bore traces of its iron blade and could be dated to the first half of the twelfth century B.C. This linked it to the initial settlement of the Philistines at Ekron.

The most pertinent parallel for this type of knife handle from excavations in Israel was found in the northeast part of the courtyard relating to the earliest Philistine temple at Tell Qasile. Similar knives with ring-shaped handles have been found in Cyprus and in the Aegean. These discoveries add to the quota of iron appearing at Philistine sites in Iron Age I and raise anew the question of the role of the Philistines in the introduction of ironworking technology.

The assemblage of iron and bronze finds, not to mention the loom-weights, in cultic contexts at Tel Miqne, added another facet to our knowledge of Philistine cultic practices and emphasized the links of this technologically and culturally advanced civilization with Cyprus and the Aegean world. In the succeeding layers we would see how the initial Aegean tradition of the earliest settlers was eventually transformed.

CHANGING INFLUENCES

Philistine material culture lost its uniqueness when the Philistines reached the peak of their prosperity and their political and military power at the end of the eleventh century B.C. This period was one in which older Aegean traditions were abandoned and new cultural influ-

Bronze linchpin from Ekron.

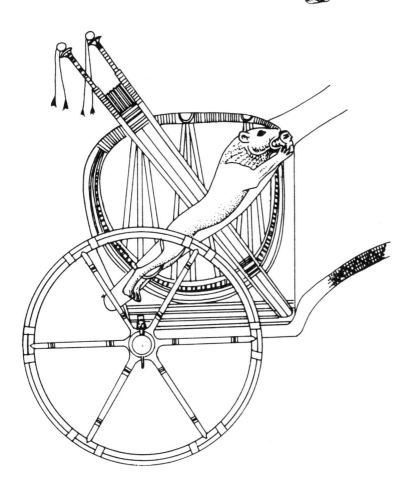

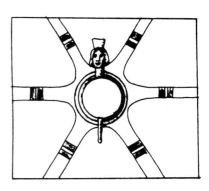

Simplified details from a painted relief, found in the Rameseum in Egypt, depicting the thirteenth-century B.C. Battle of Kadesh. Stylistically, the double heads and flat caps of the Ekron chariot linchpins strongly resemble the sphinxes that decorate wheeled ceremonial stands from Cyprus, and are clearly Aegean in origin.

251

ences, primarily Egyptian and Phoenician, took their place. On the floor of one of the main rooms of the monumental temple—apparently destroyed and abandoned in the early tenth century B.C.—we found heaps of pottery vessels, predominantly red-slipped and burnished, reflecting a transition point in Philistine ceramics: the all-over red slip heralding the Iron Age II repertoire, introduced while the last echoes of bichrome decoration were still retained. This is a unique testimony to the ultimate integration of the various styles that coexisted during the preceding centuries. Many of the vessels were miniature reproductions of standard-sized bowls, kraters, and juglets, perhaps for votive purposes, an impression reinforced by the appearance of *kernos* rings, pomegranate-shaped vessels (plate 31), goblets, chalices, and fragments of "bird-shaped" vessels, all of which were found in cultic contexts in contemporaneous levels at Ashdod and at the Tell Qasile temple.

Scattered on the floor was a cache of elaborate luxury objects that highlighted the city's contacts with the cultural fashions of Egypt during the XXIst Dynasty (c.1085–945 B.C.) and demonstrated how the different cultural strands were beginning to coalesce by the end of the eleventh and the beginning of the tenth centuries B.C. (plate 32). Among them were a carved ivory head, the ivory lid of a cosmetic vessel, a painted limestone baboon, large faience and ivory earrings, and faience pendants bearing the image of the Egyptian goddess Hathor.

DESTRUCTION AND REBIRTH

Ekron was totally destroyed and abandoned in the wave of destruction that swept over Philistia in the early tenth century B.C. It is unclear whether the responsible parties were the Israelites under David or the Egyptians under Siamun. The impact of the destruction, however, was unambiguous. The period of the city's early Philistine expansion was over, and at least two centuries would pass before Ekron would expand again. Meanwhile, the occupation of the city, as we discovered from pottery forms from the later tenth, ninth, and early eighth centuries B.C., was limited to the northeast acropolis. Sometime after the tenth-century B.C. destruction, a city wall with fine ashlar facing was constructed. This may have been the new defensive line of the city, which lay close to the border of the kingdom of Judah and was on the front line of later conflicts between the Judeans, the Israelites, and the Philistines. And we know—from the Assyrian reliefs in the palace of Sargon at Khorsabad depicting Sargon's archers and infantry attacking Ekron—that by the end of the eighth century B.C. Ekron possessed impressive fortifications.

Moshe had aleady discovered archaeological verification of the profound impact that Sargon had on the history of Ashdod after the rebellion in 712 B.C. Assyrian texts indicated that Ekron suffered a similarly disastrous conquest in the same year. In any case, while Ashdod's prosperity declined at the end of the eighth century B.C., Ekron became a large city again. Like Ashdod it became part of the Assyrian Empire and, after the campaign of Sennacherib in 701 B.C., was granted some Judean territory. Instead of a frontier town with a limited agricultural hinterland as it was before, we found evidence of the expanded extent of the city's urban core. At the end of the eighth century B.C., a new system of fortifications was erected, encircling more than fifty acres of the tell, perhaps as much as eighty acres. At the south end a six-chambered gate was linked to a massive city wall and surrounded by a belt of industrial buildings whose finds gave us an indication of the basis of the city's prosperous economy.

Even before the beginning of the excavations, a surface survey had revealed dozens of stone vats for olive pressing lying along the edges of the tell, suggesting that this was Ekron's main industry at the end of the Iron Age. But it was only when we uncovered the buildings adjoining the city gate that we began to appreciate the full extent of Ekron's olive oil industry.

In one of the rooms of this complex we discovered a complete olive oil processing installation: two presses flanking a solid stone basin close to heavy stone weights that had drawn down the press levers. Only traces of carbonized wood remained of the levers. The rest of the room was filled with the remains of large storejars and a wide variety of other pottery vessels used for manufacture and storage.

One of the most surprising discoveries in this area was the apparent connections between cult and industry in Ekron of the seventh century B.C. In a room adjoining the presses there was a well-built niche in the wall in which a small stone four-horned altar had been placed. Altars of this type found in other places were long identified as characteristic of Israelite worship practices. Yet it was clear that at Ekron they had been incorporated into the Philistine cultic tradition, which was still very much alive. This we could tell from the name of its king, Ikausu, the preservation of the earlier Philistine name from the time of the wars with the Isrealites—Achish.

At the end of the seventh century B.C., after the renaissance enjoyed by some of the cities during the period of Assyrian rule, Babylonian ascendancy over the ancient Near East augured an end to Philistine power. From the archaeological evidence it was clear that the prophet Zephaniah was not merely speculating when he warned [2:4] that "Gaza shall be deserted, and Ashkelon shall become a desolation; Ashdod's people shall be driven out at noon, and Ekron will be uprooted."

OLIVE OIL
GALORE

A PROPHECY
FULFILLED

Overlaying the industrial area and the fortifications on the southern side of the city we found a thick layer of destruction debris: the work of Nebuchadnezzar during the Babylonian campaign in Philistia in 604–603 B.C. Although Ekron is not specifically mentioned in the Babylonian chronicles, the grim situation facing the city appears in a fragmentary papyrus document found at Sakkarah in Egypt. It is a letter begging for help from Egypt to avert a military disaster. The letter was written by a King Adon, and though the name of his city is not evident in the text, a fragmentary demotic notation on the back of the document may be read as Ekron. In any event, Adon's appeal went unanswered, for Ekron was destroyed and never became an urban center of any importance again.

In the wave of conquest and mass deportations that put an end to the power of the Philistine cities and the independent existence of the kingdom of Judah, the political, economic, and social landscape of the country was changed forever. The great age of the Philistine cities, from the initial settlement of the Sea Peoples around 1200 B.C. to the time of the Babylonian conquest six hundred years later, was over. Although Gaza, Ashkelon, and Ashdod rose again to become flourishing cities in the Persian, Hellenistic, and Roman periods, their heritage was no longer strictly Philistine.

ARCHAEOLOGICAL TREASURE TROVE

Ekron, as we noted at the beginning, was an archaeological treasure trove. No other site in the vicinity could compare in size or richness. The excavation pointed to the fact that in its development, this culture paralleled the broad cultural developments throughout other parts of Philistia. Yet at the same time it was unique as an example of sophisticated urban planning in the ancient world. And since we had a continuous sequence of well-stratified Early Iron Age levels, the site provided us with a unique opportunity to examine the relationship of Mycenaean IIIC:1b ware to the later Philistine bichrome, and determine the process by which the Philistines' material culture emerged.

The great age of the Philistine cities is a chapter in the history of the country that archaeological excavations and analysis have begun to place in historical context. As the complexity of Philistine culture has become evident, so has the vital role that the Philistines played in the cultural and political development of the region throughout the biblical period. At the same time, our search for the Philistines has shed new light on a unique period of interaction between the cultures of the Aegean and the Near East.

The Ekron excavation team, sitting on the "Gates of Ekron."

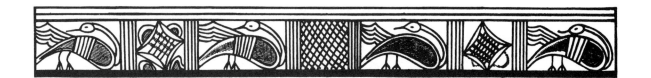

Epilogue

No archaeologist can ever complete the work of discovery and interpretation: the past can only be seen from the perspective of the present. And since the concerns of the present are constantly changing, so are the questions which must be asked about the past. In our search for the Philistines over the last forty years, many of our most exciting discoveries not only answered some pressing questions about Philistine culture but, just as importantly, raised new ones. And so it must be, and the search must continue.

Like the long list of travelers, explorers, and excavators searching for clues about the Philistines for the last four hundred years, from the intrepid Chevalier Laurent D'Arvieux in the seventeenth century through to the twentieth-century excavators of Palestine and Israel, we, too, are part of this ongoing scientific search. Although the ultimate answer to one of the central problems—the riddle of the specific origin of the Sea Peoples—is still elusive, our understanding of the character of their culture and the role they played in the emerging Iron Age civilizations of the eastern Mediterranean world is at last beginning to coalesce.

We can now see that in the close yet long-forgotten connections between Canaan and the rest of the Mediterranean world lies the true importance of the role of the Philistines and the other Sea Peoples in the history of the region. We now know that the commercial, technological, and cultural connections of the Philistines, hardly mentioned in the Bible, were far deeper and more pervasive than we could ever have imagined when we began our search. The conclusions to be drawn from the unique coincidence of pottery styles, social organization, and cultic practices can no longer be considered a regional phenomenon of interest to Egyptologists, biblical scholars, and Aegean archaeologists

alone. Their role was central in the Mediterranean during the political upheavals and population movements that marked the transition from the Bronze to the Iron Age.

The precise pattern of Philistine settlement is still somewhat enigmatic and there are variations in the different cities. One particularly intriguing question relates to the changeover from locally produced Mycenaean IIIC 1:b monochrome pottery to the characteristic Philistine bichrome. One theory suggests that there were two distinctive waves of immigration: an early group of Sea People who founded settlements at Ashdod and Ekron, and produced the locally made Mycenaean IIIC 1:b ware; and the Philistines, who arrived at the time of Ramesses III and, in the aftermath of their defeat and resettlement by the Egyptians, became the dominant ethnic element. Another theory suggests that there was only one wave of invasion by the Sea Peoples and that while the Philistines' earliest pottery was Mycenaean IIIC 1:b ware, it was slowly replaced by the bichrome style in a gradual indigenous artistic development. What is certain is that the settlement of the Philistines in Canaan was a complex process of immigration, integration, and interaction between the cultures of the ancient Near East and the Aegean that began around 1200 B.C.

What is also certain is that in the initial phases of settlement there was an *undiluted* recollection of their former cultural milieu. This we could see in the fact that their cities were well planned, that some of their important buildings contained Aegean-type hearths, and that their various industrial skills were based on an existing repertoire of models. And although they had to adapt to a new environment and to specific local conditions, the initial phase in all places excavated so far has been basically the same. Philistine settlements were always distinct from the Canaanites' city-states on which they were built: they were larger, better fortified, better planned.

We do not know as yet enough about how the ordinary Philistine lived. We do know that their social structure was based on an elite, that there were workers, and that they had an elaborate military hierarchy. Yet the relationships between the various strata of Philistine society have still to be explored as do the relations between the Philistines and the Canaanites. We know that the large residencies, containing the hearths, were focal points for meeting and were tied to cultic practices. The various iron, bronze, and ivory artifacts indicate that they enjoyed a technologically advanced standard of living. During the course of time, in the second stage of their settlement, they became prosperous and their assimilation with the local milieu—with Phoenicians and Israelites—intensified.

Among the major gaps in our picture of the Philistines is the lack of

knowledge of their language. It is also incumbent upon us to refine our
knowledge of the interrelations among all the Mediterranean cultures
of that period.

What is abundantly clear, however, is that the Philistines brought
with them a developed material culture which continued to evolve,
even as it was naturally affected by influences active in the new surroundings. They were accomplished architects and builders, highly
artistic pottery makers, textile manufacturers, dyers, metalworkers,
silver smelters, and farmers, soldiers, and sophisticated urban planners.
They played no small part in influencing the culture and political organization of their neighbors. Yet in their uneasy and ultimately violent
confrontation with the hill people known as the Israelites, the Philistines
acquired a negative image that still retains its symbolic power, despite
the archaeological discoveries of the last hundred years.

The ironies of history are hard to fathom. Indeed, the hard facts are
seldom able to alter perceptions that have become ingrained over the
centuries. From the perspective of the Bible, the Philistines were a
nation of uncouth barbarians, and remain so to the present. Yet from
the reliefs of Medinet Habu and the ruins of the great Philistine cities,
we catch glimpses of the vibrant, advanced culture that they trans-
planted from their old to their new homeland. Whether or not they
can ever shed their negative image, they have, at least, emerged from
the web of myth onto the stage of history.

CHRONOLOGICAL TABLE

BC	EGYPT Dynasties and pharaohs		ISRAEL AND PHILISTIA	GREECE
975	21st Dyn.	Siamun 978–959	Solomon 965–928	Proto-Geometric
1000			David 1004–965 David's wars with the Philistines Saul Battle of Gilboa 1020–1004	Sub-Mycenaean
1025			Battle of Eben-ezer	
1050			Wenamon's travels	
1075	20th Dyn.	Ramesses XI 1113–1085		Dark Ages
1100				
1125			Philistines' consolidation /expansion	
1150		Ramesses VI 1156–1148 Ramesses IV 1166–1160	Sea Peoples/Philistines' settlement— founding of Pentapolis: Ashdod, Ashkelon, Ekron, Gath, Gaza	Mycenaean IIIC
1175	Battle of Ramesses III, year 8, with Sea Peoples			
1200	19th Dyn.	Ramesses III 1198–1166	General wave of destruction in Levant and Aegean at the beginning of the Iron Age	End of Mycenaean palaces and maritime trade
1225		Tewosret 1209–1200 Merneptah 1235–1223	Late Bronze Age	
1250				
1275		Ramesses II 1301–1235		Mycenaean IIIB

(Spanning the Israel and Philistia column vertically: Israelite settlement: Period of the Judges)

The Egyptian dates listed above correspond to the high chronology.

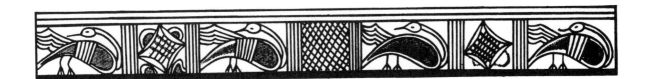

Suggestions for Further Reading

GENERAL BACKGROUND AND HISTORY

Egypt: New Kingdom

Faulkner, R. C. "Egypt: From the Inception of the Nineteenth Dynasty to the Death of Ramesses III," *CAH*, 3rd ed., Vol II. Cambridge University Press. (Egypt during the period of the coming of the Sea Peoples.)

Kitchen, K. A. *The Third Intermediate Period in Egypt (1100–650 B.C.)*. Aris and Phillips, Warminster, England, 1973. (Definitive study of the chronology and history of the period of consolidation of Philistine culture in Canaan.)

Nelson, H. H., et al. "The Naval Battle Pictured at Medinet Habu," *JNES* 2 (1943), pp. 40–55. (Detailed discussion of the naval battle between Ramesses III and the Sea Peoples.)

Stager, L. "Merneptah, Israel and Sea Peoples: New Light on an Old Relief," *Eretz Israel* 18 (1985), pp. 56–64. (Important for establishing chronology of the Sea Peoples.)

Wente, C.F. and Van Siclen, C.C. "A Chronology of the New Kingdom," *Studies in Ancient Oriental Civilization*, 39. University of Chicago Press, Chicago, 1976. (Discussion of Egyptian chronology.)

General Chronology

Åström, P., ed. *High, Middle or Low: Acts of an International Colloquium on Absolute Chronology–Held at the University of Gothenburg, 20–22nd August, 1987*, Part 1. Paul Åströms Förlag, Gothenburg, 1987.

Hankey, V. "The Aegean Late Bronze Age: Relative and Absolute Chronology," *Acts of an International Colloquium on Absolute Chronology–Held at the University of Gothenburg, 20–22nd August, 1987*, Part 2. (Correlations between the Aegean, Egypt, and the Levant.)

Warren, P. and Hankey, V. *Aegean Bronze Age Chronology*. Bristol Classical Press, Bristol, 1989. (Overall view based on Egyptian data and historical synchronism.)

SUGGESTIONS FOR FURTHER READING

Mycenaean Civilization (with special emphasis on pottery)

Desbourough, W. R. d'A. *The Last Mycenaeans and Their Successors*. Clarendon Press, Oxford, 1964. (Including the coming of the Philistines.)

Furumark, A. *The Mycenaean Pottery: Analysis and Classification*. Kungl. Vitterhets Historie och Antikvitets Akademien, Stockholm, 1941. (Basic study of typology and decorations: important for understanding Philistine pottery types.)

Heurtley, W. A. "The Relations between 'Philistine' and Mycenaean Pottery." *QDAP* 5 (1936), pp. 90–110. (One of the earliest discussions of the subject.)

Mountjoy, P. *Mycenaean Decorated Pottery–A Guide to Identification* (SIMA LXXIII). Paul Åströms Förlag, Gothenburg, 1986. (Important for understanding Aegean background of Philistine pottery.)

Mylonas, G. E. *Mycenae and the Mycenaean Age*. Princeton University Press, Princeton, 1966. (Pertinent to the study of Mycenaean archaeology.)

Renfrew, C. "The Archaeology of Cult–The Sanctuary of Phylakopi," *BSA* Supplementary Vol. 18 (1985). (Important for the study of Minoan and Mycenaean religious practices.)

Stubbings, F. H. "The Recession of Mycenaean Civilization," *CAH*, 3rd ed., Vol. II. Cambridge University Press. (Relevant to the appearance of the Sea Peoples.)

Catling, H. W. "Cyprus in the Late Bronze Age," *CAH*, 3rd ed., Vol. II. Cambridge University Press. (Close connections between the culture of Cyprus and the Philistines.)

Kling, B. *Mycenaean IIIC:1b and Related Pottery in Cyprus*. (SIMA LXXXVII). Paul Åströms Förlag, Gothenburg, 1989. (Important for the study of the early phases of Philistine cities.)

Muhly, J. D. "The Role of the Sea Peoples in Cyprus during the LCIII Period," in *Cyprus at the Close of the Late Bronze Age*, ed. V. Karageorghis and J.D. Muhly. Department of Antiquities, Nicosia, Cyprus, 1984.

The Sea Peoples

Barnett, R. D. "The Sea Peoples," *CAH*, 3rd ed., Vol. II. Cambridge University Press. (Important for historical and biblical references.)

Dothan, M. "Archaeological Evidence for Movements of the Early 'Sea Peoples' in Canaan" in *Recent Excavations in Israel: Studies in Iron Age Archaeology*, ed. S. Gitin and W.G. Dever. *AASOR* 49 (1989), pp. 59–70.

Sandars, N. K. *The Sea Peoples, Warriors of the Mediterranean*. Thames and Hudson, London, 1981. (Based on Egyptian sources and archaeological evidence, the book covers the wanderings of the Sea Peoples throughout the Mediterranean and the Balkans.)

Yadin, Y. "And Dan, Why Did He Remain in Ships?" *AJBA* 1 (1968), pp. 9–23. (Suggested identification of Israelite tribe of Dan with the Sea People of Danuna.)

The Philistines

Dothan, T. *The Philistines and Their Material Culture*. Yale University Press, New Haven, 1982. (Comprehensive study from textual and archaeological sources.)

Dothan, T. "The Philistines Reconsidered," *Biblical Archaeology Today*. Israel Exploration Society, Jerusalem, 1985, pp. 165–176. (Reevaluation of chronology and culture based on excavations.)

Macalister, R. A. S. *The Philistines, Their History and Civilization*. The British Academy, London, 1914. (A classic, the first comprehensive work on the subject by an insightful archaeologist, using biblical and historical sources.)

Malamat, A. "The Struggle against the Philistines," in *The History of the Jewish People*, ed. H. H. Ben-Sasson, pp. 80–87. Harvard University Press, Cambridge, Mass., 1976. (Historical background of the wars between the Philistines and the Israelites.)

Mazar, A. "The Emergence of Philistine Culture," *IEJ* 35 (1985), pp. 95–107. (Reassessment of the appearance and settlement of the Philistines in Canaan, based on the Tell Qasile excavations.)

Mazar, B. "The Philistines and the Rise of Israel and Tyre," *Proceedings of the Israel Academy of Sciences and Humanities* 1 (1964), pp. 1–22. (Seminal synthesis of archaeological and historical material.)

Waldbaum, J. C. *From Bronze to Iron* (SIMA LIV). Paul Åströms Förlag, Lund, 1978. (Including a discussion of the use of iron by the Philistines.)

Yadin, Y. *The Art of Warfare in Biblical Lands in Light of Archaeological Study*. McGraw-Hill, New York, 1963.

EXCAVATIONS: STUDIES AND REPORTS

Cities of the Philistine Pentapolis

Ashdod

Dothan, M. *Ashdod I* (Atiqot VII). Israel Department of Antiquities and Museums, Jerusalem, 1967.

Dothan, M. "Ashdod at the End of the Late Bronze Age and the Beginning of the Iron Age," in *Symposia Celebrating the Seventy-Fifth Anniversary of the Founding of the American Schools of Oriental Research (1900-1975)*, ed. F. M. Cross. American School of Oriental Research, Cambridge, Mass., 1979., pp. 125–134. (Discussion of the initial phase of Philistine settlement at Ashdod.)

Dothan, M. and Porath, Y. *Ashdod IV, Excavations of Area M* (Atiqot XV). Israel Department of Antiquities and Museums, Jerusalem, 1982.

Askhelon

Stager, L. "The Philistines Ruled Ashkelon," *BAR* (1991), pp. 26–43. (New large-scale excavations of the harbor city of the Philistine pentapolis.)

Tel Miqne–Ekron

Dothan, T. "Mycenaean IIIC:1b Pottery and the Arrival of the Sea Peoples at Tel Miqne-Ekron," *Sixth International Colloquium on Aegean Prehistory*. The Ministry of Culture, Athens, Greece, 1987.

Dothan, T. "The Arrival of the Sea Peoples: Cultural Diversity in Early Iron Age Canaan," in *Recent Excavations in Israel: Studies in Iron Age Archaeology*, ed. S. Gitin and W.G. Dever. *AASOR* 49 (1989), pp. 1–14.

Dothan, T. "Ekron of the Philistines, Part I: Where They Came From, How They

Settled Down and the Place They Worshipped In." *BAR* XVI No. 1 (1990), pp. 20–26.

Dothan, T. and Gitin, S. "Ekron of the Philistines," *BAR* XVI, No. 1 (1990), pp. 26–36.

Gitin, S. and Dothan, T. "The Rise and Fall of Ekron of the Philistines." *BA* Vol. 50, no. 4 (1987), pp. 197–221.

Gitin, S. "Ekron of the Philistines, Part II, Olive Oil Suppliers to the World." *BAR*, No. 2 (1990), pp. 32–42.

Other Philistine (or Related) Settlements in Canaan

Akko

Dothan, M. "Sardinia at Akko?" *Studies in Sardinian Archaeology*, Vol. II. University of Michigan Press, Ann Arbor, 1986, pp. 105–15. (Suggested identification of the Sea People settled at Akko with the Shardana.)

Beth Shean

Oren, E. *The Northern Cemetery of Beth Shean.* Museum Monograph of the University Museum of the University of Pennsylvania. E.J. Brill, Leiden, 1973. (Anthropoid coffin burials from the 13th and 12th centuries B.C., some of them identified with the Sea Peoples-Philistines in the cemetery of the ancient Egyptian garrison town.)

Deir el-Balah

Dothan, T. *Deir el-Balah* (Qedem 10). Monograph of the Institute of Archaeology, the Hebrew University of Jerusalem, Jerusalem, 1978. (Discovery of an Egyptianized cemetery and outpost near Gaza, later settled by Philistines.)

Dor

Stern, E. "Excavations at Tel Dor" in *The Land of Israel: Crossroads of Civilizations.* (Orientalia Lovaniensia Analecta 19), Uitgeverij Peeters, Leuven, 1985, pp. 169–192. (Settlement of the Tjekker at the harbor town of Dor.)

Gezer

Dever, W.G., et al. *Gezer IV: The 1967–71 Seasons in Field VI, "The Acropolis."* Annual of the Nelson Glueck School of Biblical Archaeology. Keter Press Enterprises, Jerusalem, 1986. (Recent excavations at Gezer and a discussion of Philistine settlement.)

Macalister, R. A. S. *The Excavations of Gezer 1902–1905 and 1907–1910,* 3 vols. Published for the Committee of the Palestine Exploration Fund by John Murray, London, 1912. (Early excavations of the biblical city of Gezer where evidence of Philistine culture was found.)

Lachish

Tufnell, O., et al. *Lachish II, The Fosse Temple.* Oxford University Press, Oxford, 1940. (Egyptian presence in Canaan during the reign of Ramesses III.)

Ussishkin, D. "Levels VII and VI at Tel Lachish and the End of the Late Bronze Age in Canaan" in *Palestine in the Bronze and Iron Ages: Papers in Honour of Olga Tufnell,* ed. J.N. Tubb. The Institute of Archaeology, London, 1985, pp. 213–28. (New excavations and a discussion of Egyptian and Philistine presence in Canaan.)

Megiddo

Loud, G. *The Megiddo Ivories*. University of Chicago Oriental Institute Publications, vol. LII, University of Chicago Press, Chicago, 1939. (Absolute dating from the appearance of the name "Ram.III" on one of the ivories.)

Mor

Dothan, M. "Tel Mor (Tell Kheidar)." *IEJ* 9 (1959), pp. 127–72, *IEJ* 10 (1960), pp. 123–25. (Egyptian-Philistine citadel, near the harbor city of Ashdod.)

Qasile

Mazar, A. *Excavations at Tell Qasile* (Qedem 12). Monographs of the Institute of Archaeology, the Hebrew University of Jerusalem, Jerusalem, 1980. (History of a Philistine temple area, important for study of Philistine cult practices.

Mazar, A. *Excavations at Tell Qasile* (Qedem 20). Monographs of the Institute of Archaeology, the Hebrew University of Jerusalem, Jerusalem, 1985.

Mazar, B. "The Excavations at Tell Qasile: Preliminary Report." *IEJ* 1 (1950–51), pp. 61–76, 125–140, 194–218.

Deir Alla, Transjordan

Franken, H.J. *Excavations at Tell Deir Alla*. E. J. Brill, Leiden, 1969. (Traces of settlement with "spin-off" of Philistine culture.)

Athienou, Cyprus

Dothan, T. and Ben-Tor, A. *Excavations at Athienou, Cyprus (1971–1972)* (Qedem 16). Monographs of the Institute of Archaeology, the Hebrew University of Jerusalem, 1983. (Excavations at a 12th-century B.C. settlement of a shrine dedicated to metalworking, with connections to the Sea Peoples.)

Kition, Cyprus

Karageorghis, V. *Kition IV, Ch.1: The Non-Cypriot Pottery*. Department of Antiquities, Cyprus, Nicosia, 1981. (Including a discussion of Mycenaean IIIC:1 pottery, related to the early phase of monochrome Philistine pottery.)

Maa-Palaeokastro, Cyprus

Karageorghis, V. "Excavations at Maa-Palaeokastro, 1979–1982, A Preliminary Report." *RDAC* (1982), pp. 86–108 (especially pp. 105–108.) (Discovery of Mycenaean IIIC:1 pottery at military outpost on western coast of Cyprus, related to arrival of settlers from the Aegean or from mainland Greece.)

List of Abbreviations of Journals, Periodicals, and Series

AA	Archäologischer Anzeiger
AA	Annuals of Archaeology and Anthropology
AASOR	Annual of the American Schools of Oriental Research
AJA	American Journal of Archaeology

SUGGESTIONS FOR
FURTHER READING

AJBA	Australian Journal of Biblical Archaeology
Antiquity	
Archaeology	
Archaeometry	
Atiqot	Atiqot. Journal of the Israel Department of Antiquities
BA	The Biblical Archaeologist
BAR	Biblical Archaeology Review
BASOR	Bulletin of the American Schools of Oriental Research
BBSAJ	Bulletin of the British School of Archaeology in Jersualem
BSA	Annual of the British School at Athens
CAH	The Cambridge Ancient History
Eretz Israel	Annual of the Israel Exploration Society (Hebrew and English)
Expedition	
IEJ	Israel Exploration Journal
JNES	Journal of Near Eastern Studies
JRCAS	Journal of the Royal Central Asian Society
OpAth	Acta Instituti Atheniensis Regni Sueciae: Opuscula Atheniensia
PEF Ann	Annual of the Palestine Exploration Fund
PEFQSt	Palestine Exploration Fund, Quarterly Statement
QDAP	Quarterly of the Department of Antiquity in Palestine, Jerusalem
Qadmoniot	
Qedem	Qedem. Monographs of the Institute of Archaeology, the Hebrew University, Jerusalem
RDAC	Report of the Department of Antiquities Cyprus
SCE	The Swedish Cyprus Expedition
SIMA	Studies in Mediterranean Archaeology (Monograph Series)
Tel Aviv	Tel Aviv. Journal of the Tel Aviv University Institute of Archaeology
VT	Vetus Testamentum

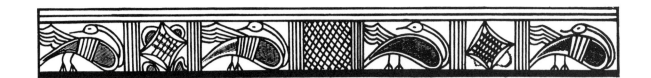

Index

Numerals in *italics* indicate illustrations.

Asia Minor, 8, 9, 23, 24, 26, 36, 45, 114, 116, 169
Assyria, 108, 137–140, 171, 213; wars with Philistines, 186–188, 252
Assyrian period, 133, 137–140, 142–157, 181, 252–253
Athienou (Cyprus), 203, 242; excavations, 193–196, *196–197*, 197–198
Aviram, Joseph, 192
Azitawatas (king of the Dannuni-yim), 215–216
Azor, 108, 199, 200, 203, 208; excavations, 108–109, *110*, 111–114, *115*, 116–117
Azor figurines, *201*
Azuri (king of Ashdod), 144

Babylonia, 137
Babylonian period, 137–140, 188, 253–254
Balkan theory of Philistine origins, 48–51
Beel-zebub, 235
Beer jugs, *90*, 134
Beersheba, 109
Beisan, 57
Bell-shaped bowls, *90*, *163*, 241
Ben Gurion University, 207
Benjamin, tribe of, 172
Ben-Tor, Amnon, 192
Berlin, 78
Besor Valley, 100
Beth Pelet, 65
Beth Shean, 65, 77, 82, 100, 103, 109, 111, 114, 172, 199, 201, 208, 229, 230; excavations, 57–59, *60–62*, 62–63, 67, 72, 88–89, 93, 109, 112, 116
Beth She'arim, 78, 80, 81
Beth Shemesh, 82, 88, 172, 235; excavations, 36–37, 39, *39*, 40, 41, 42
Beth Yerah, 80, 81
Bible, 7, 22, 25–27, 80, 117, 144; references to Sea Peoples in, 3–11, 22, 25–27, 36, 40, 57, 58, 59, 64, 65, 82, 100, 103, 106, 141, 210, 213, 215–218, 233–238, 248, 253, 256, 258. *See also specific books*
Bilbils, 192, 195
Bird motif, 85, 109, *110*, 134, 200, 229, *230*, 252
Black Sea, 10

Blanche Garde (Crusader fortress), 31–32
Blegen, Carl, 49–50
Bliss, Frederick, 31–32, 234
Boeotia, 201
Bowls, Tell Qasile, 83, *83*
Bows, *17*, *20–21*
Brandl, Baruch, 203
British School of Archaeology, Athens, 32, 34, 37, 49
British School of Archaeology, Jerusalem, 43
Bronze Age, 29, 34, 39, 40, 49, 59, 108, 121, 131, 134, 157, 188, 192, 257. *See also specific cultures, periods, and sites*
Bronze objects, 67, 82, 83, 101, 114, 122, 174, 185, 193, 202, 204, *206*, 212, 214, 225, 229, 248, *249*, 250, *251*, 257
Brosh, Menashe, 132, 177, 181
Bulging-neck jug, *90*
Bulla, 207
Burial customs, 67, 69, 72, 87, 93, 101–102, 108–116, 122, 142, 173–174, 199–208, 230; Ashdod, 142–143, 146, 173–174, 199; cremation, 114, *115*, 116–117; for cult vessels, 230; Egyptian, 67, 69, 72, 199–208; individual vs. communal, 111; mass graves, 142; mourning figurines, *200–202*, 207; for warriors, 174; *See also* Anthropoid coffins; *specific cultures and sites*
Byblos, 209, 213
Byzantine period, 8, 44, 45, 58, 59, 81, 143, 150, 177, 178, 188

Cairo, 11, 14
Calchas (Greek sage), 216
Calmet, Dom Augustin, 7–9, 34–35; *Treatises Serving as an Introduction to the Holy Scripture*, 9
Canaan, 7, 8, 9, 24, 25, 27, 39, 40, 46, 48, 55, 57–58, 92, 95, 123, 124, 135, 151, 154, 191, 192, 198, 202, 205, 206, 218; settlement patterns, 57–73, 82–83, 87–96, 99–100, 111, 135, 138, 150–151, 154, 161–170, 209–238, 256–258; *See also specific cultures and sites*
Caphtor, 5, 8–9, 11, 27, 34–35
Caphtorim, 8–9
Cappadocia, 8, 9

Carnegie Museum, Pittsburgh, 125, 171
Cephalonia, 51
Cesnola, Luigi di Palma, 191
Ceyhan River, 215
Chabas, François, 25–28
Chalcolithic period, 99, 108, 109, 237
Champollion, Jean François, 19, 22, 23, 26
Chariots, *21*, 22, *26*, 172, 250, *251*
Château des Plains (Crusader fortress), 108
Cherethites, 8
Children, 22, 26, *26*, 114, *156*
Chronicles, Second Book of, 186
Cilicia, 215
Climatic changes, 100–101
Collège de France, 23, 26
Commerce, 83–87, 99–106, 122–123, 133, 165, 169, 185, 192, 193–196
Communal tombs, 111
Composite drinking vessel, *232*
Copper industry, Cypriot, 192–198
Copper objects, 83, 192–198, 212, 214
Cosmetic vessels, 245, *246*, 252
Costumes and clothing, 15, *17–18*, 19, *21*, 22, 35, *35*, 59, 93, *94*, *95*, 109, 134, 140, 153, *200*, 204–205, 213, *214*, 215, 241. *See also specific cultures*
Council of Chalcedon, 129
Cow shoulder blades, 242, *242*
Crafts and trades, 83–85, 99, 140–142, 149, 193–198, 248. *See also specific crafts*
Cremation, 114, *115*, 116–117
Crete, 8, 9, 10, 27, 34, 35, 41, 45, 51, 64, 86, 112, 200; figurines, *201*; Knossos excavations, 34–35, *35*, 36. *See also* Minoan culture
Crucible, Tell Qasile, *83*
Crusades, 6, 41, 44, 108, 111, 131, 234; Third, 6
Cults and cult objects, 139–141, 143, 149, 153–154, *155–157*, 156–157, 166–167, *167*, 174–175, *176*, 178, 193–194, 224, *227–228*, 257; Cypriot, 193–196; Ekron, 242, *242*, 245, *246–247*, 248, *249*, 250, *251*, 252–254; Tell Qasile, 224–226, *227–228*, 229–233. *See also specific cultures and objects*

Cult stands, *227–228*, 229, *230*, 248, *249*, 250, 251
Cylindrical bottle, *90*
Cypro-Mycenaean scripts, 153, 186
Cyprus, 23, 30, 46, 51, 84, 87, 89, 91, 95, 105, 122, 123, 145, 153, 154, 155, 162, 166, 168, 169, 187, 191–198, 200, 212, 218–219, 230, 233, 242, 248, *249*; excavations, 191–208, *249*
Cyprus Department of Antiquities, 192, 193

Daggers and knives, *67*, 174, 250
Dagon, 5, 134, 156–157, 159, 175, 216
Dagon, Temple of (Ashdod), 7, 159, 173, 174
Dan, tribe of, 108, 117, 216–218
Danaans, 26
Danaoi, 215
Danites, 117
Dannuna (Sea People), 117, 210, 213, 215–217
Dardanians, 25, 49
D'Arvieux, Laurent, 7, 48, 256
David (king of Israel), 65, 85, 138, 171, 172, 179, 181, 182, 183, 229, 252
David and Goliath, 5, 6, 10, 27, 159, 175, 235
Dayan, Moshe, 203, 205
Deir el-Balah, 203; excavations, 203, *203*, 204–206, *206*, 207–208, 223, 233
Deity figurines: Ashdod, 153–154, *155–156*, 156–157, 159, 160, 174–175, *176*, 200; Tell Qasile, *231*
Denon, Dominique Vivant, 14–15, 19, 22
Denyen (Sea People), *18*, 23, 26, 27
Derden (Sea People), 25, 49, 209
DeRouge, Vicomte Emanuel, 23–27; *Fouilles à Thèbes*, 24
Desaix, General, 14
Description de l'Égypte (architectural study), 13–14
Dessueri (Sicily), 116
Deuteronomy, Book of, 8, 169
Diadems, 93, *94*
Dikaios, Porphyrios, 193
Dinaric class, 113
Djahi, 23–24
Dominican École Biblique et Archéologique, Jerusalem, 61
Dor (city), 210–211, 213

Dorians, 34
Dunayevsky, Immanuel, 81–82
Dunes, drifting, 100–101, 129

Early Bronze Age, 59, 80, 101, 132
Early Iron Age, 48–49, 57, 67, 70, 72, 88, 91–96, 102–106, 113, 121, 157, 161, 211, 229, 254
Ebenezer, 172
Egypt, 6, 8, 11, 13–28, 30, 43, 57–73, 81, 83, 95, 100, 101, 103, 114, 120, 122–125, 132, 133, 138, 151, 164–165, 169–170, 182–185, 188, 191, 195, 199–208, 210, 211–214, 219, 233, 250, 252, 254; –Aegean connection, 24–25, 30–55, 57–73, 122–125, 152, 199–208, 211–215; architecture, 58, 103, 124, 133, 206–207; art and pottery, 13–14, *15–18*, 19, *20–21*, 22–27, *26*, 28, 30, 35, *60–62*, 63, 67, *68*, *71*, 72, 83, 88, 90, 91–93, *94*, 95, 102, 108, 109, 110, 114, 121, 122–125, *152*, 154, 164–165, 169, 183, 185, 200, *200–201*, 201–208, 212, *214*, 250, *251*; and Beth Shean excavations, 57–59, *60–62* 62–63, 67, 72, 93, 109, 116; burial customs, 67, 69, 72, 199–208; XVIIIth Dynasty, 42, 67, 122; XIXth Dynasty, 58, 122; XXth Dynasty, 169; XXIst Dynasty, 182, 252; XXIInd Dynasty, 185; French archaeological expeditions to, 13–28; Hyksos rulers, 103, 122, 164; language, 22; Middle Kingdom, 15, 30, 211; mummies, 59, 70, 72, 93, 204; navy, *16–17*, *20–21*; New Kingdom, 34, 40, 164, 195, 202, 204, 211; wars with Israel, 131, 160, 185, 199, 205; wars with Sea Peoples, 15, *15–18*, 19, *20–21*, 22–28, 30–31, 58–63, 82–83, 122–125, 169–170, 213, *214*, 238, 252
Eilat, 186
Ekron, 8, 145, 172, 217, 219, 235–255, *240*, *243*, 257; excavations, 235–242, *241–244*, 245, *246–247*, 248, *249*, 250, *251*, 252–254; shrines, *244*, 245, *247*, 248; Stratum IV, 238; Stratum VII, 237–238; Stratum VIII, 237
Ekwesh (Sea People), 48, 210
Elam, 146

Enkomi (Cyprus), *95*, 192, 195, 213–214, 225, 242, 248; excavations, 192–193
Esdraelon Valley, 6, 57, 61, 100, 103, 104, 114, 172, 173
Ethnika (Stephanus of Byzantium), 8
Etruscans, 25
Evans, Arthur, 34–36, 39, 50
Execration Texts, 211
Exodus, Book of, 205
Ezekiel, 8, 9
Ezion-Geber, 186

Facial features, 15, *61–62*, 69, *70*, 112–113, 140, *176*, *200*
Famine, 165
Fayum culture, 30
Feeding bottle, *90*
Female figurines: Ashdod, 153–154, *155–156*, 156–157, 159, 160, 200; Tell Aitun, 200, *200*, 201; Tell Qasile, *231*
Ferembach, Denise, 113
Fertility goddessses, 200, *231*
Figurines, 177, 200, *200–202*, 225; Afula, *105*; Ashdod, 153–154, *155–156*, 156–157, 159, 160, 174–175, *176*; Ekron, 241, 242, *251*; mourning, *200–202*, 207; musician, *140*, 174–175, *176*, 177; Perati, 201, *202*; Tell Aitun, 200, *200*, 201; Tell Qasile, 225, *231*
First Olympiad, 29
Fish decorations, *163*, 200
Fisher, Clarence, 58, 59, 61, 63
Fourmant, Étienne, 9–10; *Reflections on the Origin, History, and Genealogy of Ancient Peoples*, 9
France, 9, 13–14, 19, 22; archaeological expeditions to Egypt, 13–28
Freedman, David Noel, 125, 131, 144
French Center for Scientific Research, Jerusalem, 109
Funerary mouthpiece, 114
Furtwängler, Adolf, 30, 33, 34
Furumark, Arne, 85, 89, 91

Games, Egyptian, 205
Garfinkel, Yosef, 237
Garstang, John, 43–47, 69, 96, 100, 210–211
Gate complexes, Ashdod, 183–184, *184*, 185, 186–188

Thebes, 13–27, 34–35, 182, 207

Thiersch, Hermann, 32–34

Third Crusade, 6

Tholoi, 111

Thucydides, 29

Thutmosis III, Pharaoh, 30, 34, 64, 103, 211

Tiglath-Pileser III, King, 144

Timnah, 172

Tin, 174

Tiryns drawing, *246*

Tjekker (Sea People), *18*, 23, 26, 27, 210

Tombs. *See* Burial customs; Cemeteries

Tos, 178

Trade, 35–36, 40, 44, 57, 63, 70, 80, 83–85, 87, 96, 102–106, 111, 122–125, 131, 165, 169, 172, 182, 183, 185, 186, 187, 192, 193–198, 211, 212, 214, 218, 237; modern, 120; routes and patterns, 99–106. *See also specific cultures and trades*

Trojans, 9, 10, 25, 29–30

Trojan War, 24, 25, 29–30, 34, 35, 48, 91

Troy, 9, 10, 25, 50, 219, 237; fall of, 29–30; Schliemann's excavations of, 29–30

Turkey, 215

Tursha, 25

Tyre, 80, 248

Ugarit, 193, 211, 213, 219

Ugaritic documents, 132, 164–165, 211

United Monarchy, 185

University Museum, Philadelphia, 57, 89

University of California, Lawrence Berkeley Laboratory, 168

University of Chicago, 103; Oriental Institute at, 72, 89

University of Istanbul, 215

University of Jena, 11

University of London, Institute of Archaeology at, 88, 93

Upper Galilee, 107

Uzziah (king of Judah), 133, 138, 185–186

Valley of Rephaim, 172

Varuna, 11

Via Maris, 101–104, 108, 132

Vincent, Hughes Père, 61–63, 69, 92, 208

Wace, Alan, 49–50

Warriors, *16–18*, *20–21*, *95*, 172–174, *214*

"Warrior Vase," 46, 47, 213

Weaponry, *17–18 20–21*, 22, *26*, 35 *35*, *47*, 65, *67*, 83, 84, *95*, 142, 153, 174, *214*. *See also specific metals and objects*

Welch, F. B., 32, 33

Weshesh (Sea People), 23, 37, 210

Wheels, 248, *249*, *251*

Wigs, Egyptian, 59, 93, 204

Women, 19, *21*, 22, 26, *26*, 153, 212; deity figurines, 153–154, *155–156*, 156–157, 159, 160, 200, *200–202*, *231*; as rulers, 212

World War I, 43, 65

World War II, 73, 78

Xanthus, 216

Yadin, Yigael, 95, 96, 105, 183–184, 191, 192, 215, 216, 217, 218

Yair, David, 121

Yamani, 186

Yarkon River, 80, 99, 172, 217, 223

Yarkon Valley, 229

Yavne Yam, 101

Yom Kippur War, 206

Yugoslavia, 48; Glasinatz excavation, 48–49

Zechariah, 138

Zephaniah, 8, 9, 138, 253

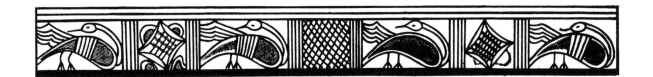

Illustration Credits

BLACK-AND-WHITE ILLUSTRATIONS

Pages 4 and 79: Carta Publishing Company Ltd., Jerusalem. Page 15: Nancy Sandars, *The Sea Peoples*. London: Thames and Hudson, 1978. Pages 16, 17, 18, 20, 21, 26, 33, 37, 38, 39, 46, 52 (right), 54, 66, 68, 70, 71 (right), 90 nos. 1–5 and 7–10, 94 (bottom), 95, 110, 164, 201, 203, 211, 214: T. Dothan, *The Philistines and Their Material Culture*. Jerusalem: Israel Exploration Society, 1982. Page 35: drawn after photograph in S. Marinatos, *Crete and Mycenae*. London: Thames and Hudson, 1960. Page 47: courtesy National Museum of Athens. Page 52 (left): drawn after photograph in G. Jacopi, "Nuovi Scavi Nella Necropoli Micenea di Jalisso," *Annuario* 13–14 (1933–40). Page 53: courtesy of G. Edelstein and S. Aurant, "The Philistine Tomb at Tel 'Aitun," *Atiqot* XXI. Israel Exploration Society. Pages 60 and 62: A. Rowe, *The Topography and History of Beth-Shean*, vol. I. Philadelphia: University of Pennsylvania Press, 1930. Page 61: F. W. James, "Beth Shean," *Expedition* 3 (1961). University Museum. Philadelphia. Pages 67, 71 (left), and 167 (top): courtesy of Israel Authority of Antiquities. Pages 83 and 84: B. Mazar, "The Excavations at Tell Qasile: Preliminary Report," *Israel Exploration Journal* 1 (1950–51). Page 90 no. 6: A. Mazar, "Excavations at Tell Qasile," part 2, *Qedem* 20 (1985). Institute of Archaeology, Hebrew University, Jerusalem. Page 104: drawn after photograph from Oriental Institute, Chicago, Megiddo Expedition. Page 95 (left): drawn after photograph in A. S. Murray and H. B. Walters, *Excavations in Cyprus*. London, British Museum, 1900. Page 95 (right): drawn after photograph in P. Dikaios, *Enkomi Excavations 1948–1958*, vol. IIIa. Mainz am Rhein, Verlag Philipp Von Zabern, 1973. Page 104: drawn after photograph in M. Dothan, "Excavations at 'Afula," *Atiqot* 1 (1955). Israel Authority of Antiquities. Page 105: drawn after photograph in M. Dothan, "Excavations from Azor, 1960," *Israel Exploration Journal* 11 (1961). Page 115: M. Dothan, "Excavations from Azor, 1960," *Israel Exploration Journal* 11 (1961). Pages 123, 151, 154, 166, 167 (bottom), 176, 184: M. Dothan, Ashdod Excavation, Department of Antiquities, Israel. Pages 130 and 138: M. Dothan, "Ashdod I, The First Season of Excavations 1962," *Atiqot* 7 (1967). Pages 132, 139, 140, 155, 156: M. Dothan, "Ashdod II–III: The Second and Third Seasons of Excavations, 1963, 1965, Soundings in 1967," *Atiqot* 9–10 (1971). Page 152: B. Brandl, "The Scarabs and Bulla from Ashdod—Area G (1968–1969)" (in press). Page 163: M. Dothan, "Relations between Cyprus and the Philistine Coast in the Late Bronze Age (Tel Mor, Ashdod)," *Praktika* 1 (1972). Pages 196 and 197: T. Dothan and A. Ben-Tor, "Excavations at Athienou, Cyprus, 1971–1972," *Qedem* 16, Jerusalem, 1983. Pages 200, 201, 202: T. Dothan, "Another Mourning Figurine from the Lachish Region," *Eretz Israel* 11 (1973). Page 206: T. Dothan, "Excavations at the Cemetery of Deir el-Balah," *Qedem* 10 (1979). Pages 224, 226, 228, 230, 231, 232: A. Mazar, "Excavations at Tell Qasile, pt. I—The Philistine Sanctuary: Architecture and Cult Objects," *Qedem* 12, Jerusalem, 1980. Page 227: courtesy of A. Mazar, Tell Qasile excavation.